CHEAPER BY THE HOUR

CHEAPER BY THE HOUR

Temporary Lawyers and the
Deprofessionalization of the Law

Robert A. Brooks

TEMPLE UNIVERSITY PRESS
PHILADELPHIA

Robert A. Brooks is Associate Professor and Chair in the Department of Criminal Justice at Worcester State University in Massachusetts.

TEMPLE UNIVERSITY PRESS
Philadelphia, Pennsylvania 19122
www.temple.edu/tempress

Library of Congress Cataloging-in-Publication Data

Brooks, Robert Andrew.
    Cheaper by the hour : temporary lawyers and the deprofessionalization of the law / Robert A. Brooks.
        p. cm.
    Includes bibliographical references.
    ISBN 978-1-4399-0285-1 (cloth : alk. paper) — ISBN 978-1-4399-0287-5 (e-book)
    1. Lawyers—Employment—United States. 2. Temporary employment—United States. I. Title.
    KF299.T46B76 2011
    331.25'729—dc22
                                                                2010028450

♾ The paper used in this publication meets the requirements of the American National Standard for Information Sciences—Permanence of Paper for Printed Library Materials, ANSI Z39.48-1992

Printed in the United States of America

2 4 6 8 9 7 5 3 1

To all those working on the "concourse level"

Contents

Preface

I had never heard of a "temporary attorney" during the eight years I spent in law practice. Looking for work while writing my dissertation, I responded to help wanted ads in the *Washington Post* and eventually found myself working on document review projects alongside dozens or hundreds of other temporary attorneys. I soon learned that temporary attorneys were big business, and that many large firms regularly enlisted the services of placement agencies to staff massive projects; in fact, one of the firms I worked for in 2004 was employing more temporary personnel than permanent workers. Realizing I had stumbled onto a gold mine of data, I began taking notes of my experiences and interviewing fellow temporary attorneys.

Despite the significant size and scope of the temporary attorney industry, it has received little attention from both academia and the public press. Although the legal press has devoted more coverage to the topic, it has been largely uncritical; many articles are authored by placement agency personnel, few have included the perspective of temporary attorneys, and only a handful have specifically examined document review work (the subject of this book). Two prior books have looked at temporary lawyering. Deborah Arron and Deborah Guyol (2004) wrote a how-to book aimed mainly at lawyers and law firms. It portrays temporary lawyering as a largely positive phenomenon and is not intended to provide any larger social analysis or contextual depth. Jackie Krasas Rogers's (2000) work is an academic analysis; however, it devotes just one chapter to a study of contract lawyers and another chapter to comparing contract lawyers with the clerical temporaries the author studied.

Cheaper by the Hour is the first detailed, critical look at the world of the temporary attorney, from the inside out. It is also one of the few book-length workplace ethnographies to study professional work of any kind.

The document review work that is described in this book, and the conditions under which it was performed, will likely surprise many readers. Most people probably picture attorneys' work to be intellectually challenging, autonomous, and interesting. Document review is none of these; rather, it involves one narrow task within a larger, typically very complex case. The work is significantly deskilled and deprofessionalized, and it is perceived as mostly boring and tedious. It provides little opportunity for learning new skills or securing permanent employment. The work is also sometimes performed under miserable conditions—in warehouses or condemned buildings, and for sixteen or more hours per day.

Rogers's book as well as Kevin Henson's (1996) provide fascinating looks at the difficulties and deprivations of clerical temping. *Cheaper by the Hour* draws many parallels with those authors' findings, and this may raise eyebrows. Should the reader have sympathy for the complaints of an attorney who is being paid upwards of $25 per hour, plus time and a half for overtime? Surely there are many people who are being paid much less to work under worse conditions. However, the reader should keep in mind that deprivation is relative. Imagine recent law school graduates from "good schools" who might have had visions of starting out at a Wall Street firm making $160,000 per year, and more important, starting up the ladder to partnership. They might have thought the best initial use of such a salary would be to pay off their student loans that could run into the six figures. These new attorneys also might have imagined taking on increasingly challenging tasks as they learned new skills and began to develop a client base. Instead, they find themselves stuffed into rooms on the "concourse level" (the law firm's basement) reading documents and making little marks on coding sheets, with any notion of applying their law school training gone. In addition, many associates (and even some partners) who lost their jobs due to firm mergers, dissolutions, or corporate downsizing—and who already had experienced challenging legal work—could find themselves alongside these new graduates.

We might be tempted to ask whether they have a right to complain. However, it seems that there are more interesting questions: How do temporary attorneys make accommodations to the lowered expectations and stigmatization that the work brings with it? How do they cope with the tedium and the time demands of the work? Are the ways that these attorneys relate to their work similar to and different from those of temporary workers in other sectors? Do traditional models of control over professional work apply here, and would temporary attorneys offer resistance to these controls? More generally, does the work described in this book represent the leading edge of a new, deprofessionalized legal "underclass"?

This Research

Much of the literature on deprofessionalization/proletarianization is theoretical and speculative in nature (e.g., Haug 1975; Ritzer and Walczak 1988; Rothman 1984; Spangler and Lehman 1983). Some of the more empirical literature draws its conclusions from analyzing macro trends such as changes in the percentage of professionals employed by organizations, or shifts in measures of employment satisfaction. The insecurity literature has few studies of temporary professionals, and only one prior study, by Jackie Krasas Rogers (2000), involves interviews of temporary attorneys.

The research for this book draws on participant-observation work, as well as interviews of temporary attorneys, involving work quite unlike that performed by Rogers's (2000) attorneys. While this sample is necessarily limited in time and place, the richness of data from the interviews and participant observation should provide welcome insight into the effects of deprofessionalization on work processes and on attorneys' work experiences, relationships, and identities.

Methods

This research involved two parts: The first employed participant-observer methods. While enrolled in a doctoral program in sociology and after completing required course work, I worked as a temporary attorney on seventeen projects on behalf of nine different law firms in Washington, D.C. My period of employment began in April 2000 and ended in August 2004. I worked a combined total of approximately thirty-six months, with breaks in between some of the projects in order to write my dissertation, which was on a different topic. The identity of the particular matters, the clients, the agencies, and the law firms are confidential; however, I can report the following information about the projects with which I was involved (further details of each assignment are contained in Appendix A): All of the matters involved document review. Eleven of them concerned either Federal Trade Commission or U.S. Department of Justice "Second Requests" involving corporate mergers in the sectors of oil and gas, beverages, electronics, medical devices, entertainment, and defense. (The process of document review, including responding to federal government Second Requests, is explained in Chapter 3.)

The other six projects involved antitrust and consumer class action litigation, and there was also one state criminal investigation. Most of the law firms I worked for were large firms based in Washington, D.C., or they were D.C. outposts of large national firms, although I also worked at one medium-sized local firm. The projects lasted from two weeks to nine months, with the median project lasting approximately eight weeks. The number of attorneys employed on the projects varied; on the smallest, I was one of six attorneys, while the largest involved several hundred. I was registered with eight temporary attorney placement agencies, and received work from five of them. During the course of my work, I took regular notes of my experiences. Sometimes these were handwritten or typed into e-mail messages, but mostly they were spoken into a handheld recorder and later transcribed.

The participant-observer work was supplemented by interviews of twenty temporary attorneys, conducted between January 2002 and July 2004. The format was a semistructured interview and included questions about why the subjects were doing temporary work, how they experienced the work, and their relationships with law firms and placement agencies. The questions also included background on schooling, family, and employment history. (The categories of questions are reproduced in Appendix B.) The research was approved through the Institutional Review process at American University, and all subjects were assured of confidentiality. I selected subjects with the intent to have a sample that would represent variety in length of temporary attorney experience, gender, age, race/ethnicity, and sexual orientation. (A brief biographical description of each attorney is contained in Appendix C.) In addition, I attempted to choose some attorneys who—voluntarily or involuntarily— appeared to have made a "career" out of being a temporary attorney. Only one attorney turned down my request for an interview, citing concerns with being tape-recorded. The interviews were conducted off-site, usually in a restaurant during lunch. The subjects were not compensated for their time, although I did offer to pay the cost of their lunch. Interviews lasted from just under one hour to one and a half hours. I later transcribed the interviews and sent them to the subjects via e-mail to give them an opportunity to correct potential errors.

Organization of the Book

Chapter 1 provides an overview of two processes that are changing the nature of work. The chapter first reviews the evidence concerning Harry Braverman's (2004) degradation of work hypothesis with an emphasis on deskilling and task unbundling, and then analyzes claims of increasing insecurity of work over the past forty years. Each of these processes is examined in the context of professional work, with particular emphasis on legal work, which some claim is subject to powerful forces that are deprofessionalizing and proletarianizing it. The Chapter emphasizes that although much work has become degraded and insecure, workers and management continue to engage in a struggle of control and resistance that is constantly enacted on a frontier of mutually reinforcing behavior.

The rise of the temporary attorney industry is chronicled in Chapter 2. Initially, temporary legal work was designed by a handful of women entrepreneurs for women lawyers. However, after layoffs and disruptions in the legal market in the late 1980s, it became apparent that male attorneys were at least as interested as their female counterparts in obtaining temporary work. Firms were at first reluctant to employ temporary attorneys due to stigma and ethical concerns; however, intensive marketing by placement agencies and demands from large institutional clients led to eventual widespread acceptance of the practice. Placement firms also marketed themselves to potential attorneys, suggesting that temporary work would give overstressed lawyers greater flexibility and control over their careers and their working hours, provide an interesting variety of work, and offer a "test run" toward a permanent job. However, none of these promises held true for my sample. Most interviewees were "involuntary" temporaries who felt that temp assignments were inflexible, the work was tedious and deskilled, and extended legal temping hurt, rather than helped, their job prospects. Thus, these experiences were much more similar to those found in studies of low-skilled temporary work than in other temporary technical and professional assignments.

Most studies of temporary work do not require a lengthy description of the type of work performed because it typically involves relatively straightforward tasks that are familiar to most readers, such as clerical work. Temporary legal work, however, requires a detailed explanation. The process of obtaining temporary work is detailed, and Chapter 3 also explains the specific type of temporary legal work and the organization of the work—document review—that I and my fellow temporaries were performing. The work is found to be largely deprofessionalized, fragmented, deskilled, intensified, and regimented.

Control and resistance are explored in Chapters 4 through 6. Chapter 4 involves conflict over the work process. Some suggest that "responsible autonomy" would provide sufficient control over temporary professional work. However, my observations and interviews clearly demonstrate that this is not the case in document review projects. Attorneys engaged in numerous acts of resistance (including work avoidance and soldiering) to elongate projects or to increase their control over the flow of work. Because these practices arose from "hidden knowledge," temporary attorneys were able to effectively disguise these behaviors. Other types of resistance—including humor, cynicism, and "bitching"—also were used widely.

One aspect of professionalism involves control over one's time, including the pace and timing of work. Placement agencies promise additional temporal control due to the "flexibility" that temporary work affords. However, Chapter 5 demonstrates that temporary attorneys experience a great deal of conflict around time, conceptualized here as both "external" and "internal" conflicts. External conflicts involve continual searching for work that offers the most overtime, attempting to maximize the time spent at work, and billing the maximum possible number of hours. Temporary work is a "feast or famine" existence, sometimes requiring a great deal of hustling to find work, which might involve registering with half a dozen or more agencies. Attorneys reported that they took jobs they did not really want for fear that turning down work would cut them off from future assignments. Internal conflicts involve the struggle to tolerate the tedium of the work and the long hours, and the toll the work takes on both one's psyche and relationships. The relenting sameness of the work leads temporary attorneys to a variety of coping strategies, both individual and collective.

Control and resistance involving identity is the focus of Chapter 6. The basic question is whether temporary attorneys identify more with their status as a "temporary" or as an "attorney." The answer varies somewhat within the sample, but it appears that the status of "temporary" has a strong effect on identity, whether attorneys attempt to "own" the label or to reject it. For many, indications of Erving Goffman's (1963) "spoiled identity" were readily apparent, a finding consistent with ethnographies of clerical temporaries. Temporary attorneys either attempted to neutralize and rationalize the stigma, or they internalized it, using a variety of techniques.

Chapter 7 returns to a discussion of the deprofessionalization of the law. It explores the potential future of commodity legal practice, including document review. It suggests that document review is not an isolated example and that other types of legal work also will be deprofessionalized—deskilled, unbundled, and performed by less-expensive labor. Demands for greater efficiency and increasing competition will continue to drive this process. However, rather than a large-scale "deprofessionalization," the practice of law will become "reprofessionalized" and further stratified. The chapter concludes with a consideration of the costs and benefits of this process on attorneys, clients, and the public interest.

This work would not have been possible without the cooperation of the temporary attorneys who took the time out of their day to talk with me about their experiences. I thank them for their openness, and I dedicate this book to them. I also thank my editor, Mick Gusinde Duffy, for his invaluable input, as well as the anonymous reviewers who were very helpful in revising the manuscript. Finally, I am grateful to my mother, Sue, who taught me early on the significance of the written word, and to Alain, who kept my spirits lifted during the research and writing of this book.

CHEAPER BY THE HOUR

1

Degraded and Insecure

The "New" Workforce

R ick had this to say about his first experience working on a document review project as a temporary lawyer: "I thought it was a little stultifying, you know, frankly. I thought it was kind of a waste of time and effort and money. . . . I thought it was a little odd that we were just expected to fill out sheets and code them and separate them into one stack or another, as opposed to actually functioning as temporary litigators, looking for documents that would assist in the prosecution or defense of the case."

Many of the attorneys I interviewed reported similar feelings. They had come to temporary attorney work as recent law school graduates or because of disruptions in their lives—the closing of a practice, a layoff, or a move to a new town. Most expected that they would be doing traditional legal work on a contingent basis; instead, they were performing tasks that were tedious, repetitive, highly regimented, and well beneath their abilities. Sometimes they worked in warehouses, basements, and even condemned office buildings. The fact that the work was temporary made the situation even more difficult—attorneys were always looking for the next project, they lacked benefits such as health insurance, and they knew that temporary work was hindering their professional advancement. Some of them responded with a stiff upper lip, hoping that a permanent job was just around the corner. Others were barely able to stand the work and felt diminished and demeaned by it. Vince told me that as a result of doing temporary work he had lost his sense of pride in being an attorney and now felt like a "slave" or a "drone."

Being a professional was not supposed to be like this. These attorneys should have been doing interesting, challenging, socially useful work in an atmosphere that was collegial and at the same time autonomous. They should have been providing individualized services with significant client contact; instead, they were performing a deskilled and regimented task that had been split off ("unbundled") from the larger case. They performed the work in factory-like conditions, with their discretion strictly limited. They were attorneys in name only.

Although the work was very tedious, it also intrigued me because I was a doctoral student in sociology. On one level, I noticed how poorly the projects were managed, and I wondered why law firms believed that attorneys needed to do this work. On a broader level, I became interested in how the temporary legal industry had arisen and what it meant for the future of the legal profession. Was document review work some strange but insignificant exception to traditional legal practice or was it a harbinger of a creeping deprofessionalization of the law? Over time, I began to view the work we were doing as part of a historical process that began with industrialization and was now affecting the professions. Professional work (or at least some aspects of it) was becoming more like other types of work—increasingly degraded and insecure.

Has Work Been Degraded?

Understanding what is "really" going on in the world of work can be a confusing enterprise. Broadly speaking, there are two opposing visions that are articulated in both academic and popular analyses. One of them sees workplaces filled with empowered, autonomous employees applying complex skills in the postindustrial "knowledge economy." The other sees work as deskilled, intensified, and performed in virtual Panopticons,[1] where management control has been perfected through technologies that are frequently disguised.

The degradation of work hypothesis is best captured by Harry Braverman's *Labor and Monopoly Capital* (1974). Braverman resurrects Karl Marx's

---

[1] The Panopticon is a type of prison building envisioned by the philosopher Jeremy Bentham, although its exact form was never realized. It is designed so that all inmates can be observed by guards without the inmates necessarily being aware that they are being watched. The metaphor of the Panopticon is employed by Michel Foucault (1977) in describing the "discipline" of contemporary society in which citizens are turned into "docile bodies" through constant observation and molding of behavior.

thesis (e.g., Marx [1889] 1967) that the imperative of capitalist production is to maximize profits, in part by reducing the cost of labor. This is accomplished by making work more routine and increasing management control. Braverman analyzes the shift from craft production (where workers use advanced skills to create products largely by hand) to industrial production (dominated by automation and an extreme division of labor). Through industrialization, worker autonomy is reduced by separating the conceptualization and planning of work from its execution. Work is also deskilled as "the automation of processes places them under the control of management engineers and destroys the need for knowledge and training" (Braverman 1974, 225).[2] As skills become less scarce, a wider labor pool is available; at the same time, the efficiencies of machines make fewer workers necessary. An intensified division of labor makes it possible to pay low wages for low-skilled work, and higher wages for the few higher-skilled jobs that remain, a realization of the "Babbage principle."[3] Each of these factors contributes to driving down labor costs.

Of course, the subjective qualities of work also suffer. Work processes are routinized and intensified; the worker is subordinated "ever more decisively to the yoke of the machine" (Braverman 1974, 231) and workplaces become "dehumanized prisons of labor" (p. 233). Scientific management, pioneered by Frederick Taylor, represents "nothing less than the explicit verbalization of the capitalist mode of production" (p. 86).[4] In its maximally efficient division

---

[2] This analysis has not gone unchallenged. For example, Braverman has been accused of romanticizing craft work, as well as nineteenth-century clerical work (see Littler 1978); such work was rarely fully autonomous and unregimented, and was standardized and controlled at least in some respects (Littler 1982). Some point out that certain types of craft work survived industrialization, while others (e.g., Adler 2007) challenge Braverman's basic assertion that capitalistic production necessarily drives deskilling, a point taken up further in this chapter.

[3] Braverman (1974) describes the work of Charles Babbage who in 1832 posited that it is more efficient to divide a manufacturing process into various tasks, each necessarily requiring different degrees of skill and strength. The manufacturer can then purchase only the exact quantity of each type of labor power that is needed, saving money because "dividing the craft cheapens its individual parts" (p. 80). Braverman sees this process as fundamental to the development of labor under capitalism. While capitalists claim that the Babbage principal "preserves scarce skills," according to Braverman it in fact "destroys all-around skills where they exist," shapes remaining skills to capitalist needs, and distributes technical capacities on a "need to know basis" (p. 82). Labor power thus becomes a commodity, organized according to the needs of its purchasers rather than its sellers.

[4] Frederick Taylor (1911) believed that the then existing means of production—based on tradition and rules of thumb—resulted in wasted work. The goal, then, of scientific management

of labor, its shifting of control from worker to management, and its dehumanizing tendencies, scientific management represents to Braverman the epitome of the degradation of work.[5]

Braverman's thesis gave new energy to critical labor studies and led to a great deal of refinement, elaboration, and contention.[6] Several challenges to

---

(or "Taylorism," as it came to be known) was optimum efficiency. Its means included a careful study of all the steps in the work process, the development of highly specific standardized procedures ("the one best method") to perform the work, and the selection of appropriate persons to complete each procedure. Taylorism was meant to replace the judgment of individual workers with "science," and thus had the effect of transferring control over work process and output from the worker to management. Some of Taylor's writing appears to the modern ear as quite ruthless. For example, he suggested that in assigning the task of handling pig iron, management should select a man who is "so stupid and so phlegmatic that he more nearly resembles in his mental make-up the ox rather than any other type. The man who is mentally alert and intelligent is for this very reason entirely unsuited for work that, for him, be the grinding monotony of work of this character" (Taylor 1911, 41). Nevertheless, Taylor's principles were broadly accepted at the time and widely applied in workplaces throughout the twentieth century, in the United States and elsewhere. This resulted in huge increases in productive capacity and a rising standard of living; however, it also created a fair amount of misery. Application of Taylor's "scientific" principles in today's fast-moving economy is arguably a "recipe for disaster" because they hamper an organization's ability to adapt quickly (Freedman 1992, 6).

[5] Braverman has been criticized for conflating capitalism with Taylorism, and thus ignoring other forms of management control. However, Braverman (1974) does in fact address bureaucratic and some postbureaucratic measures at length (e.g., pp. 35–37), but ultimately finds them to be Taylorist in intent, application, and result.

[6] Three rather distinct threads have emerged in response to Braverman's 1974 work, *Labor and Monopoly Capital* (see Sawchuk 2006). The first directly challenges Braverman's theories, for example, by arguing that capitalist production does not necessarily lead to deskilling, intensification, and other outcomes negative to workers. The second mitigates what many see as Braverman's deterministic tendencies, for instance, by giving more weight to worker subjectivity (resistance and dissent), to localized factors, to other large-scale processes (such as globalization), and to the effects of social stratification (aside from class). Most recently, poststructuralist theories have gained prominence; these are based on Foucault (1977), Marcuse (1964), and others. Broadly, these reject Braverman's suggestion that control is possessed by one party to wield against the other. Rather, control emerges as relative "power" rather than as hegemonic "exploitation" and is created and maintained through processes of language ("discursive practices"). In addition to theoretical and methodological concerns, one must acknowledge that the partial eclipse of Braverman is also rooted in the "defeat of the left" over the past thirty years (Hassard, Hogan, and Rowlinson 2001). Braverman tapped into the then prevailing zeitgeist of general economic uneasiness and concern with the state of the working "man." Today, his hopes for class consciousness seem hopelessly romantic. Yet at the same time, he continues to be relevant because of his recognition of several factors: (1) the negative effects that late capitalism may have on workers' skills and quality of life, (2) the central importance of control in understanding the labor process, and (3) the polarization and proletarianization of at least some labor sectors.

Labor and Monopoly Capital seem particularly relevant in this context. These suggest that work in recent decades has actually become more—not less—skilled; that post-Taylorist methods have made work more humane and more autonomous; and that worker resistance, largely overlooked by Braverman, plays an important role in understanding the labor process.

Upskilling in the Information Economy

Braverman (1974) suggests that deskilling is the inevitable outcome of capitalist production. However, the best evidence is that large-scale deskilling does not seem to have occurred in recent decades (see Form 1987; Spenner 1979, 1983). Some believe that the postindustrial "knowledge economy" has created more complex work environments that demand greater technical and social skills from workers (see Bell 1973; Castells 1999; Frenkel et al. 1999). In this new economy, "even" factory workers and providers of basic services must become knowledge workers (Hirschhorn 1984; Zuboff 1988). In fact, some research has found evidence of "upskilling," whether localized (e.g., Fernandez 2001) or more broad-based (e.g., Kim 2002).

However, the development of a knowledge economy has been uneven at best. For example, there is evidence that deskilling has occurred, at least for some workers in some sectors (see Hecht 2001), and certainly there are workplaces that still rely on Taylorist management practices and industrial era technology. Even where knowledge-intensive work is growing, it appears that certain population segments are not being integrated, such as the urban poor (Lewis 2007). In addition, it appears to be simplistic to equate advances in technology with an automatic upskilling of jobs. New technologies represent a double-edged sword; while they may provide a platform for the exercise of advanced skills, they can simultaneously be deployed by management to increase the division of labor and to deskill some tasks, resulting in skill polarization (e.g., Gallie 1991; Penn, Rose, and Rubery 1994). We are all familiar with the concept that as information technologies become more complex, they also become easier to use. Thus, increasingly greater skills are required to *design* technological systems (requiring relatively few workers), but fewer skills may be needed to *operate* them (involving jobs performed by the mass of workers).

The polarization hypothesis is theoretically appealing for several reasons. It implicitly recognizes that new technologies are continually being deployed in the workplace, and thus generalized deskilling is implausible. It also acknowledges marked societal divisions in access to training and education (Lewis 2007), as well as increasing divisions between standard and nonstandard employment

(Standing 1999). Skill polarization also has empirical support. There is evidence that much of the growth in "knowledge workers" has occurred in relatively low-level information handling positions (e.g., Fleming, Harley, and Sewell 2004; Thompson, Warhurst, and Callaghan 2001). Such positions are not entirely devoid of skill; neither are they highly credentialed, terribly complex, or well remunerated. In his 1991 work, Robert Reich estimated that only 20 percent of future jobs would be truly knowledge-centric; his prediction was recently deemed optimistic (Fleming, Harley, and Sewell 2004). Skill polarization is also supported by findings that indicate an increasingly "hourglass-shaped" society, where the proportion of workers in both higher- and lower-paying jobs has increased both in the United Kingdom (Anderson 2009) and in the United States (Massey and Hirst 1998).[7]

Changing Forms of Control

Taylorism is a type of direct control over work processes, and it was initially deployed in industrial settings. As nonindustrial sectors expanded, and as organizations enlarged and became more rationalized, bureaucracy (and its partner, human resources management) replaced Taylorism as the chief form of direct control. However, other forms developed to control the work of managers and professionals, which tends to have less structure. Andrew Friedman (1977) labels one of these "responsible autonomy," an indirect form of control wherein workers have some freedom to decide how their work is conducted but are held accountable if they fail to perform adequately. This form is most often employed with professional workers; it is useful for management because it heads off potential resistance that workers might employ against direct methods.

An additional form of indirect control has arisen, found in postbureaucratic structures. "The distinguishing feature . . . is the creation of shared meaning, which obviates the need for the principles of hierarchy and explicitly rule-governed behavior" (Sewell 1998, 408). Such postbureaucratic structures and methods typically exist within or alongside bureaucratic ones (Fournier 1999), but this alliance may be rather uneasy (Hodgson 2004).

---

[7] An hourglass-shaped wage spread does not necessarily mean that skills have been polarized in the same pattern, for at least two reasons: First, skill and pay are not perfectly correlated (although they tend to be positively related); second, "skill" is a socially constructed measure, while "pay" is an objectively measurable one. In addition, the hourglass economy has not been found in all nations or all sectors within nations. Anderson (2009) finds that in the United Kingdom, male pay rates are hourglass-shaped, while women's display a more traditional, "pyramid" shape.

These post-Taylorist, post-Fordist, and postbureaucratic practices are said to empower workers by giving them more control over work processes and working conditions. However, some see these new forms as representing "the transformation of people issuing from the same capitalist need as the transformation of other production inputs" (Lewis 2007, 402). They can serve as new, disguised forms of control through identity shaping; they are the "Trojan horse" by which management delivers control in the guise of participation (Yates, Lewchuk, and Stewart 2001).

Management control over knowledge-centric skills may be more difficult to achieve than over manual ones. However, researchers (e.g., Gutek 1995a; Hecht 2001) and popular press accounts (e.g., Fraser 2001) have demonstrated that white-collar work also has been increasingly deskilled, intensified, and surveilled.

Worker Resistance

Braverman (1974) sees the worker as an inert object of hegemonic management control. Many have criticized this view as deterministic and have taken pains to locate the "missing subject"—the worker. Michael Burawoy (1979) shows how management achieves control through gaining workers' consent, and others (e.g., Edwards 1979; Friedman 1977) stress the importance of considering worker resistance. Control and resistance have come to be conceptualized as part of a symbiotic process that is constantly being enacted on a "frontier" of mutually reinforcing behavior between managers and employees (Edwards 1990, 130). Thus, put simply, "control is the outcome of struggle" (Gottfried 1994, 105). Workers are not passive recipients of employer rules; rather, they are constantly "adapting, interpreting and challenging those rules, in part because they are orienting their conduct to a conception of informal norms, and in part because it is a product of a relationship—albeit unequal" (Ackroyd and Thompson 1999, 29). Worker resistance in turn shapes management response, which leads to new or altered types of resistance.

Conflicts between employer and employee can be conceptualized in four different realms: work output, time, product, and identity (Ackroyd and Thompson 1999). Within each of these spheres, employers make demands while employees attempt to "appropriate" more of that sphere to themselves. Employee resistance also can be classified as either formal or informal, and either type can be individual or collective. Formal types of resistance include strikes, grievances, and worker protests. Informal resistance has a myriad of forms, including sabotage, absenteeism, resignation, noncooperation, humor, "bitching,"[8] and even violence. The specific forms that control and resistance take are shaped by the organization of the work process, its physical location, and relative access of the various parties to information. Patterns of control and resistance may lead to the formation of particularistic employee "subcultures" that differ in material ways from the "management culture" (see Ackroyd and Thompson 1999). Thus, patterns of employee behavior—including resistance—can become quite entrenched and self-perpetuating.

Many have noted (and some have bemoaned) the decline of collective, formal employee resistance, and some even have gone as far as to suggest the "end" of employee dissent, citing a number of external and internal factors. External factors include increasing competition causing the restructuring of labor markets, the shift from manufacturing to services and from blue-collar to white-collar work, increasing use of contingent labor, and state regulation that has become opposed to organized labor (Ackroyd and Thompson 1999). Internal factors include postbureaucratic management practices that attempt to align workers' views with those of management, thus obviating dissent. Within this framework, some see both individualized and informal resistance as inferior, reactive, accommodative behavior that seeks only to adapt to management rules rather than to fundamentally change them. However, a rich body of work is developing on "everyday acts of resistance," which shows that even in the most stringent work environments, employees can exert at least some degree of autonomy in the employment relationship (Ackroyd and Thompson 1999; Tucker 1993). For example, workers can resist direct attempts at control through work limitation, relying on the "hidden knowledge" they have acquired about work processes (Kusterer 1978).[9]

---

[8] Complaining to other employees about management or the work process in general is, of course, a time-honored practice. In one study, undergraduate students were surveyed about how they dealt with complaints involving their employment (Tucker 1993). The most common mechanism, reported by half of the respondents, involved discussing their complaints with others, usually coworkers. James Tucker (1993, 31) views complaining (which he labels "gossip") as a form of informal resistance—"a type of settlement behavior," where employers are tried for their wrongs *in absentia*. Tucker found that these student employees rarely took the problem up with their employers after discussing it with someone else. Thus, it appears that gossip served the function of a "safety valve," providing employees an outlet for their frustration while sparing them the risk of confronting their employers. It is also possible that fellow employees served as a sounding board, encouraging employees to drop complaints they thought lacked validity or significance.

[9] Work limitation is one type of employee resistance that has been studied at length. Stephen Ackroyd and Paul Thompson (1999, 26) write that "[w]ork limitation is in many ways an obvious recourse for people because they retain degrees of control over their activities at work,

They may also resist ideological control by resorting to humor or cynicism.[10] However, much informal and individual worker resistance is difficult to locate and assess because it is hidden from public view, and even if it is observed, it can appear ambiguous. For example, the same employee behavior can be perceived by different viewers as either "resistance" or merely "coping" (Prasad and Prasad 2000). Thus, identifying and evaluating informal resistance requires some familiarity with the workplace and the employee subculture. Participant-observer methods provide one way of gaining a nuanced perspective of worker behaviors and group dynamics (Tope et al. 2005).

Thirty-five years after the publication of Braverman's *Labor and Monopoly Capital*, debates continue about skill, control, and resistance in the workplace. Given all the competing theories and evidence surrounding Braverman's legacy, one author finds the research at an impasse, with "roughly equal proportions of persuasive work/skills research demonstrating that disempowerment and resistance occur, new forms of technological and socioemotional control occur, rising educational requirements and attainments continues [*sic*] to occur, de-skilling occurs, and up-skilling occurs—all with little agreement as to their inter-relations" (Sawchuk 2006, 594).

The challenge to understanding work in the twenty-first century is to reconcile these contradictions. This would involve delineating the ways that opposing trends are simultaneously occurring, and exploring differential outcomes through testing a host of macroeconomic and situational variables, including patterns of stratification (e.g., race, gender, education) and state

---

however tightly their work is specified or closely their activities regulated." One type of work limitation is "soldiering," a term coined by Frederick Taylor (1911) in his famous study of the Midvale Steel Works. Taylor believed that workers naturally choose to perform their tasks at the slowest speed they can get away with. He observed employees deliberately slowing down work while at the same time hiding their knowledge about work processes from management, thus limiting the ability of managers to even diagnose the work limitation as a problem. Taylor interpreted soldiering behavior as rational—not for the purpose of raising wages or serving other employee interests, but rather as a response to inefficient or unplanned management action. Thus, Taylor thought that soldiering would stop once management had learned and applied scientific principles. Taylor, of course, failed to realize the myriad other reasons why employees might want to regulate the flow of work.

[10] Gideon Kunda (1992) describes attempts by a U.S. computer company to impose a new set of corporate values. Middle managers resisted these attempts through humor, parody, and irony. However, and as an interesting illustration of the dialectic of control/resistance, upper management co-opted these efforts, redefining them as evidence that management valued the open expression of disagreement.

interventions (or lack thereof).[11] It would also require consideration of an additional factor—the decline in workers' security.

Is Temporary Work Particularly Degraded?

When Braverman wrote of the degradation of work, he did not focus much on employment insecurity. (One exception is his description of the "reserve army of labor," a segment of the working population that possesses few skills and is irregularly employed.) This lack of attention is understandable because the United States was still experiencing relatively high levels of job security in the early 1970s. However, various measures of security have declined significantly since then. One such indicator is a rise in temporary and other nonstandard employment.

Increase in Temporary Employment

Throughout the nineteenth century and into the Great Depression, work was relatively insecure for most American workers. Wages were unstable and benefits were uncommon (Edwards 1979), and there were few legal protections for workers (Jacoby 1985). The 1930s ushered in a wide range of worker protections including unemployment insurance, the right to collective bargaining, and minimum wage laws. From the 1940s through the 1970s, there was a period of relative employment stability and security, particularly for unionized labor and middle-class white-collar workers. Large organizations made use of "internal labor markets," whereby entry-level employees were hired, trained, and then promoted to fill vacancies. This resulted in minimal churning of employees (Stone 2007). The norm was the "standard employment arrangement," where work was done on a fixed schedule at the employer's

---

[11] Such an effort also would involve addressing some of the theoretical challenges involved in defining skill, and the methodological difficulties in measuring it (see Form 1987). Paul Adler (2007) identifies autonomy and complexity as the components of skill. However, Braverman (1974) recognizes that "skill" is a social construction and thus cannot be objectively measured, a point that others have continued to forcefully make (e.g., Littler 1982). Perceptions of "skilled" work are gender-bound, tending to favor traditionally male work over traditionally female work (Phillips and Taylor 1980), and also class-bound, neglecting to account for the "hidden knowledge" or "tacit skill" contained in the most apparently basic work (see Kusterer 1978; Peña 1996). Measuring skill also presents challenges. Using job categories such as "professionals" as a proxy for higher skill can be misleading (Fleming, Harley, and Sewell 2004). Using education as a proxy can be similarly problematic because skill resides in the job and not in the worker (Lewis 2007).

place of business and with an expectation of continued employment (Kalleberg 2000).[12]

Beginning in the 1970s, global competition, rapid technological change, and shifting markets created greater uncertainty. Businesses were encouraged to adopt new flexible forms such as the "core/periphery" framework, whereby key functions are performed in-house and the remaining functions are externalized (Atkinson 1985). While there is debate regarding the extent to which such new organizational structures were implemented, there is little question that businesses were successful in shifting more risk onto workers (Stone 2007). One result was a sharp increase in nonstandard work arrangements, which grew at an annual rate of 11 percent from 1972 to 1998 (Kalleberg 2000). By 1995, only 65 percent of American workers were employed in a standard full-time job (Kalleberg, Reskin, and Hudson 2000), less than 20 percent of U.S. employers used only full-time workers, and more than half used some sort of staffing intermediary for at least some work (Kalleberg, Reynolds, and Marsden 2003). The use of temporary workers has become a central personnel strategy for many businesses (Nollen 1996). Some employers continuously employ the same "temporary" workers for many years, and such workers may make up a substantial percentage of total personnel. For example, temporary workers at Microsoft at one time accounted for approximately 40 percent of the employees at its headquarters (*Washington Post* 2000).[13]

While some workers seek out nonstandard work for its flexibility or other perceived benefits, it is clear that most part-time and temporary workers are

---

[12] "Nonstandard" work, then, lacks any or all of these components. It can involve use of independent contractors, temporary direct-hire, temporary agency-hire, and contract workers, or some combination of these (Kalleberg 2000).

[13] Claims about the current "age of insecurity" should be carefully considered because there is a tendency to see the current moment as a pivotal one (see Nuñes 2007). Some believe that employment insecurity is just a "moral panic" (see Heery and Salmon 2000) or an overblown "nightmare" scenario (Fevre 2007) concocted by social scientists with little objective basis. For example, the apparent growth in temporary employment may be explained by businesses' greater reliance on agency temporaries rather than on direct-hire temporaries; thus, the numbers reflect a shift, not a growth (Polivka 1996). Some believe that the growth in temporary workers was real, but was itself temporary (see Green 2007). Others point out the variation in insecurity across particular sectors and occupations (du Gay 2004). However, most others (e.g., Crain 2004) recognize that while there may be quibbles about particularized effects, the overall evidence of a decline in security is quite substantial. It can be seen across a host of factors, such as the increase in nonstandard employment, a decline in the size and power of unions, the elimination of defined-benefit pension plans, greater job "churning," and widespread downsizing and layoffs.

in such arrangements involuntarily (e.g., Cohany 1998; Golden 1996; Golden and Appelbaum 1992; Tilly 1996). Thus, the growth in temporary and other nonstandard employment is best explained by its benefits to employers. Through externalizing employment, firms experience three types of flexibility: (1) numerical (using temporary, part-time, or contract workers for peak-period staffing), (2) financial (reducing overhead costs for administration and worker benefits), and (3) functional (temporarily tapping special expertise that is not regularly needed) (Broschak, Davis-Blake, and Block 2008). In addition, employers can test-drive potential employees without the risks that a longer-term promise contains. They also can shift unpleasant work to noncore workers, thus maintaining morale among their core workers (Parker 1994).

Arguably, the increase in nonstandard work also has been encouraged by changes in labor laws designed to protect permanent employees (Lee 1996), as well as by the increasing costs of providing benefits such as health care (Magnum, Mayall, and Nelson 1985). In addition, the temporary help services industry itself appears to have been a key player in creating demand for its services, as well as in heading off legislation that could constrain its growth (Gonos 1997, 2001; Ofstead 1999; Parker 1994). Vicki Smith and Esther Neuwirth (2008) detail the ways that temporary agencies sold the ideal of the "good temp" (compliant, efficient, capable) to potential employers and to prospective temporary workers, much as a business would market any new product. Thus, the growth in temporary employment is "not the result of inexorable economic forces, but rather the mobilization of well-organized political forces" (Stone et al. 2006, 235).

The Qualities and Effects of Temporary Employment

Is *non*standard work necessarily *sub*standard? This question is difficult to answer in the abstract because nonstandard employment is highly heterogeneous. For example, independent business consultants who apply advanced skill sets and command high pay surely have very different work experiences, attitudes, and behaviors compared to day laborers or clerical temporaries. Thus, it is important to distinguish between the various forms that nonstandard work can take. Temporary work, particularly agency temporary work, tends to be associated with a high number and greater intensity of "bad job" characteristics. Jackie Krasas Rogers (2000, 5) asks whether it is the "temporary" or the "work" that makes it so bad. The answer seems to be "both."

Certainly, the quality of temporary *work* tends to be particularly degraded—deskilled, fragmented, and intensified—as compared to work performed in standard employment. Fragmentation of work occurs both spatially and functionally. Spatial fragmentation occurs when temporary workers are physically placed to have little interaction with each other and with standard workers (Gottfried 1994). Through task fragmentation, assignments are unbundled and given to temporary workers, resulting in tasks that are simple and narrowly prescribed, allow little autonomy, and prevent the temporary worker from having an overview of the total work process. In addition, this task unbundling allows the more unpleasant, monotonous, or (sometimes) dangerous tasks to be reserved for the temporary worker. Because much temporary work has been simplified and fragmented, it is also intensified and thus can be more easily supervised and controlled: It is easier to place a quota on typing one hundred letters or filing one hundred documents than to put output demands on a multitasking employee, particularly if that employee is involved in creative tasks. In his interviews with temporary clerical workers, Kevin Henson (1996, 95) found that "much of the job has been so routinized that one can tell from observing (or listening) to a temp whether the temp is actually working, or how hard they're working."

The *temporary* nature of the work also leads to "bad job" qualities. Employers do not need to offer loyalty incentives; thus, temporary workers earn less pay and receive fewer benefits such as health insurance and pension plans (Kalleberg, Reskin, and Hudson 2000). They receive little or no training (Nollen 1996; Dale and Bamford 1988), and there are few opportunities for advancement. While some temporary workers are able to transition to a standard job within the same organization (see Broschak, Davis-Blake, and Block 2008), ethnographic studies (Henson 1996; Rogers 2000) indicate that low-skilled temporary work typically does not provide an easy stepping-stone to permanent employment, and if a worker *is* offered a permanent position, it is likely doing the same routinized work he or she had been doing as a temporary employee.

One might assume that these "bad job" aspects of temporary work would contribute to a number of direct and indirect negative effects for workers. Temporary workers might be expected to have more job stress, less organizational commitment, less job satisfaction, and poorer well-being than workers in standard arrangements. Temporary workers also might experience broader "employment strain" from "the constant search for new employment, the effort to keep employment, the need to ensure a positive employer assessment of work performance and, for some workers, the effort to balance demands from multiple job holdings and multiple employers" (De Cuyper et al. 2008, 29). However, a recent review of the literature indicates that findings have been inconsistent, with studies (mostly in Europe) indicating temporary workers are variously worse off, better off, or no different when compared to workers in standard jobs, on a number of outcome variables (De Cuyper et al. 2008).[14]

Notwithstanding this divergence in findings, temporary employment clearly is associated with characteristics of "bad jobs" and has negative effects on at least a significant subset of temporary workers. The fact that a high percentage of temporary workers are "involuntary" is further cause for concern. In addition, the growth of temporary work has pernicious social outcomes. Women and ethnic and racial minorities are more likely to be performing low-wage, low-skilled temporary work (Kalleberg, Reskin, and Hudson 2000). The potential collective organization of temporary workers is limited due to both an absence of legal protections and the social fragmentation of the work. Laws that allow temporary agencies to be the legal ("de jure") employer of temporary workers suppress those workers' wages because of the "cut" that the agency receives from the client, typically 30 to 40 percent of the amount the client pays the agency for the worker's services (Gonos 2001).

Ethnographic studies of low-skilled temporary work clearly show the significant negative subjective effects on workers, including stigmatization and alienation. For example, Henson (1996, 98) studied temporary clerical employees and found that temporary work "frequently did not satisfy workers' needs for meaningful employment." This is because the work has been so routinized and deskilled that the temporary worker gains neither satisfaction from its completion nor any connection to the larger project or to the organization. Temporary workers also face considerable stigma about their abilities, intelligence, and commitment. They are seen as being "flaky and simple tasks are overexplained" (p. 148). They are depersonalized and often referred to as "the temp." The source of this differential treatment is located

---

[14] This multiplicity of findings likely has a variety of causes. For example, insecurity in temporary work is assumed to lead to lower job satisfaction; however, it may be that workers in *standard* arrangements would be more affected by insecurity because their "psychological contract" would be violated (Nolan, Wichert, and Burchell 2000). The lack of consensus also may be explained by the heterogeneity of temporary work. For example, some temporary workers have a clear opportunity to move into a standard work arrangement; thus they may adopt attitudes and performance patterns similar to those of standard workers, perhaps because of "anticipatory socialization" into the organization (Broschak, Davis-Blake, and Block 2008). Temporary workers who are highly skilled and experience high autonomy—"free agents"—also might be expected to fare better on various outcomes. One study (Kunda, Barley, and Evans 2002) finds such workers to be more satisfied with their incomes, but also to experience significant anxiety about locating work.

within the nature of temporary work itself, but the deviant label also arises from gender-laden assumptions about the temporary worker.[15]

Developing a coherent and stable identity in such an insecure work context would appear to be difficult. Researchers have found that workers in nonstandard work arrangements can develop work-based identities, particularly if they are performing skilled work (Van Wijk and Leisink 2004; Westenholz 2004). However, the work identity of temporary clerical workers seems to be formed mostly in opposition to the stigma that is attached to the work (Henson 1996; Rogers 2000).

Control and Resistance in Temporary Employment

The structure of temporary work provides special challenges to, but also unique opportunities for, employee resistance. As discussed previously, temporary work is highly fragmented. Employees are typically scattered geographically and placed individually at work sites. Thus, the potential for formal collective action—such as strikes or other organized protest—is severely limited (Gottfried 1994; Henson 1996). In addition, the stigmatized nature of temporary work militates against employees identifying with the role and seeking to protect its status (Rogers 2000). Most temporary workers—including the attorneys I interviewed—are well aware of their "second-class" status. Some types of informal resistance employed by standard workers may also be unavailable. Quitting or complaining are perceived by the temporary worker to be futile (because the worker is easily replaced) or even self-defeating (because workers may harm their chances for future assignments). Other acts of individual resistance such as absenteeism or tardiness also are not effective because the temporary worker is only paid for actual time at work.

The dispersion and isolation of temporary workers usually benefits both the agency and the employer. For example, temporary workers may be unable to absorb group norms on work restriction (Gottfried 1994). At the same time, the dispersion of workers creates challenges to control because the agency cannot directly observe the worker. Thus, agencies have developed

---

[15] Kevin Henson (1996, 27) finds that temporary workers in placement agency literature are described through gendered categories including the "gregarious grandma" and the "chipper coed." In the media, a temporary employee may be gender-stereotyped as a "vixen" or a "ditz" (pp. 28–29). The implication is that primarily women are interested in temporary work, and that they take on the work for "extra" money. Jackie Krasas Rogers (2000, 132) also uncovers a highly gendered depiction of temporary work, beginning at least with "Rosie the Riveter," where temporary work is feminized and portrayed "as supplemental to a male 'permanent' income."

various control mechanisms, such as offering higher pay for better performance or promising return engagements (Henson 1996). Agencies also rely on more indirect methods of control, such as an appeal to professional norms in the case of skilled workers (see Peck and Theodore 1998), or discursive control through ideological indoctrination in the case of less-skilled workers (see Rogers 2000).

Another challenge to control lies in a unique aspect of temporary work that involves duality of control—the agency is the de jure employer while the client is the employer-in-fact. (With attorney temporaries, this becomes a four-part relationship involving the attorney, the law firm, the placement agency, and the law firm's corporate client.) Thus, both entities can exert control over the worker. Intensification of work seems an obvious outcome, and it might appear that opportunities for resistance would be limited. However, there is a tension inherent in this duality that involves a divergence of interests: the client wants to maximize work effort, while both the temporary agency and the worker want to maximize time at work (Gottfried 1994). This duality can be exploited by the temporary worker to extend assignments. Where temporary workers are placed together, the potential for group soldiering exists; where there is spatial fragmentation, individual soldiering also can occur. One study (Henson 1996) found that temporary workers rationed the flow of work while making sure to appear busy. Rogers (2000) found a similar phenomenon in her study of clerical temporaries. Since they could not predict the flow of work, some would do their own work, sleep, or "cruise" (work very quickly for a while, then take breaks).

Degradation and Insecurity in the Professions

The professions are different from other occupations in their public prestige, remuneration, credentialing, and degree of independence and autonomy. The professions of law and medicine stand out as the "purest" form of the professions, given their extensive use of peer review, lengthy education and training, and high proportion in self-employment. Professional services tend to be highly individualized, with their delivery tied to a specific time and place; thus, they would appear to be resistant to deskilling, management control, intensification, and commoditization. However, various social and economic factors have been combining to make professional work more like other employment. For example, insecurity appears to be increasing. Formerly independent professionals are being absorbed into bureaucratic organizations, subjecting them to the same risks of downsizing or externalizing that apply to other types of workers.

Nonstandard professional work arrangements are also on the rise. There are now a number of agencies that specialize in placing physicians in temporary positions (so-called "locum tenens" appointments). The field is small but growing—total billings were estimated to be $1.5 billion in 2005 (Skidmore 2006). The expansion of the legal temporary services industry has been even more significant; its origins and growth are discussed in some detail in Chapter 2.

Besides becoming more insecure, some professional work is also becoming degraded, deskilled, and intensified. Professionals are proletarianized as they are increasingly employed by large organizations, and their work is deprofessionalized as it becomes subject to the same drive for economic efficiency that characterized the shift from craft work to industrial work. These processes are likely to be as complex and uneven as the patterns of work degradation in other employment sectors. Some professionals likely will see upskilling, some deskilling, some will experience increased autonomy as part of a new "professional-managerial class," and others will find their jobs highly regimented.

Theories of Professionalization

There are two basic, competing views regarding professionalization, identified as "functionalist" and "revisionist" (Spangler and Lehman 1983). Functionalists define an occupation as a profession if it possesses certain characteristics such as extended formal training, autonomy, self-governance, and an ethical code. Functionalists believe the professions arose because scientific and technical expertise was needed by increasingly complex, rationalized societies (see Bell 1973). In this view, the professions are relatively immune from the degradation of work that Braverman (1974) outlines. Skill expropriation and standardization are unlikely because of the professions' monopoly, autonomy, and possession of specialized and abstract knowledge. In fact, some have predicted that the professions will expand and achieve even greater dominance in the "postindustrial" society (Bell 1973) because capitalism requires constant innovation that originates in large part in the work of professionals and other knowledge workers (see Adler 2007). Thus, professionals will thrive because they are needed.[16]

---

[16] Over the last several decades various occupational groups have increasingly sought to claim the status of "profession" (see, e.g., Pulskamp 2005, discussing computer programmers). However, their lack of autonomy, monopoly, or both, renders claims to professional status rather hollow (see Wilensky 1964).

Revisionists reject the notion that there is anything inherently unique about the professions that separates them from other occupations, and they seek to demystify professional knowledge, authority, and status. Marie Haug (1975, 211) asks: "What then is the difference between a plumber and a urologist?" Her answer: "Both require training, both deal with pipes. Neither works for nothing." Revisionists do not define a profession in terms of static qualities but rather advocate a "professional dominance model." This historical and process-based view emphasizes that the professions were active in developing a monopoly over their services (or, in Eliot Freidson's [1994] term, a "market shelter"), sometimes even before they had developed *effective* services.[17] The professions must constantly work to protect their monopoly from encroachment by other groups—Carol Kronus (1976) terms this "boundary maintenance." The professions also have been successful in reserving autonomy in the way their monopolized services are performed and delivered. "Autonomy" refers to collective freedom from outside interests dictating the form and content of professional work, as well as autonomy of the individual to work in his or her own way. Revisionists question whether autonomy is truly a necessary component of professional work, or if it is simply a privilege that comes with professional power (see Larson 1977). Another difference is that while functionalists believe the professions serve the greater good by providing needed public services, revisionists believe that professional monopolies may sometimes harm both public and professional interests, for example, by stifling innovation (Timmermans 2008).

Within the revisionist view, three relatively distinct theories have emerged: *re*professionalization, *de*professionalization, and proletarianization. These claims are not entirely new,[18] and they are not limited to the legal

---

[17] Crain (2004, 549) distinguishes between three potential types of monopoly control: economic monopoly (over "recruitment, training and credentialing"), political monopoly ("over areas of expertise"), and administrative monopoly ("over determining what standards shall apply to practitioners"). The legal profession exercises all three.

[18] Sociologists since Durkheim have been "intrigued" with professional work (Haug 1975, 198), including claims of its demise. Within the law, such concerns have occurred in several cycles (see Nelson and Trubek 1992, 177–78). John Heinz and associates (2005, ii) quote an author who wrote in 1905 that lawyers were more part of "the great organized system of industrial and financial enterprise" than members "of a distinct professional class." Similarly, Harlan Stone wrote more than seventy-five years ago: "The rise of big business has produced an inevitable specialization of the Bar. The successful lawyer of our day more often than not is the proprietor of a new type of factory, whose legal product is increasingly the result of mass production methods" (in Katherine Stone 2004, 6–7). These concerns seem quaint in light of the current and potential application of information technology to legal work, discussed briefly in this chapter and explored in more detail in Chapter 7.

profession.[19] The first predicts rather subtle shifts, while the other two portend major disruptions that include the degradation of professional work, echoing at least to some extent Braverman's thesis. Those who advocate reprofessionalization acknowledge that the professions are changing, but assert that their core aspects will stay largely intact for two main reasons: (1) the professions will continue to exploit their control over expert knowledge that others need but do not have (a difference Talcott Parsons [1970] refers to as the "competence gap"), and (2) professional organizations are highly resilient and possess significant social power to maintain their monopoly and autonomy. Freidson (2001) suggests that greater bureaucratization will lead to further stratification of the professions and the ascent of a professional-managerial class that will serve as a point of contact between corporate and professional interests. He suggests this process will strengthen professionals' hold on both monopoly and autonomy.

Others predict less-significant changes, in such aspects as "opportunity structure, the terms and loci of employment, and salaries" (Anleu 1992, 200). Generally, authors such as Eliot Freidson and Sharon L. Roach Anleu see the professions as having a great deal of control in crafting responses to changing market and regulatory conditions; regardless of the specifics, they see reprofessionalization as defensive adaptation, never co-optation (e.g., Muzio and Ackroyd 2005). For example, some (e.g., Adler, Kwon, and Heckscher 2008) predict that professionals will resist certain aspects of rationalization by turning to more collaborative forms of organization.

The deprofessionalization hypothesis suggests that a variety of structural and cultural factors will combine to seriously erode the monopoly and autonomy of professional work. These include increased competition between professions, the diffusion and routinization of expert knowledge, a decline in public trust, absorption of professionals into bureaucratic organizations, government deregulation, and less solidarity caused by intensified intraprofessional stratification. Haug (1975) predicts that technology will combine with an educated, increasingly skeptical populace to more broadly allocate expert medical knowledge.[20] Robert Rothman (1984) foresees deprofessionalization

---

[19] Deprofessionalization concerns have been raised in nearly every professional or quasi-professional category, including physicians (McKinlay and Arches 1985), teachers (Filson 1988), college professors (Krier and Staples 1993), and social workers (Carey 2007). The issue also has been raised regarding various occupations that have struggled to be recognized as professions, including law enforcement (Sharp 1982).

[20] Scholars continue to debate the extent of deprofessionalization among physicians. Most seem to agree that fundamental shifts are occurring in medicine, such as changes in technology, in physician self-employment, in government regulation, and in the rise of rationalized practice norms such as "evidence-based medicine" (see Timmermans 2008). However, there is

of the law caused by increasing competition among legal services providers, the demystification of legal knowledge, and advances in technology.

The proletarianization argument suggests that professionals will slowly lose autonomy, status, and reward as they are absorbed into large bureaucratic organizations (see Oppenheimer 1973). Charles Derber (1983) refines this view by distinguishing between two types of proletarianization—ideological and technical. Technical proletarianization—the type emphasized by Braverman (1974) and discussed above—involves workers losing control over the *means* of work (i.e., their skills). This occurred to craft workers under industrialization. Conversely, ideological proletarianization is a process by which workers lose control over the *ends* of their labor—the uses to which their labor is put. This results in a "powerlessness to choose or define the final product of one's work, its disposition on the market and its uses in the larger society, and the values or social policy of the organization which purchases one's labor" (Derber 1983, 313). Drawing on Stephen Marglin's (1975) historical analysis, Derber writes that ideological proletarianization happened to skilled workers first through the "putting out" system whereby merchants took control of the market for products produced by skilled labor, and even of the final form of the finished product. However, the worker maintained control over the *means* of the work for some time after. It was only through the factory that technical control over the means of labor was achieved.

There appears to be broad agreement that professionals are experiencing ideological proletarianization because of their increasing employment within hierarchical organizations.[21] Derber (1983) finds this troubling because professionals can be reduced to mere technicians whose work is drained of freedom, creativity, and a connection to the larger community. At the same time, he

---

disagreement as to the likely outcome. Some see proletarianization and deprofessionalization as inevitable outcomes (e.g., McKinlay and Arches 1985; Ritzer and Walczak 1988). Others (e.g., Filc 2006; Pickard 2009) predict a reprofessionalization and further stratification of the profession. Law appears to be somewhat better equipped than medicine to resist standardization. First, even though medicine also involves confidential services, it leaves a more public "trail" because of third-party billing. Second, there is a greater emphasis on development of a single "standard of care" for particular diagnoses, and thus, governmental entities, consumer interest groups, and professional bodies can more easily facilitate standardization.

[21] Physicians and attorneys always have been much more commonly self-employed than members of other professions, and therefore have been referred to as the "free professions" (Gerth and Mills 1946). Thus, a tendency toward more bureaucratic employment would affect the autonomy of these two groups most significantly. However, even among those professions with a history of organizational employment (such as architects and university teachers), a greater "intensity" of bureaucracy (in terms of specialization and control) could also have significant effects on professional autonomy.

believes that technical proletarianization has not yet been realized because professionals continue to maintain control over the *means* by which their expert knowledge is applied. He sees two potential future outcomes: In the first, professionals will continue their current bargain with management, ceding ideological control in return for technical control. In the second, management will successfully appropriate and control expert skills; such "technical proletarianization may be introduced with surprising speed in the coming decades" (p. 316).

Rethinking Deprofessionalization and Proletarianization

Whether reprofessionalization, deprofessionalization, or proletarianization is occurring has obvious implications for professionals' identity, autonomy, quality of work, remuneration, and job satisfaction. It also may have profound social effects. Professionals play a role in generating and diffusing innovation and contribute to the general welfare of society (Adler, Kwon, and Heckscher 2008). Some professional work contains a public service component, and this could be altered or "hijacked" by other interests, to social detriment. Notwithstanding these ramifications, there has been an apparent decline in interest in this area in recent years. This book is in part intended to reenergize this debate. This section addresses three factors that have been explored in prior theory but rarely have been fully realized in their potential future implications, especially for legal practitioners.

The Corporatization of Law Practice

Historically, the dominant form of organization for attorneys was the solo practice, and the legal profession was relatively stable. Beginning in the 1970s, a number of factors—including the complexity of the legal and regulatory environment, competition, technological change, and globalization—led more attorneys into law firms, as well as into government service. Law firms dramatically increased in size and complexity. By 1987, Baker and McKenzie became the first law firm to employ 1,000 attorneys. By 2008, it had 3,627 lawyers, while another megafirm, DLA Piper Rudnick, became the largest firm, with 3,785 attorneys (*National Law Journal* 2008). Baker and Mackenzie also was the first firm to reach $1 billion in annual billings, in 2001; by 2007, there were ten additional firms in that category.[22] Law firms

---

[22] While large corporate law firms such as Baker and McKenzie are quite large, they employ a relatively small percentage of the total number of licensed attorneys in the United States. However, their influence is felt beyond their numbers. Their practices "trickle down" to smaller firms, they tend to represent the largest corporate clients, they hire from the most

increasingly began to resemble the corporations they served—employing nonlawyer managers, outsourcing their noncore functions, and downsizing when faced with reduced demand, such as during recessions (Gross-Glaser 1990).[23] During periods of growth, they competed for the best law school graduates; salaries increased nearly tenfold from 1969 to 1989 and then nearly doubled by 2007, reaching $160,000 (without bonuses). Firms' billing rates also increased at a pace faster than inflation, year after year.

Firms also changed their internal organization. For many years, they employed the "Cravath model," named for one of the first and premiere New York law firms, Cravath, Swaine, and Moore. The Cravath model involves two tiers of attorneys—equity partners and associates. The equity partners have an ownership interest in the firm, and the associates march, lockstep, on a "track" toward eventual partnership. (If associates are not voted in as partners, they are asked to leave the firm.) The partners' income is supported by "leveraging" of associates, ideally more than one associate per partner. The associates together produce more revenue than the partner but are paid significantly less, thus supporting the partner's higher income. This model could not hold as firms ballooned in size; thus, firms began to create additional hierarchies, adding non-equity partners, "of counsel" attorneys, staff attorneys, and senior attorneys.[24] It also became much more common

---

"elite" law school students, and they are frequently profiled by the media and thus shape public expectations (Johnson and Coyle 1990). Many observers therefore believe these large corporate law firms hold disproportionate influence in their ability to shape policy. Many of them also commonly utilize temporary legal help, another reason for a particular focus here on their practices.

[23] Notwithstanding their size, income, power, and increasingly corporate organization, prohibitions remain on the public ownership of law firms in the United States and many other nations. However, in 2007, an Australian law firm became one of the first to offer public stock (see Susskind 2008).

[24] Non-equity partners earn a salary rather than own shares in the partnership, but they are allowed a vote on management issues. Senior attorneys are ex-associates who were not asked to become partners (perhaps because they were not considered sufficient rainmakers), but are asked to stay on as salaried attorneys because they offer useful skills to the firm. Staff attorneys are junior attorneys who are hired to perform specific and limited types of work such as project management or litigation support. They are not considered associates and thus have no potential to become partners. Of counsel attorneys are neither associates nor partners, but are otherwise affiliated with the firm in one of several ways permitted by an ethics ruling from the American Bar Association (1990). They may wish to work part-time or may have retired from the firm but want to maintain a connection with it. The status also may be conferred on attorneys who are brought in laterally with the expectation that they will soon become partners, but of counsel attorneys also may occupy positions between associate and partner, with no expectation of advancement.

for partners and associates to decamp to other firms, sometimes taking entire practice groups (and clients) with them.

The effect of these changes has been debated. For example, most seem to agree that more bureaucracy in law firms decreases ideological autonomy because each individual attorney has less power to influence the organization's direction, focus, and engagement with clients and other groups. However, the effect upon technical autonomy is less clear. Some (e.g., Harrison 1994) point out that an organization's structural form (such as bureaucracy) does not translate neatly into a prescribed set of work practices, especially where professional work is involved. Enhanced division of labor (such as in legal specialization) may mean gaining and using more esoteric knowledge, not deskilling and loss of autonomy. More hierarchy may mean an enhanced need to coordinate with others, but still may leave attorneys relatively free to design the timing and process of their work (Anleu 1992).

However, others claim that bureaucracy is ultimately a form of control. It is "softer" than scientific management and thus may appear to be a set of neutral rules, yet it tends to subtly shape individual behavior toward organizational objectives (Derber 1982) and therefore has negative effects on professionalism (see Freidson 2001; Liecht and Fennell 1997). It also may lead to a loss in collegiality and an intensification of work. Marion Crain (2004) notes that as firms became larger, annual billable hour requirements increased from a mean of 1,100 in 1950 to 1,900 in 2000. Factors such as these are blamed for the decline in lawyers' work satisfaction that has been found in some studies (see summary in Johnstone 2008, 741n15), but not others (e.g., National Association for Law Placement 2004). Associates who work for large firms are particularly dissatisfied with the intellectual challenge of their work. This may be because they take on more responsibility at a slower pace than at smaller firms; also, it may be because attorneys hired by large firms have higher expectations and therefore are more susceptible to frustration and discontent (see Sterling, Dinovitzer, and Garth 2007).

While bureaucracy itself may not reduce technical autonomy, it can provide the necessary *framework* for the regimentation and standardization of work when combined with technology, management practices, or client demands. For example, public sector lawyers experience more standardization of work because of increased hierarchy and required application of lengthy, elaborate rules (e.g., Eisenstein 1978). This is perhaps expected from the "heavy hand" of government; however, decreased technical autonomy also can occur in private lawyers' work when market pressures combine with advances in technology.

Efficiency Pressures

Competition in legal services began to increase in the 1970s. Law experienced some erosion of its borders as nonattorneys began to perform some law-related services. For example, realtors in some states won the right to draft property transfer documents (Rothman 1984). Competition between attorneys also intensified. In separate opinions, the U.S. Supreme Court struck down limits on law firm advertising and on fixed-fee arrangements. Opening up competition among attorneys, or between attorneys and other professional groups, theoretically could have driven down fees, which in turn could have forced law firms to be more efficient, leading to greater standardization. However, the areas of practice most affected by increased competition involved consumer legal services, which were already relatively standardized. Thus, for some, the lasting importance of these rulings is that the Supreme Court for the first time clearly labeled law as "commerce" and therefore made it subject to the same freedoms and limits that apply to the buying and selling of nonprofessional goods and services.

A much more significant pressure toward deprofessionalization in recent years has come from perhaps an unlikely source—the corporate client. The great majority of work done in private law practice is billed by the hour; at worst, this leads to overbilling and at best, it encourages inefficiency as firms repeatedly "reinvent the wheel" for each client facing similar issues (see Susskind 2008). Until recently, most clients had little leverage concerning billing issues because law firms usually have better information than clients about what sorts of resources legal matters require. However, this balance began to shift in the late 1980s. Legal fees rose dramatically, and corporate executives ordered their legal divisions to cut costs, much as they had required their other corporate divisions to do. Many in-house counsel previously had worked for private law firms and thus had insight into how cost savings could be achieved. Some corporations hired outside consultants to help them reduce their legal costs. Law firms cooperated with these measures because waves of corporate mergers left them with fewer available large clients.

These efforts took many forms. DuPont decreased the number of law firms it employed and required the remaining firms to institute a number of cost-cutting policies (*Metropolitan Corporate Counsel* 2002). General Electric farmed out some domestic legal work to its operations in India, saving $1.7 million per year (Reisenger 2003). Some of these savings were achieved by reducing technical autonomy, including more standardization. For example, Cisco Systems entered into a fixed-fee arrangement (rather than hourly billing) for all of its litigation. This forced its outside counsel to be more efficient and resulted in the hiring of temporary attorneys for some work (Susskind 2008). At the urging of their corporate counsel, firms began to adopt a variety of commoditizing practices, including the unbundling of legal services that is described in the following section. By the end of the 1980s, it was noted that even in large law firms "[p]ressures favoring conformity and assembly-like standardization are readily apparent" and work within law firms was becoming boring, dehumanized, routinized, and fragmented (Johnson and Coyle 1990, 397).

Technological Innovations: Unbundling and Multisourcing

Even among those who acknowledge that stratification, bureaucratization, and competition are reshaping aspects of professional work, there is a tendency to believe that professionals will not lose technical control. For example, Sharon Anleu (1992, 200), in considering legal practice in the United States and Australia, writes that "although professional employees are required to conform to organizational procedures and to coordinate work with other employees, they maintain exclusive control over their knowledge base, which preserves their autonomy and reduces managerial encroachments." Others similarly acknowledge that bureaucratization might lead to a narrower division of labor and thus to greater specialization, but not to deskilling.

However, these pronouncements and others like them make two related errors: First, they overstate the actual expertise involved in much professional work. Second, they assume that professional work is "unitary"—that it cannot be isolated into its constituent components, with the less-skilled parts reallocated to more-efficient and therefore cheaper labor. As to the first issue, many commentators (e.g., Susskind 2008) have pointed out that there is a great deal of mystification of legal work, through use of jargon and other means. In fact, a fair amount of legal work is rather rote and standardized. This includes various types of consumer law, such as wills, property transfers, uncontested divorces, and simple bankruptcies (see Derber 1983). Some of this work is even performed by franchise law firms in near "factory" settings, with legal secretaries doing much of the drafting of documents and lawyers seeing clients during fifteen-minute meetings (Van Hoy 1995). There is also much standardization of simple criminal matters, and the term "assembly line justice" has become a commonly used phrase (Wheeler and Wheeler 1980). However, it is not just in traditionally understood "commodity" legal work that one finds the potential for commoditization through standardization and routinization. Even the most complex legal process potentially can be unbundled; advances in information technology make this increasingly easy to do (Crain 2004).[25] Commoditization would obviously change the *form* of legal services, but it would also affect the *process* through which such services are delivered. For some, the attorney-client relationship would mutate from a professional one rooted in mutual trust to an "encounter relationship" based on speed, efficiency, and uniformity (see Gutek 1995b).

Conclusion

Paul Adler (2007) is not quite right when he claims that capitalism needs knowledge *workers*; rather, it simply needs their *knowledge*, just as industrialists needed craft workers' knowledge in designing more efficient means of production. Put another way, professionals possess a monopoly over knowledge that capital needs, and capital will find a way "to take measures to control and constrain that monopoly" (Crain 2004, 553), that is, by appropriating it for itself. Chapter 7 explores potential future applications of unbundling, multisourcing, and other deprofessionalizing practices while Chapters 2–6 describe in detail how unbundling currently is being widely deployed in document review and management.

Thus, it appears that the proper questions to ask are not whether work in general is deskilling or whether "law" is deprofessionalizing or proletarianizing, but *which aspects* of legal work are or are not, and *which lawyers* are likely to be most affected. We also might wonder how the legal profession is responding—and will likely respond—to the forces causing deprofessionalization. Thus far, individual law firms have been fairly reluctant to unbundle and multisource. This may be due to attorneys' well-documented risk aversion or simply to their protecting traditional income streams (Susskind 2008). At the same time, there has been little organized resistance. Perhaps some attorneys believe their practices are too complex and customized to ever be unbundled; others may feel they have little choice but to unbundle if their corporate clients insist on it. In any event, bar associations have permitted the use of offshore lawyers and temporary lawyers with few conditions, and have allowed nonlawyers to conduct legal research as long as a licensed attorney

---

[25] Of course, attorneys have long delegated work within their firms among partners, senior associates, and junior associates. More recently, attorneys have made more use of paralegals and highly skilled legal secretaries. This type of shared work is quite different in both quantity and kind from unbundling. Unbundling involves a much-heightened division of labor and may involve entities outside the firm delivering or coordinating services (e.g., through "multisourcing" [see Susskind 2008]). It is also quite different from outsourcing back-office functions like human resources, accounting, or photocopying, because it involves the delivery of core legal services.

prepares the actual court pleadings and provides the ultimate advice to the client.

It remains to be seen how much *individual* resistance will be encountered. The legal profession has largely relied on professional autonomy as a means of control. However, the unbundling of tasks has the potential to largely deskill the work through extreme standardization and routinization. Attorneys could become bored, frustrated, and resentful, and their professional identities could become eroded. This could be particularly true where the work is being done on a temporary basis, because attorneys' connection and commitment to the law firm and to the corporate client would be even more attenuated.

In such a setting, several questions arise: Will responsible autonomy be sufficient to control attorneys' labor? If not, must management more directly control work process and output, perhaps by taking advantage of the extreme division of labor and greater intensification of work inherent in unbundled tasks? Even if such controls are attempted, will attorneys find space for individual resistance, for example, by relying on the "hidden knowledge" that Kenneth Kusterer (1978) finds in even the most seemingly routinized labor? Finally, even if informal resistance occurs, will it really "matter"—is having *some* control over the flow and output of miserable work any kind of victory for a professional worker?

2

"Basically Interchangeable"

The Creation of the Temporary Lawyer

The temporary attorney industry began with a handful of one-person agencies in the 1980s in New York City and Washington, D.C., and it is now a national, $1.5 billion per year business. Law firms were initially resistant to using temporary attorneys, but their use is now widely accepted. Thus, of particular interest here is the marketing of the temporary lawyer, which involved both the legal press and placement agencies, whose apparent goal was to change the perception of the temporary attorney from "damaged goods" to a legitimate, professionalized category (Agger 1997; MacLachlan 2001). This process was quite similar to the way placement agencies have marketed the "good temp" in clerical temping (see Smith and Neuwirth 2008). However, one difference is that large corporations were also part of the "push" toward temporary lawyering because they were keen on reducing their legal fees. This marketing was occurring in the midst of economic and structural changes in law firms. Shifts in demand for legal services, an increase in the size and complexity of cases, technological change, and the growing size and bureaucratization of large law firms created conditions under which firms became more open to the use of temporary lawyers.

Temporary lawyering was presented in the legal press by both placement agencies and corporations as a "win-win" for lawyers and their employers, both of whom could gain greater flexibility and use temporary lawyering as a dry run toward permanent employment. Temporary attorney work was widely described as having a great deal of variety and allowing the learning of new skills. While the legal and popular press frequently depicted temporary lawyering as being largely driven by the lifestyle needs of individual attorneys, such claims often lacked both a logical and an empirical basis. It appears that—just as in other types of work—temporary lawyering arrangements largely benefit employers and staffing agencies. This finding is supported by data from my sample of temporary attorneys. Most of them reported that they were doing the work "involuntarily" and not for lifestyle reasons. Most of them also did not find the work flexible, interesting, challenging, or a stepping-stone to permanent employment.

The "Push" toward Temporary Lawyering

Before beginning a detailed discussion of the temporary attorney, it must be pointed out that attorneys have long been employed through various contingent work arrangements, whether on a temporary or a continuing contract basis.[1] Typically, two types of work are involved: The first, known as "overflow" work, occurs when a small firm or solo practitioner has more work than the firm can manage, so the firm hires an outside attorney and pays that attorney by the hour to complete the work. Many solo practitioners actively network to keep a steady supply of overflow work while they build their practices or sustain themselves during lean times. The other type of contingent lawyering involves "appearance work." Attorneys who are required to be in court for a hearing on one of their clients' matters, but have another conflicting obligation (or simply find it more economically advantageous) hire another attorney—again, usually a solo practitioner—to appear at the hearing on the client's behalf. In both cases, the contract attorney is paid a per-hour (or per-appearance) fee, which the originating attorney then bills to the client, sometimes directly as a "pass through" cost and sometimes with a markup. These practices are widespread and, in fact, there are some small law firms that cater only to other attorneys, rather than directly to clients (see Robinson 1996).

However, the kind of temporary lawyering that began to occur in the late 1980s was on a very different scale. It involved large law firms and major

---

[1] I have chosen the terms "temporary lawyers" or "temporary attorneys" throughout this book in order to differentiate between attorneys who work directly for small firms (whom I call "contract attorneys") and attorneys who work for firms through placement agencies (whom I refer to as "temporary attorneys" or "temporary lawyers"). I understand that there is a stigma associated with the term "temporary" (in fact, I avoided it when I was doing the work myself); however, the term is widely used and is more precise than other options. Later, in discussing the more specific work (known as "document review") that I and the other attorneys did, I use the term "project attorneys."

corporations, and resulted in an entire new subindustry in the temporary help field. Before the advent of temporary lawyering, many law firms had become accustomed to outsourcing their back-office, secretarial, or word processing functions. Beginning in the 1980s, firms began to unbundle even some of their core legal functions, to be completed more cheaply and efficiently by contingent workers. The following sections describe the origins of this new type of temporary lawyering and chart its course from initial resistance to generally widespread acceptance, or at least tolerance.[2]

"Kelly Girls" for Lawyers?

Demand for temporary lawyering was driven by a number of factors. Law firms utilized leaner staffing after some were forced to downsize following the 1987 stock market falloff; this left them unable to address large, temporary upswings in demand. The increasing size and complexity of cases, and a rise in corporate merger activity also contributed.[3] Temporary attorney placement agencies first began to form in the mid-1980s.[4] Four women attorneys, acting independently, were particularly involved in the formation of this market. In Washington, D.C., in 1984, Janis Goldman founded

---

[2] The sources cited in this chapter were located using the LexisNexis database (student edition) of all popular and legal press databases in the United States. The temporal span was from 1987 (the first mention of agency temporary lawyering that I located) through 2008. Search terms initially included combinations of various forms of the word "temporary" with the words "attorney" or "lawyer." Early searches using just these terms resulted in many thousands of irrelevant sources because "temporary" is a word often used in the law (e.g., "temporary restraining order," "temporary injunction"). Thus, the search that was ultimately employed used the initial terms plus "[not] injunction," which made it manageable while excluding an insignificant number of relevant articles.

[3] There was also an explosion in other categories of temporary legal personnel, especially paralegals. While this book concentrates on the temporary lawyer phenomenon, I note that many of the same factors fueled the rise in both employment categories.

[4] Temporary legal placement agencies operate similarly to those in other sectors. The agencies recruit attorneys through advertising or word of mouth and market themselves to law firms and corporations. They screen potential applicants, place them with firms for particular projects, and earn a fee as a percentage of the hourly wage paid to the temporary attorney. The amount these agencies charge their clients is a closely kept secret, just as it is in other sectors, and the agencies prohibit both law firms and temporary attorneys from discussing fees, compensation, and billing. However, it has been reported that agencies earn from 20 to 35 percent of the amount they bill the firm. Hourly rates vary extensively, depending on the legal expertise required. Temporary attorneys typically earn $20 to $35 per hour for document review (which constitutes the "bread and butter" for many placement agencies) and $50 and up for more specialized work.

Lawyer's Lawyer, Inc. and Rita Jensen created Law Clerk Temporaries.[5] In 1987, Shelley Wallace founded the Wallace Law Registry and Lesley Friedman formed Special Counsel, both firms initially serving the New York City market. Both Wallace and Friedman were quoted as saying they formed their agencies at least in part to provide opportunities for other women lawyers, particularly those with small children, who were having a difficult time reconciling their professional and personal lives (see Frey 1989). An article from the early days suggests that many of the first agencies' temporary lawyers were "new mothers or retired attorneys who don't want to stop working but need flexible, limited hours" (*Crain's New York Business* 1987). Temporary lawyering was seen as a way to allow women with small children the opportunity to "keep their feet wet" by participating part-time in legal practice. These early placement firms were even referred to, rather derisively, as "Kelly Girls for lawyers" (Cameron 1984; Scheffey 1995).

However, it quickly became apparent that temporary lawyering was not a panacea for overburdened new mothers. Lesley Friedman said in 1996 that most working mothers want regular, part-time, temporary work, but that she had "had only 'about three' jobs become solutions for the Supermom syndrome" (Scheffey 1996). She added: "In practice, employers want interim workers, but at a full-steam 40-plus-hours-per-week pace." One writer agreed in 1994 that "temping is not an outlet primarily for women trying to balance careers and a family" (Duncan 1994). These early placement firms also quickly discovered that new mothers were not the primary group looking for temporary work. In 1989, Shelley Wallace said that 75 percent of her applicants were "men who are either between jobs or want to pursue other interests, like writing" (Frey 1989). The recession and attendant layoffs had glutted the market with unemployed attorneys—of both sexes—who, unable to find associate positions, were willing to work on a temporary basis. It was apparent from statements by agency personnel that men made up a majority of temporary placements in the mid-1990s, and the head of one placement agency in Washington, D.C., said in 1999 that only 15 percent of his agency's temporaries were young mothers (Goldhaber 1999).

---

[5] Many believe that Janis Goldman's agency may have been the first. However, the District of Columbia Bar issued an ethics opinion in 1977 that cleared the way for a law referral agency to place attorneys in temporary assignments and then charge a fee (see Johnson and Coyle 1990). It is unclear whether this agency actually went into business or, if it did, whether it successfully placed any attorneys.

Initial Resistance

Large firms were at first reluctant to hire temporary attorneys, for several reasons. Law firms tend to be conservative and resistant to innovative practices. As a Motorola attorney said: "Once again, lawyers are simply behind the trend" (Scheffey 1995). There were also specific objections raised to temporary lawyering. First, there was a stigma associated with the temporary attorney that reflected concerns over quality of the work product, reliability of the attorneys, and concerns over possible character flaws. One commentator wrote that "'[l]egal temps' had enjoyed about the same status in the law as faith healers in the American Academy of Neurosurgeons" (Margolick 1988). Questions abounded: Were temporary attorneys law firm rejects who could not hack it in the real world? Were they "flaky" and unreliable (after all, what type of attorney would not want to commit to a law firm 24/7)? One law firm partner at a small New York City firm said in 1988: "I asked to see six or seven people [from the placement agency] because I thought fifty percent would be losers" (Berkman 1988). The managing partner at the New York office of the Los Angeles-based firm Latham and Watkins said in 1989: "They're just not your people. . . . I don't think they have the same incentive to do as good a job as our people" (Frey 1989).

Firms also expressed concern about potential damage to their reputation, to the firm's culture, and to employee morale (Cherovsky 1991). One law review article by Vincent Johnson and Virginia Coyle (1990, 404) raises concerns about "inter-group jealousy and non-cooperation, accompanied by lack of institutional loyalty and diminished motivation." For example, permanent employees may resent "the scheduling courtesies extended to temporary employees." The authors believe these potential problems can be headed off by making sure that permanent employees know they have a greater stake in the firm, for example, by minimizing pay and benefit disparities between temporary and permanent employees and by treating temporary attorneys with "appropriate professional respect" (p. 406). They also recommend that the law firm only hire attorneys who really want to work temporarily. (The irony of these observations and recommendations becomes readily apparent as the actual work experiences of my temporary attorney sample are detailed throughout the book.) Johnson and Coyle raise an additional fear that widespread use of temporary attorneys might create a two-tier system, with the added possibility that women and members of racial/ethnic minorities would be disproportionately represented in the bottom tier. However, they believe this would be unlikely because attorneys are well educated, have more access to power than people in other professions, and would sue if this did happen.

But the greatest apparent concern—expressed by Johnson and Coyle (1990) and throughout the legal press (e.g., Blodgett 1985)—was a variety of potential ethical problems that might arise from the use of temporary attorneys. These included concerns about client confidentiality, conflicts of interest, fee splitting, malpractice, licensure, disclosure, and supervision. For example, would the temporary attorney—who might work for many clients at a number of law firms in a short period of time—lead to conflicts of interest and thus disqualify the law firm? Would client confidences be more vulnerable to disclosure given increased numbers of personnel—who have little loyalty to the firm—with access to client files (see Eastin 1997)? And should (or must) law firms inform clients that they are employing temporary attorneys on client matters?

Some questioned whether these were genuine concerns or rather attempts by the legal aristocracy to prevent the profession from becoming "degraded." Stephen Gillers, a professor at New York University Law School, said that attorneys "live on the aura of specialness," and "[t]he mere suggestion that some portion of their work could be done by rented lawyers may not fit within the image they want to promote" (Walsh 1997). Law firms rely as much on their image as they do on their work product. Maintaining this image involves an "elite convergence"—hiring attorneys from the top-ranked law schools and serving prestigious corporate clients—that "continues to provide law firms with their own status and underwrites their ability to retain and bill corporate clients" (Dinovitzer and Garth 2007, 43). If some legal work is degraded and deprofessionalized, the entire "brand" may become tarnished, and attorneys will continually be asked to justify their staffing decisions, work allocation, and billing rates.

Growing Acceptance

Given large law firms' concerns about these and other matters, the first agencies in the New York City market initially placed most temporary attorneys in small- and medium-sized firms and in corporations. Corporations were drawn to the cost savings and many smaller firms were already accustomed to some forms of contract lawyering. However, resistance from even the large firms slowly gave way. Quality concerns were mostly allayed when a flood of highly qualified attorneys entered the market because of firm downsizing in the late 1980s and early 1990s. In an article from 1992, a placement agency director is quoted as saying: " 'Even a year and a half ago, the idea [of hiring temporary lawyers] was offensive' to some partners. But once temporary agencies showed their attorneys are 'from firms like yours, that argument started to fall apart'" (Adams 1992). In addition, firms realized that unbundling some of the least desirable work and giving it to temporary attorneys might actually *increase* morale—and therefore retention—of their associates. One law firm partner was quoted as saying that "many of the tasks [assigned to temporary attorneys] are too mundane to contribute to young lawyers' development" (Heller 1991). A partner at another firm said that using temporary lawyers allowed his firm to "hand off some of the more unwelcome tasks" (Jones 2005). Brian Uzzi, a Northwestern University sociologist who studies the legal profession, said: "Temps are good for any kind of work that's boilerplate. They're basically interchangeable in quality or features, no matter what the work" (Myers 2005b).

It also was suggested that the use of temporary attorneys might increase morale because permanent associates will presume themselves to be at less risk of layoff during lean times—the firm "politely show[s] the temps the door" when the project wraps up (Sullivan 1995). In addition, it is likely that the law firm personnel changes that had occurred (described in Chapter 1) also created an internal psychology that was more open to the use of temporary attorneys. One corporate counsel said in 1991: "It's a natural evolution from nonpartnership-track to second-tier attorneys to contract lawyers" (Lucas 1991).

Most ethical concerns were addressed and resolved by a series of state, local, and national bar association rulings. One of the first was an initial ruling in 1988 by the New York City Bar, which found that temporary attorney placement agencies might violate "fee-splitting" rules that prohibit attorneys from sharing fees with nonlawyers. The New York City Bar was concerned "that an agency might urge a lawyer to finish a project quickly in order to undertake a more lucrative project" (Blum and Cox 1988), and therefore required that placement firms charge a fixed fee rather than a percentage of hours worked. Because the three agencies then operating in the New York City market all charged firms a fee according to the number of hours worked, the ruling effectively stopped them from placing temporary lawyers. The Wallace Law Registry challenged the ruling, which also had been ridiculed by many observers, and the New York City Bar reversed itself.

Soon afterward, the American Bar Association (ABA) issued an ethics opinion that said the use of temporary attorneys is an "efficient and cost-effective way for law firms to manage their work flow and deployment of resources" (see Marcotte 1989). The opinion provided that employment of temporary attorneys would not generally violate ethical rules, as long as sound professional judgment was exercised. The ABA did not require firms to disclose to clients their use of temporary attorneys if the firm was directly supervising their work. This opinion also opened the door for firms to bill out the work of temporary attorneys at up to three times the hourly rate they were paying those attorneys or their agencies. Over the next few years, state bars tended to agree broadly with the ABA that the employment of temporary lawyers would not create unmanageable ethical issues. These bar associations suggested that with appropriate contracts between the parties and proper disclosure to the client, firms could employ temporary attorneys and not violate ethical strictures.

Another factor that led to greater use of temporary attorneys was pressure from clients. Corporate clients (who had been among the first to use temporary legal help) began to demand that law firms also use temporary help to hold down billings. Lesley Friedman credits the 1987 stock market crash with heralding the success of legal temporary placement agencies because of corporations' "pressure to push the work down to the lowest-cost service provider" (Scheffey 1996). In the legal press, the point was made frequently that the client benefited economically because the work of the temporary attorney is generally billed out at less than the average rate for an associate. An assistant general counsel of Nissan was quoted as saying that "you can hire top legal talent without paying silk stocking prices" (Ors 1993).

Increased efficiency also was emphasized. Articles pointed out that the large swings in demand for legal services and the increase in the size and complexity of cases—particularly involving the management and review of huge numbers of documents—made it impossible to efficiently staff these large cases solely with permanent personnel. Temporary staffing avoids the direct costs of permanent employees (such as taxes, benefits, training, and recruitment), as well as their indirect costs (paying idle attorneys' salaries or suffering damage caused by laying off associates). The law firm needs to pay the temporary attorney only for the actual hours worked. At the same time, however, the law firm may bill out the work of the temporary attorney at a rate exceeding the firm's actual cost. The firm makes money because, even with the agency markup, it is paying out less than it would for the pay and benefits of associates.

Large markups—a practice that appears to have declined in recent years (see Triedman 2006a)—can result in temporary attorneys becoming a major profit center for the firm. This last point is a controversial topic and has led to some public flare-ups between law firms and their corporate clients. For example, the law firm Chadbourne and Park was employed by Brown and Williamson Tobacco Company to oversee its document repository regarding the various tobacco lawsuits it was defending. The *American Lawyer*, quoting an unnamed former partner of the firm, reported that the firm was billing Brown and Williamson $1 million per month in legal fees, an amount allegedly three to four times what it was paying the twenty to thirty attorneys and sixty to eighty clerks who were working at the facility (Crawford 1998). The *American Lawyer* said that Brown and Williamson took the firm off the case because it thought the fees were excessive. Chadbourne and Park denied this, claiming that it marked up the work only to cover overhead costs plus "a small profit" (Bezanson 1998).[6] In another case, a media company fired a New York City firm for staffing a case with temporary attorneys because it believed that legal assistants could have performed the work at half the price. It was a sign of the maturation of the temporary attorney industry when a writer referred to this incident and claimed that "the quality of temps is not the central issue; clients care most about full disclosure and who realizes the savings—the law firms or themselves" (Davis 1996).

Initially, the temporary attorney market was centered in the New York City area, but placement agencies soon appeared in Los Angeles, Washington, D.C., and other cities. Eventual acceptance of temporary lawyering around the country was slow and uneven; however, a pattern emerged that was generally similar to what occurred in New York City. One or more temporary agencies would open up in a new market. Most of the original clients were corporations or small- and medium-sized law firms, with large firms at first resistant. The legal press is replete with examples of the initial skepticism of law firm partners in various cities, some of which now make extensive use of temporary attorneys. The New York City firm Skadden, Arps, Slate, Meagher, and Flom was said to be a late holdout to hiring temporary attorneys, and the managing partner of the Washington, D.C., firm Cleary Gottlieb said in 1995: "We recruit the best lawyers and offer the best training. . . . We couldn't do that with temporary attorneys" (Sullivan 1995). However, by the time I was conducting my research, both firms had given in to the practical and economic realities of staffing large-scale document review projects; they had each begun to make extensive use of temporary attorneys and had devoted large suites of on-site offices in Washington, D.C., to these efforts. Skadden has since moved to hiring "permanent" staff attorneys to conduct its document review work at its New York City office (Triedman 2006b).

---

[6] In another tobacco-related case, attorney Peter Angelos was hired by the state of Maryland to represent it in the multistate tobacco litigation. Temporary attorneys were responsible for one-quarter of the 34,000 hours racked up by attorneys on the case. Angelos's firm paid the temporary attorneys $12 per hour in 1998 (the agency was paid $21 per hour), and was asking for a total fee of about $1 billion, claiming it had a 25 percent fee agreement with the state (Associated Press 2000).

As the temporary attorney market spread beyond New York and Washington, D.C., reports in the legal press quoted attorneys in areas such as New Jersey, Philadelphia, the Twin Cities, Atlanta, and Baltimore who believed that the market there was "too conservative" for temporary lawyering to succeed. However, and sometimes under pressure from their corporate clients, one or more major firms in the area would eventually try out temporary attorneys, which led to greater acceptance and more firms willing to hire them. Nevertheless, this progress toward acceptance appeared to be slowed by the unwillingness of many firms to admit that they used temporary lawyers at all. One recruiter in Washington, D.C., said in 1996: "I think the firms still have a view that this is like illicit sex. It's really good, but they don't think they should be doing it" (Davis 1996).

Not everyone has jumped on board the temporary lawyer bandwagon. As late as 2006, one writer proclaimed: "Temporary/contract lawyers can help partners boost profit margins, but at what cost? Many law firms eschew contract lawyers, believing that the hired gun concept runs counter to their culture, evokes images of a sweatshop, and contributes to a general sense of unease among full-time members of the firm and clients" (*Partners Report* 2006). However, many of the initial skeptics have been won over due to the factors discussed previously—the availability of "quality" attorneys willing to do temporary work, appropriate management of ethical issues, practical demands of large cases, and significant economic benefits to both firms and their clients.

Intensive marketing by placement agencies also appears to have played an important role in the acceptance of the temporary lawyer. This is similar to findings that the temporary help industry created demand for its services (Parker 1994), assured potential clients of the quality of those services (Smith and Neuwirth 2008), and guaranteed favorable legislative treatment for employment agencies (Gonos 1997). Lesley Friedman, an early innovator in the field and the founder of Special Counsel, is the daughter of a Los Angeles lawyer. She told of using her contacts to get meetings at New York City law firms, where she would arrive wearing her mother's fur coat to send an implied message of her agency's success. She said that within a year she had broken into the market (Fox 1994). Agency directors also authored dozens of articles in the legal press extolling the virtues of hiring the temporary lawyer while minimizing any downsides. In order to head off quality concerns, they also advertised themselves as hiring only the best attorneys. For example, Special Counsel claimed that its roster of attorneys included a former U.S. Supreme Court clerk (Mansnerus 1991), and another agency claimed to hire only "the top 15% from the top 15% of law schools" (Kuntz 1994). Central to their mission, apparently, was a desire to reduce stigma and normalize the job of temporary attorney. For example, two agency executives wrote that "contract work is a legitimate, acceptable option" (Molloy and Heilman 1999), and another agency said: "These are not people who are incompetent or bad lawyers, they are individuals driven to do their own thing" (Livingston 1998).

The Maturation of the Temporary Attorney Industry

Notwithstanding lingering resistance, the temporary attorney placement field reached critical mass in the mid-1990s. Between 1993 and 1995, industry billings increased 400 percent according to *Forbes* magazine (Wolf 1997). By 1995, dozens of temporary attorney placement agencies had sprung up, in all major U.S. metropolitan areas, and tens of thousands had registered with these agencies, including reportedly forty thousand with the Wallace Law Registry (Scheffey 1995) and twenty-five thousand with Special Counsel (Fox 1994). Agencies expanded by opening offices in more cities—the Wallace Law Registry had offices in fifteen cities by the end of 1995 (Scheffey 1995)—and other agencies merged and consolidated.

This highly lucrative and growing market quickly caught the attention of national staffing companies. In 1995, Lesley Friedman sold Special Counsel to AccuStaff, a Jacksonville, Florida, firm that was one of the largest providers of temporary workers in the nation. Friedman was reportedly paid $21 million in stock and cash for Special Counsel; she says that she later sold the stock "after about an 800% increase in value" (Chudicek 1996). AccuStaff did not stop at Special Counsel—during the following few years, it purchased several other temporary attorney placement agencies in Baltimore, Atlanta, and Los Angeles. Interim Services of Fort Lauderdale bought Of Counsel, a publicly traded temporary attorney placement agency in 1996. In 1995, in a move tinged with irony, Kelly Services (it had changed its name from "Kelly Girls" in the late 1960s) bought the Wallace Law Registry, keeping Shelley Wallace on as the new division's president. She left in 1997, citing "irreconcilable differences" (Scheffey 1998). Commenting on Wallace's departure, Bryce Arrowood, founder and owner of Washington, D.C.'s Law-Corps, said that such takeovers "almost always end in disaster [because] the corporate culture changes radically" (Scheffey 1998). In 2003, Arrowood sold LawCorps to Special Counsel's parent firm, reportedly for more than $14 million (Greene 2003). One observer speculated that this rash of acquisitions and consolidations "could mark the dawn of a McLegal Job Market" (Bowling 1995). As of 2000, the entire legal temporary placement industry had about

$800 million in annual revenue. The industry continued to grow at breakneck speed; by 2005, annual billings had reached about $1.5 billion (Triedman 2006b).

Notwithstanding this rash of consolidation, today more than one hundred temporary attorney placement agencies exist across the United States, both in major financial centers and in smaller markets such as Columbus, Ohio, and Boise, Idaho. Some law firms make extensive use of temporary help, particularly those involved in antitrust, large-scale litigation, and other matters that require processing and review of massive numbers of documents. Surveys of large law firms found that use of temporary attorneys doubled between 2002 and 2003, rose another 48 percent the following year, and then 13 percent the year after (see Lewis 2006). At one Washington, D.C., law firm where I worked, I learned from an associate that the number of temporary personnel they employed in 2004—secretaries, paralegals, and attorneys—actually exceeded the number of permanent staff.

The "Pull" of Temporary Lawyering

The discussion so far is based on the many factors that "pushed" law firms into greater utilization of temporary legal help and led to the creation of a *bona fide* temporary attorney industry. As discussed in Chapter 1, temporary employment agencies regularly claim that temporary work fulfills the needs of both their workers and their clients—employees seek out temporary work so that they can fulfill other obligations or pursue lifestyle interests. I observed a strikingly similar process in the "selling" of temporary lawyering. The legal press and placement agencies claimed that the increase in temporary lawyering was mostly a response to the needs of individual lawyers who were "pulling" the law toward more contingent employment.

Many times, temporary employment was extolled as a "win-win" situation for the temporary attorney, as well as for the law firm. For example, one article profiled "Nat," a temporary attorney who volunteered as a social worker, saying: "Nat gets to pursue his ideals—and perfect his rumba—while his firm avoids overhead. And if recession hits, the firm won't be saddled with dead weight" (*Metropolitan Corporate Counsel* 1998). This marketing project invoked many of the same "ideologies" that researchers also have highlighted in the temporary clerical employment literature (e.g., Rogers 2000). The "ideology of flexibility" and the "ideology of the stepping stone" are identified and explored below, and they are also tested against findings from my own sample of temporary attorneys.

The Ideology of Flexibility

The legal press and placement agencies typically promoted temporary lawyering as a way for attorneys to maximize flexibility. No longer tied to the day in, day out demands of the law firm or corporate law department, temporary lawyers could be freed to pursue other obligations or interests. One agency executive wrote: "Many project attorneys today have the qualifications to work in any large firm, but have chosen temporary work for lifestyle reasons" (Yodh 2004). An in-house attorney at DuPont said that he preferred to work with temporary attorneys rather than law firm associates on document review projects because the temporary lawyers "are usually doing the [work] by choice, whereas law firm associates are not" (Deger 2003).

This emphasis on choice is also found in the only previous academic study of contract or temporary lawyers. Jackie Krasas Rogers (2000) interviewed fourteen contract attorneys in Los Angeles in the mid-1990s as part of a larger project that also involved interviews of temporary clerical workers. The attorneys in Rogers's sample were mostly hired for "overflow" work (described earlier) from small- or medium-sized firms. Rogers found that most of the clerical temporaries she interviewed were longing for the relative security of permanent employment, but for the attorneys she spoke with, working "in a law firm, large or small, held little attraction" (p. 153). Rogers sees this distinction largely in terms of class; she suggests that attorneys' specialized education and training allowed them the freedom to perform temporary work that was relatively high paying, autonomous, and personally rewarding. Rogers concludes that "[l]egitimation crisis and work flexibility may be luxuries of the professional class" (p. 153).[7]

The Selling of Flexibility

The "flexibility" in temporary lawyering as outlined in the press and promoted by placement agencies encompassed at least three facets. First, as one agency director in Toronto claimed, temporary attorneys could generally "accept and reject jobs as they wish" (see Szweras 1993). Janis Goldman,

---

[7] However, Rogers also acknowledges that law firms had been cutting back on hiring and even had been laying off associates, and she quoted a 1991 survey of temporary attorneys that found about 70 percent of them would have preferred permanent work (Rogers 2000, 129). Thus, the attorneys she interviewed may not have been representative of most attorneys doing temporary work. The differences between Rogers's attorneys and the ones I interviewed are explored further in later chapters.

founder of Lawyer's Lawyer in Washington, D.C., similarly said: "They love this lifestyle. . . . They work when they want to" (Del Villar 1989). Second, when temporary attorneys *did* choose to work, they could set limits on the amount of hours or choose particular days. One agency director in Philadelphia said: "If you only want to work three days a week, that's the availability you give to the agency. If you want to leave at five o'clock, that could be part of your agreement" (Agger 1997). Temporary lawyering was frequently written about as requiring significantly fewer hours per week than the average law firm required—it was ideal for hypothetical "women with families who didn't want a 60-hour week at a firm" (Vielmetti 1989) or lawyers who chose temporary employment "rather than work 90 hours a week" (Del Villar 1989). Temping always implied a "less hectic schedule" (Berkman 1988), and some articles even seemed to equate being a temporary attorney to working part-time (e.g., Sandburg 2000). Location was the third type of flexibility sometimes mentioned. Many articles—particularly those written by agency directors (e.g., Janczak 1997)—suggested that temporary attorneys could work from home.

The press and placement agencies frequently went beyond invoking choice and flexibility and actually glamorized the position of temporary lawyer. One article began: "Psst. Wanna make up to $175 an hour and name your own hours? This is not an infomercial come-on or a hallucination. . . . It's a real job description that attracts former law partners, Fortune 500 counsel and at least one assistant attorney general of the United States. It's called temping" (*Metropolitan Corporate Counsel* 1998). The same article claimed that one attorney made "close to six figures temping half-time." Another temporary attorney was said to be earning $60,000 annually working only twenty weeks per year (Loomis 1999). One writer gushed that a lawyer could "earn as much as $100,000 a year as a part-time attorney" while still free "to pursue Pulitzers, Oscars, Tonys, Emmys, and Grammys" (Margolick 1988). Another reported that "stories abound" about attorneys who pursue exciting outside interests, such as supporting a microbrewery business (Livingston 1998). Attorneys more prone to travel than ambition could do some contract work "in between trips to Florida" (Griffin 2005), work hard for three months "and then spend the next three sleeping on a beach in Jamaica" (Fernandez 2005), ski six months out of the year (Livingston 1998), sail in the Caribbean for the summer (Del Villar 1989), or just "go off to London for a week" (Lucas 1991). A partner at a Detroit, Michigan, law firm said that "there's something alluring about a contract attorney's career. It's a lifestyle. . . . I sometimes want to be a contract attorney. Take two months off. Come back. Work really hard for two months and then take two more months off. Let me do it, please" (Callahan 2005).

This glamorizing appeared to be driven at least in part by agency marketing. However, it also reflected the perception at the time that many lawyers—especially those at large firms—were experiencing deep dissatisfaction with their jobs, as law firms became increasingly bureaucratized and billable-hour minimums continued to rise. Lauding attorneys who were "making it" outside of the traditional, increasingly stressful law firm allowed readers to experience vicariously the pleasure in leaving that environment behind without considering the attendant risks. (Such stories were not limited to temporary attorneys; one article [*Bloomington Pantagraph* 1999] admiringly profiled an attorney who left the law to pursue his dream of joining the circus, where he put on a dog show every night.)

This yearning for a more balanced life outside the law also was reflected during this period in the many books that appeared about how to use one's law degree other than to practice law. Seminars were regularly marketed to attorneys who wanted to change careers. Even though temporary lawyering was still "lawyering," it was almost universally viewed as less stressful than other options. One temporary lawyer said: "It's so liberating. I don't have to work around politics or kowtow to anyone" (*American Lawyer* 1988). The temporary lawyer also did not have to worry about office administration, client development, or billing.

Within the ideology of flexibility, five contract attorney "types" tended to be invoked. I have labeled these the "new mother," the "dual-interest attorney," the "budding solo practitioner," the "burnout," and "attorneys in transition." (A sixth type—the "socially impaired"—was seen very rarely.) Frequently, many types would be invoked within a single article. As discussed earlier, when the field of temporary lawyering first began to form, the temporary attorney was frequently depicted as a mother with small children at home who did not want to stop working but needed more limited hours (e.g., Temes 1990). However, as more men than women registered with placement agencies, and it became obvious that part-time temporary work was not in great supply, emphasis shifted to the other types.[8]

---

[8] It is not possible to know, but interesting to speculate as to other reasons that the emphasis on temporary lawyers shifted away from mothers with children. Social science researchers (e.g., Fernandez-Mateo 2009; Standing 1999) have emphasized that women are overrepresented in temporary work, especially clerical positions. This is frequently cited as a reason that the work is devalued. It would appear that as the temporary attorney market developed, it would have been beneficial to the placement agencies to be seen as much more than "Kelly Girls" for attorneys. True "professionalization" (and concomitant destigmatizing) of the temporary attorney would require that it be deemed a category fully embracing men attorneys.

The type mentioned most often is one I call the "dual-interest" attorney, frequently referred to by the press and placement agencies as having chosen temporary work in order to explore "lifestyle interests." The legal and popular press profiled dozens of temporary attorneys who were pursuing outside interests such as film production, acting, writing, dancing, or stand-up comedy. One temporary lawyer finished producing a seven-part Public Broadcasting Service (PBS) documentary and then returned to contract work (Livingston 1998). Another landed a part in the Al Pacino film *Scent of a Woman* and left the law altogether (Duncan 1994). Frequently, the same temporary attorneys were profiled in different articles at different times, suggesting that the placement agencies made particular attorneys available to the media. For example, several articles (e.g., Friedman 1990; Nance 1989; Temes 1990) included comments from a particular temporary attorney who was attempting a second career as a legal journalist. At other times—such as in the case of the oft-mentioned (but unnamed) attorney who spent half the year skiing—it was unclear if such a person actually existed.

The ranks of temporary attorneys also included those who were trying to build a solo practice. Another type was the "burnout"—the attorney who no longer wanted to endure the pressures of working for a law firm. The director of the Atlanta office of the Wallace Law Registry described them as "people who have decided their lifestyle is not going to be 2,400 hours a year at a large firm" (Brickley 1996). An article in a business newspaper invoked "dot-com refugees who don't want 90-hour work weeks" (Fernandez 2003). Agency directors reported that a significant percentage of their temporary attorneys fell into this category. Lesley Friedman said in 1994 that 35 percent of temporary attorneys registered with Special Counsel were burnouts— she referred to them as "professional temps" (Fox 1994).

Another type of temporary attorney encompassed those "in transition." This catchall category included those who were preparing to leave the law for another career. For example, one was attending divinity school (Drell 1997), another the John F. Kennedy School of Government at Harvard (Pristin 1998), and a third had started a dog-walking service (Murray 2000). This group also included recent graduates who took temporary work while looking for a permanent legal job, women who were returning to law after taking time off for family reasons, relocating attorneys, and retired lawyers seeking to supplement their income.

There was a sixth and final type of temporary attorney, encompassing those with personality problems or who were otherwise socially impaired. This type was almost never directly invoked, but sometimes appeared to be alluded to through use of terms like "reliability," "communication skills," or "compatibility." One general counsel said that the permanent attorneys in his workplace were "very sharp" and he was therefore careful not to hire temporary attorneys who "can't communicate or can't get along" (Samborn 1994). One of the few articles to address this type head-on said law firms should understand that temporary attorneys "often have different academic and personal qualifications from permanent attorneys." The article continued: "For instance, project attorneys who will not have client contact may need not fit the same personality standards that may be required of full-time attorneys. Their technical expertise, ethical standards and reliability will, however, be of great importance" (Bellon and Alexander 1990/1991). Similarly, a partner at a law firm who had worked with "about a dozen" temporary attorneys said that some attorneys do contract work "because they do not fit into a normal working situation." He continued: "You might well decide . . . that you wanted to hire someone who was brilliant but flaky to help draft some motion papers and yet not want to take the person on on a long-term basis" (Mansnerus 1991).

Questioning "Choice"

With the possible exception, then, of recent law school graduates—or the rare "socially impaired" individual—being a temporary attorney was nearly always referred to in the language of "choice." However, beginning in 1991 and continuing through 1997, the legal press noticed another subtype of lawyers in transition—including "victims of downsizing" or, more generally, "lawyers between jobs"—who were effectively *involuntary* temporary attorneys. Lesley Friedman said in 1991 that up to 50 percent of Special Counsel's attorneys in New York City were looking for full-time jobs (Mansnerus 1991), with the percentage even higher in other major markets. Discussing this subtype of lawyer in transition, some articles recognized that an oversupply of attorneys had been created due to economic recession and law firms' restructuring, merging, and dissolving (or "rightsizing," as one agency director put it [see Molloy 1997]).

However, in some cases, these "push" factors were followed up within the same article with the "pull" language of employee flexibility. For example, one article said that "the past recession and the glut of lawyers have pushed temp lawyers into boardrooms and the marble-filled suites of law firms" and then went on to quote a partner at a Detroit law firm who said that "[f]or lifestyle reasons, [temporary attorneys] have chosen that route" (Sherefkin 1995). Another wrote: "At the same time that firms are seeking to rein in costs and have more flexibility, 'the pool of lawyers desiring only part-time or intermittent work continues to grow'" (Strahler 2005). No data was cited for the proposition that attorneys actually desired more contingent work arrangements; if the statement is true, it is certainly convenient that law firms' needs for efficiency dovetailed with lawyers' sudden desire for more flexible employment. Many of the most positive "win-win" articles appearing in the legal press were either written by managers or owners of temporary attorney agencies (e.g., Evers 1992; Junge 2004), or used such managers or owners as primary sources (e.g., Mansnerus 1991).

Even when external or internal economic forces were cited as reasons for the increase in attorneys willing to do temporary work, this fact was often "spun" to be a positive factor in three different ways. The first supposedly inured to the benefit of the law firm, while the last two were said to favor the out-of-work attorney. First, agency directors used the fact of layoffs to promote the increased numbers of "quality" temporary lawyers that had become available. Second, layoffs and recessions were reframed as a "good" reason to try temporary lawyering, either as an interim solution—Shelly Wallace said that in the face of recession, "temporary placement has become a welcome way to secure a decent living" (Scheffey 1995)—or as an opportunity for lawyers to rethink their work choices and perhaps satisfy other interests they had ignored. Lesley Friedman, then head of Special Counsel, said: "Many sort of used the recession to do something they'd always wanted to do. . . . It's a time to redefine oneself and explore" (Duncan 1994). (Interestingly, a few years earlier, she had said that "lawyers who have been laid off yet still want to be lawyers do not have the luxury of being flaky or pleading artistic interests" [Mansnerus 1991].) Third, some suggested that because of firm restructurings and layoffs, many attorneys had given up for good on the notion of permanent employment; one agency director in Texas said that because of this, many attorneys were now "available, even eager, to serve as temporary contract attorneys" (Carter 1997). Thus, even the basically involuntary choice to become a temporary attorney was loaded with references to autonomy.

Most contract attorneys who were interviewed for this research fit into the category of "involuntary" temporary lawyers, doing the work because they could not find permanent work elsewhere. Most were also in transition. Some were recent law school graduates, two were attorneys in later life (late fifties and early sixties) who felt they would never find permanent work because of their age, several had lost their jobs when firms downsized, some had quit their law firm jobs, and others relocated to Washington, D.C., and took up temporary work when they could not find positions.

Susan (all attorney and law firm names used herein are pseudonyms), who was let go from a position, said that she was doing contract work because "I really need the money and I have not gotten a permanent job yet that I wanted. Well, no, I have not gotten a permanent job offer in a year." Melinda was in her late twenties and had quit her job at a law firm. I asked her why she was working as a temporary attorney, and she said: "I really have no choice if I want to do anything legally related because I've sent out resumes for positions posted in-house. I've sent out resumes to agencies and companies that I've found doing searches online, and I haven't gotten any feedback. The only feedback I get is from these placement agencies." Rick was in his sixties when I interviewed him. He had moved to Washington, D.C., several years before, after having closed down his law firm. He said:

I haven't been able to break out of the cycle and find something permanent or satisfying or at least reasonably satisfying. So I'm doing [temporary work] because frankly the opportunities are fairly limited at this point. [At my age] I'm not likely to be hired into a permanent position somewhere else, and I need the work at least for the next ten years. Fortunately, in the D.C. area . . . there's a sizable need for pools of temporary workers; for temporary workers, an opportunity exists to at least do the job.

Only four of the twenty attorneys I interviewed said they were not looking for permanent work in the legal field. Julie, single and in her fifties, was doing contract work because her investments had lost value, and Maya was a new mother in her thirties who saw contract work as a way to "get some adult interaction" and make extra money for the household. Lynn was in her thirties and had been a litigator for a small law firm. She got tired of the "day-to-day drudgery" and found herself fantasizing about other professions. She said: "And I realized that I'm wishing that I'm doing everything but what I'm doing." So Lynn quit her job and started doing temporary work to earn a living while she thought about how she could take her career "in a different direction." Mitch is a former solo practitioner in his forties who had closed his practice; out of the twenty attorneys I interviewed, he was one of the few who could see himself being comfortable with "temping" indefinitely.

This voluntary/involuntary proportion appeared similar to the temporary attorneys I met but did not interview. Most of those attorneys seemed to have the goal of obtaining full-time, permanent legal employment, although many had given up on snagging associate positions with large corporate firms.

I met a handful of attorneys who were pursuing solo practices, and there were also some who had "dual interests"—one of them was a lawyer, well known in temporary attorney circles, who was pursuing an acting career and also had appeared on *Who Wants to Be a Millionaire?* I was taking on project assignments myself, in between periods of writing my dissertation. And I did meet some law firm "burnouts" who appeared to have accepted (and occasionally even embraced) their destiny as "permatemps."

I also observed some temporary attorneys who fell into the "socially impaired" category. These attorneys appeared to me to have personal or social problems to the extent that they probably could not survive (or *had not* survived) in a traditional law firm or corporate environment. For these attorneys, temporary work was probably their long-term answer to not "fitting in" elsewhere in the legal world. I asked Frances if she thought there were a lot of "social misfits" in project work. She laughed and said: "Absolutely." When I asked her why, she answered: "I think that there are those who don't interview well and can't find jobs that way, or don't necessarily get along in that atmosphere and either can't keep them or just can't get those kind of jobs, and so contracting—you don't necessarily have to be the gregarious, over-the-top personality to be employed."

While I did not find such attorneys to be numerous, they did tend to stand out. One was rumored to have had a "nervous breakdown" while employed as an associate at a large firm (thus, he also could fall into the "burnout" category). Many times, I observed this attorney at the buffet table picking up food, sniffing it, and then placing it back. Another attorney would go into long periods of "social hibernation." On one project, he stopped talking to everyone in the room when he felt that people had been "ganging up" on him, and I heard the same thing had occurred on a different project. Another was a pop culture trivia expert—it appeared to me that he also might have a minor case of Tourette syndrome—who tended to talk all day about such things as the names of all four members of the Monkees or which currently famous television star had appeared in a guest spot on *The Brady Bunch*. While I did not necessarily question these attorneys' legal ability or intellectual capacity, I had trouble picturing them as associates—much less partners—at a law firm.

Questioning "Flexibility"

While the legal and popular press did not effectively challenge whether temporary lawyering was always a fully voluntary choice, there were some scattered references to that effect. One aspect was related to the insecurity of temporary work and was raised in several different ways. First, some noted the initial barrier to even registering with a placement firm. For example, Special Counsel at one time claimed to be receiving resumes from twenty to twenty-five attorneys per week, but would interview only five to seven of them (Parks 2004). Second, assuming that an attorney successfully registered with an agency, the notion that work was so plentiful that many attorneys were free to work whenever they wished was questioned, although sometimes obliquely. Lesley Friedman of Special Counsel was quoted as saying that she had "approximately 225 applications on file for every position she can fill" (Mandelbaum 1995), a ratio that works out to 0.4 percent. Similarly, the Wallace Law Registry claimed to have 40,000 resumes on file, while it placed about 450 temporary lawyers per day (or just over 1 percent) (Scheffey 1995/1996). Even assuming (probably correctly) that most temporary attorneys were listed with multiple agencies, and also assuming (probably incorrectly) that most temporary lawyers did not want to work most days, the figures still suggest that temporary work was relatively scarce. One article about a placement agency in Detroit confirmed this directly, saying: "Given today's tight job market, it cannot possibly place [all of its temporary attorneys] or even keep its top temps in steady work" (Barringer 1996). Only a few articles quoted temporary attorneys themselves. One said: "Contract work is a feast or famine existence" (Hodges 1995). Another attorney lamented the large gaps between her assignments (Ramsey-Lefevre 1997), and a temporary attorney in Washington, D.C., said that during one period of two and a half months, he had only worked 150 hours (or an average of 15 hours per week) (MacLachlan 2001).

Sometimes there was an acknowledgment that once a project began it could be shut down at any time or it could be contracted with little or no warning. Crowell and Moring, a D.C. firm, was said to have taken certain temporary attorneys' work badges one evening as they left a particular project, indicating that those individuals should not return the next day (Triedman 2006b). In addition, a few articles mentioned that even when work *was* available it did not always fit the desired schedules of temporary lawyers. Very little of it, for example, was part-time (as noted earlier), and sometimes the work was most available during unappealing times, when permanent employees did not want to work. Agency directors advertised their temporary attorneys as being "available immediately" and able to "fill in late at night or on weekends" (Friedman 1989). Also, the end of the year holiday period was said to be a busy time for temporary attorneys (e.g., Brede 1995/1996). When an agency director in Washington, D.C., said that temporary attorneys have sometimes even worked on Christmas Day, "but not a full eight hours," Lesley Friedman responded, perhaps in jest: "That's 'cause they are in

D.C. In New York, the firms work round the clock on the holidays" (Torry 1996).

Two authors of an early law review article wrote that "because use of temporary lawyers sometimes requires firms to adjust their demands to the unique needs or limited availability of those interested in taking such positions, there is a modicum of hope" that firms would become more flexible with their full-time employees (Johnson and Coyle 1990, 399). In hindsight, this article appears hopelessly naïve. It is based on the assumption that law firms would actually be *more* accommodating to their temporary employees than to their permanent ones. This assumption fails to take into account the reported experiences of temporary workers in other sectors (discussed in Chapter 1) who have found little actual flexibility in their employment, and also ignores the broader economic realities of supply and demand.

Most of the temporary attorneys I interviewed for this project reported high levels of insecurity and very low flexibility in their temporary work. While some reported that they were confident they would continue to receive temporary assignments for the foreseeable future and could ride out any downtime in between, many considered the unpredictability of the work a real problem. Frances called it "disruptive" and Julie called it "nerve-racking." Attorneys reported that they sometimes took whatever project was offered to them, even if they did not believe the location was convenient or the pay sufficient. Several attorneys—particularly the most recent graduates—told me that they had taken temporary paralegal jobs that paid significantly less than attorney assignments because they could not find other work or they felt pressured by their agencies. Evan, in his twenties, said that his agency sent him out repeatedly on paralegal assignments, which earned him $15 to $18 per hour. After several of these assignments, he said to his agency: "I'm not getting paid enough for what I do here. . . . You know, I've just gone to too many schools to be doing data entry." Kathy, a recent graduate in her thirties, also accepted paralegal work, explaining: "Beggars can't be choosers. I can sit [at home] and watch Jerry Springer all day or I could work and make a little less than I'd want to."

In addition, attorneys were frequently called on very short notice and rarely had a clear sense of how long the project would last. For example, when I worked on one project for a Washington, D.C., outpost of a major New York City law firm, we were notified at 6:00 P.M. on a Friday that we should not report to work the following Monday. (Two hours earlier, out of loyalty to the firm, I had turned down an offer of a new project to start at a different firm the following Monday.) Flexibility also was not apparent in the way the work was organized and performed. Because these attorneys were doing a particular type of temporary work called "document review" (described and explained in Chapter 3), the work was performed on-site and had relatively rigid hours. It was also deskilled and routinized, and involved detailed, inflexible procedures. Thus, ideological autonomy was nonexistent, and technical autonomy was strictly limited.

The Ideology of the Stepping-Stone

Temporary lawyering was often portrayed in the press as a great way to get exposure to a variety of work settings and substantive practice areas, and to take on interesting and complex assignments. Through temporary work, the attorney supposedly could gain new skills and new experience, thereby making him or her more marketable. Thus, temporary lawyering was almost always depicted as commonly leading to permanent employment. One agency director wrote that "temping is a great way to try working with several firms on the way to finding a long-term position" (Taylor 1995). Another wrote that through temping, an attorney "can get his or her foot in the door that would be otherwise closed" (Evers 1992). At the same time, the employer could use the assignment as a "testing ground" (Kensik 1998) to learn more about the temporary attorney. One corporate counsel called it "the equivalent of an extended interview" (Mandelbaum 1995) and one article said firms could "try before they buy" (Agger 1997) by evaluating temporary attorneys' skills, as well as their "fit" with the firm.

Questioning the Stepping-Stone

These claims about variety, training, and a stepping-stone to permanent work were rarely tested, even though it appears they were illogical. First, it is unclear why law firms and corporate legal departments would not keep the most interesting and challenging work for their own attorneys. Articles occasionally cautioned the temporary attorney about this possibility—one attorney in Chicago who had completed temporary assignments at sixty law firms was quoted as saying: "Law firms only give out what they don't want to keep for themselves" (Wells 1987). Another article said that "temporary lawyers may find themselves performing exclusively the more onerous tasks of law practice—document production and due diligence reviews" (Connolly 2007). However, such comments were infrequent. Second, law firms and corporate legal departments are filled with busy people who do not have a great deal of time to mentor new attorneys, even among their own in-house staffs. Certainly, there is no incentive to train temporary lawyers, who are only with the firm briefly and then would take that training to other firms when they leave. One rare blast of truth from an agency director strongly cautioned against the expectation of learning new skills as a temporary attorney: "The employer of temporary attorneys is seeking individuals with legal expertise to solve an immediate workload crisis. The best candidate is the highly experienced attorney who can step in and handle the matter with little or no training" (Friedman 1990). Friedman added that an "attorney's chance of securing a temporary job is enhanced if she is willing to perform work below her skill level."

However, temporary lawyering was more commonly depicted as a stepping-stone to permanent employment, even though good empirical evidence was lacking as to the actual extent to which attorneys had converted from temporary to permanent status at the same law firm. Certainly, many individual examples were provided by the legal press. However, agencies only occasionally reported specific figures. For example, Special Counsel claimed that a 1993 survey showed that 25 percent of its temporary attorneys had converted to permanent status over a six-month period (compared to just 2 percent two years prior) (*New York Law Journal* 1993). Bryce Arrowood, the president of LawCorps in Washington, D.C., estimated in 1999 that 10 to 15 percent of LawCorps' attorneys had converted to permanent positions, and a placement firm in Detroit estimated its conversion rate at 10 percent in 1999 (McCracken 1999). More frequently, agencies made much more general claims about how widespread the stepping-stone phenomenon was. An agency director in Texas said it happens "often" (Shiffler 1998), one in Chicago said it "happens very often" (Pessin 2005), and other agency heads claimed that "many" attorneys had moved from temporary to permanent status while working at a firm or corporate legal department (King 1999).

Only a few observers raised doubts as to whether temporary lawyering was a fruitful avenue to permanent employment. Deborah Arron, coauthor of *The Complete Guide to Contract Lawyering*, said in 1999 that temp-to-perm conversion was "unusual" (Goldhaber 1999), and another commentator said it happened only "on occasion" (King 2004). One corporate lawyer cautioned that temporary lawyering is not a reliable route to permanent work, saying "there are three jobs and 2,300 people who want each job" (Mansnerus 1991). Some noted that the frequency of conversion from temporary to permanent attorney could differ based on the type of employer and the legal market. One agency director pointed out that the stepping-stone is more common in small companies than it is in larger corporations, and added that in New York City and in big firms, "it is difficult" (*Metropolitan Corporate Counsel* 2001).

The legal press also failed to explore the tension between the ideology of flexibility and the ideology of the stepping-stone. As detailed earlier, most articles presented temporary lawyering as a "win-win" for the attorneys and their employers. Law firms and corporations were increasing the use of contingent work arrangements for economic reasons, and attorneys were choosing it to suit their needs for flexibility and variety. However, if temporary work fit the needs of these attorneys, why would they *want* permanent work? We know, of course, that many attorneys—including most of the ones I interviewed—were doing the work "involuntarily" because they were unable to find permanent legal jobs. Also, if law firms were increasing their use of contingent workers, this would have meant that many permanent jobs were drying up and were not available, even if the temporary attorneys wanted them.

The Stepping-Stone in Washington, D.C.

During the time I worked as a temporary attorney, I never witnessed a case in which a temporary attorney was offered a position as an associate at the firm where he or she was temping. However, I did see a few temporary attorneys hired into staff attorney positions that offered no chance for advancement to partnership and involved supervising the work of temporary attorneys on the same types of cases that the new staff attorney already had been working on—a rather dead-end position. These positions also paid significantly less than the salary of a starting associate at the same firm. However, they usually required less annual billable hours, provided benefits, and were more secure than temporary attorney work.

The attorneys I interviewed, as well as those I spoke with more informally, believed the stepping-stone to be a myth. It was widely understood as nearly impossible to go from a temp to an associate, at least at any of the Washington, D.C., firms where we worked. Vince came into temporary lawyering thinking that it was a way of "learning a new skill to make you more marketable," and Evan thought that after doing good work as a temporary attorney, someone at the firm would ask him: "Hey, you know, do you want to be hired?" Both of their hopes were quickly extinguished.

Frances's experience illustrates the difficulty inherent in attempting to make a temp-to-perm transition. She had helped to manage an enormous, very complex, and lengthy temporary attorney project right out of law school. Later, she did temporary work at a prominent D.C. firm and was well liked there. In fact, after her first project ended, partners at the firm kept finding more work for her to do. However, Frances eventually decided to stop working for the firm so she could concentrate on studying for the bar examination. After she had passed the exam—she said she "blew it out of the water"—she applied for an associate position at the same firm, but was turned down. She said: "We all know how that happens. It's really difficult to get hired from a contractor to a permanent employee." She continued: "And so even though my entire [practice] section was behind me, the hiring committee just wouldn't budge because there's such a stigma." Frances's job saga continued. Unable to find a job as an associate, she began doing contract work for another prominent D.C. law firm. When the work was finished, Frances told one of the firm's partners that she would love to stay and work directly for the firm, but that she couldn't because the project had ended. This partner—who was one of the more powerful members of the firm—said to Frances: "This is an outrage. You should be here. Come work for me." He then "leaned on" the hiring partner to allow him to hire Frances to work for his practice section. The hiring partner agreed to hire Frances, but told her that under no circumstances would she ever be an associate at the firm. The partner she worked for thought that Frances could become an associate if she worked hard enough, but as it turned out, the economy soured and she lost the support of the partner she had been working for, so the firm let her go.

Frances correctly identifies "stigma" as one of the reasons that law firms were so reluctant to consider temporary attorneys for associate positions. Even though some of the temporary attorneys I worked with graduated from respected law schools, earned good grades, and served on their schools' law reviews, their stint as temporary attorneys seemed to torpedo any chances they had of being hired by the "prestigious" firms for which they were temping. And the assumption among the attorneys I worked with was that the longer one temped, the less likely one was to be hired at *any* firm. The head of Meridian Legal Search in New York City echoed this when he said: "If you start to pile up temp positions, you might be perceived by employers as either not good enough to hold a permanent job or only suited to temp" (King 2004).

However, another likely reason that temporary attorneys I worked with were not frequently hired full-time is because of the type of work they were asked to do. If temporary work frequently represents the dregs of legal work—a charge that has been increasingly common to hear—then few temporary attorneys really get a chance to "shine" and impress the law firm. If "a monkey can do it" (as several of my fellow document review attorneys often put it), then it is difficult to stand out as particularly smart and competent. And if temporary attorneys are frequently working below their skill level, as has been suggested, then they are likely bored and disinterested, qualities that also will not draw much positive attention.

The attorneys in my sample were performing "document review," a kind of work that was particularly deprofessionalized. Because the work was highly deskilled and routinized, it was even less autonomous and flexible than other types of temporary attorney work. In addition, we were frequently squirreled away in offices apart from the rest of the firm and had almost no contact with law firm partners who make hiring decisions. Being a "star" document reviewer might get one invited back for another document production, but not for an associate interview. The nature and purpose of document review, and the experience of performing it, is explored in Chapter 3.

3

Life on the Concourse Level

Doing Document Review

Publisher Mortimer Zuckerman, who was trained as an attorney but never practiced, said that law is the opposite of sex: "Even when it's good, it's lousy" (Paumgarten 2007). When it's bad, then, it must be miserable. This research involves a particular type of miserable work that is commonly performed by temporary attorneys: document review.[1] Document review involves the reading and coding of documents relating to a legal matter, typically in advance of producing the documents to an opposing party. This work is particularly deprofessionalized, even in the context of temporary attorney work: it is deskilled, intensified, routinized, and controlled. Temporary attorneys have little (formal) technical autonomy over work conditions, organization, pace, or content of the work. Document review is sometimes performed under very unpleasant physical conditions, and project attorneys find the work to be highly tedious and unrewarding.[2] These findings are more typical of studies that involve clerical temporaries than professional temporaries.

---

[1] Temporary attorneys can perform a wide variety of work, from covering court appearances to drafting complex contracts. Attorneys can sometimes work several months or even years for the same firm in a full-time "temporary" arrangement. Document review is only one type of work performed by temporary attorneys, but it appears to represent the majority of billings in the D.C. market.

[2] In the remainder of the book, I refer to attorneys doing document review as "project attorneys" to reflect this particular type of work.

The Purpose and Nature of Document Review

The exchange of documents between parties is a common process in many legal interactions. In litigation, this process is known as "discovery"; in corporate transactions, it is known as "due diligence"; and in governmental regulatory actions, it goes by a variety of other names. In each of these cases, the law allows one party to request relevant documents from a second party and requires the second party to "produce" those documents (with some limited exceptions) on a particular date. The purpose of such a request is either to find evidence that tends to support a party's legal claims or to help a client make an informed business decision.

This process can be illustrated with two examples of differing complexity. First, assume that a home owner is unhappy with the quality of work that a contractor did on remodeling her bathroom. Unable to settle with the contractor, the home owner retains an attorney and files a lawsuit. The home owner (now the "plaintiff") will serve a "discovery request" on the contractor (now the "defendant"), seeking documents relevant to the lawsuit. Such documents might include all evidence of written communications between the contractor and subcontractors, including such things as change orders, invoices, cancelled checks, and written evidence of oral conversations. The plaintiff also might ask for documents relating to any similar disputes with other customers in the past. With this relatively small case, the number of documents would be fairly limited and probably easily managed by a solo practitioner.

As the complexity of a case increases, so do the effort and expense involved in document production. One of the most complex and costly construction projects in U.S. history involved replacing an elevated highway in Boston with a 3.5 mile long tunnel. This megaproject, known informally as the "Big Dig," cost more than $14 billion, took more than ten years to complete, and involved dozens of contractors and subcontractors. The Big Dig was plagued with cost overruns, use of substandard materials, and thousands of leaks; after its completion a concrete ceiling tile fell on an automobile, killing a passenger. If the Commonwealth of Massachusetts decides to sue the contractors involved, the parties would serve discovery requests on each other. The documents produced from these requests would likely number in the millions of pages. This mountain of documents would require advanced technical capability (computers and software), as well as a large number of legal personnel (clerks, paralegals, and attorneys) to review and organize the materials. Depending on the capacity and capabilities of the law firms involved and the economics of the case, it is likely that some of this reviewing and organizing would be handed off to temporary attorneys.

Huge numbers of documents are not just produced in litigation, however. Government regulatory action, particularly antitrust review, also can result in massive discovery requests. The Hart-Scott-Rodino Act (HSR) lies at the heart of U.S. government oversight of corporate mergers. When corporations that meet a certain size or dollar threshold agree to merge, the HSR requires that they notify the U.S. Department of Justice (DOJ) and the Federal Trade Commission (FTC) of their intent to merge. Then, during a waiting period of thirty days, the FTC and the DOJ decide whether to request further information from the parties about the proposed merger. If either agency decides it wants more information—which means it has determined that the merger may unduly reduce competition and therefore harm consumers or other businesses—it may file a "Second Request" addressed to the parties to the proposed merger. A Second Request is very wide-ranging and asks for documents relating to the proposed merger itself, as well as documents involving the companies' markets, competition, sales, pricing, business plans, research and development, and other matters. The request specifies a time period for such documents (typically from two to five years back) and asks that the documents be produced to either the DOJ or the FTC by a certain date.

For large corporations, a Second Request is extremely burdensome and time-consuming. Typically, copies of the Second Request are distributed company-wide, and particularly to those persons or divisions that the DOJ or FTC have specified. All potentially responsive documents must be gathered and reviewed. While most people think of a "document" as a paper copy containing text, the definition of "document" in most discovery requests is much more expansive and also includes such things as photographs, e-mail, computer files, and voice mail messages. Thus, complying with a discovery request usually involves a great deal of work by information technology specialists within the companies. Attorneys representing the corporations are sent out to offices around the country (and sometimes outside the United States as well) on a "document pull" to collect the documents so they may be reviewed and organized. Paper documents are photocopied and electronic documents are either printed out or saved electronically. Typically, a third-party vendor is hired by the law firm or the corporation to organize and manage the documents. The documents are then either uploaded in electronic form for later review on computers, or they are printed out and put in boxes so they may be physically reviewed. Similar processes are involved in matters involving due diligence or litigation.

The size of document review matters has greatly increased in the past twenty years, largely due to two factors: First, the size and number of corporate mergers has increased substantially. For example, in the oil and gas industry alone, a wave of consolidations occurred in the late 1990s and early 2000s. British Petroleum merged with Amoco, Exxon with Mobil, Texaco with Chevron, and Philips Petroleum with Conoco. Each of these deals was valued at more than $10 billion, and each subjected the companies to the Second Request process, resulting in lengthy government review. Consolidations have swept other industries in recent years, especially the financial and telecommunications sectors. Of the seventeen temporary projects I worked on, eleven involved FTC or DOJ Second Requests, and two more matters I worked on involved private antitrust litigation.

The second reason is decidedly more prosaic—the number of corporate documents has greatly increased due to the digital data revolution (Wiggins 2003). As recently as 1990, the majority of corporate documents were retained on paper; by 2000, 80 to 90 percent were in electronic form (Triedman 2006a). This shift to digital media has resulted in the creation and retention of more documents than under paper-based systems. For example, matters that would have been discussed on the telephone or in person are now conducted through e-mail. In addition, electronic media allow multiple drafts of a document to be easily retained and widely shared. And the physical costs and constraints involved in retaining documents are much less in digital data than they are in paper documents, providing less incentive to cull old documents. All of these factors have led to a rise in the complexity and cost of discovery.

Reviewing a massive number of documents is work ideally suited to the use of temporary employees. The work is high-volume, involves tasks that associates do not want to do, is project-specific (and is therefore subject to peaks and valleys in demand), and can theoretically be done without a great deal of direct supervision. Most major document review cases are handled by law firms in Washington, D.C., and New York City because firms there have the greatest expertise in these matters. Firms in D.C. are close to the requesting government agencies, and firms in New York City tend to represent the largest corporate clients. Therefore, New York and D.C. also have the largest concentrations of temporary legal placement agencies.

Getting the Work

The attorneys I interviewed were introduced to legal temping in various ways. About a third of the attorneys, like I, first learned about legal temping from reading a classified advertisement, either in the *Washington Post* or the *Legal Times*. Most of the attorneys who found temporary work through classified ads were initially looking for permanent work and did not expect to find the option of temporary employment; Melinda said she was surprised to see an ad that mentioned an agency with both "temporary and permanent divisions." About another third of the attorneys heard about temping through friends. Betsy told a friend she was having a difficult time securing a job and her friend suggested that she move to D.C. and temp until she found regular employment. Larry said that while he was still in law school, an acquaintance told him how some large law firms, "when they have a large case, can't afford to give it to their associates, and they need to farm it out to people who will work cheaper." A friend told Kathy that temporary work as an attorney was available; she later told me: "I thought it was very strange. I mean, I just—I'd never heard of it before and—but it was good, because then I thought: 'Oh, good. 'Cause maybe I can actually do something as a lawyer—that I didn't have to go back to, you know, typing eighty words a minute.'" Three of the attorneys heard about temping through the career counseling office at their law school, and Roger and Lynn were working as law firm associates when they heard generally about law firms hiring temporary help.

After learning about the existence of temporary work, the attorneys sent their resumes out to various agencies. Some of them received an immediate response; Larry remembers that the first agency he contacted called him in and placed him on a project within two weeks. Mitch's introduction was even quicker; he faxed his resume to an agency on a Monday afternoon and was working on a project the next morning, without having met face-to-face with anyone from the placement agency. Bernice had a similar experience. She sent her resume to twelve placement agencies in D.C., unknowingly "right in the middle of the mother of all document reviews," a huge defense industry merger. She was hired almost immediately.

For others, the process was more protracted. Bill, a recent law graduate in his twenties, told me that he initially faxed his resume to several agencies, and "nothing happened." He remembered thinking: "Man, is it that bad? Like, are my qualifications that bad? Like, you know, I haven't heard anything." He continued, punctuating his comments with laughter:

> I treated it as if it were like a normal job. You know, I called to follow up about the resume, and to check in with them. And I got nothing, for like the first month and a half. And then, you know, I looked back in the paper, and the next week, I was like: "These sons of bitches! They've got another ad out!" And I was like: "God damn them!" You know, I took it pretty personally. I was like: "These guys are just taking

my resume, looking at it, throwing it out." I sent it in one more time, and then randomly, you know, someone called me, and that was it.

My experience was similar. I faxed resumes to several different agencies, but initially got no response. I later learned that agencies value attorneys who take the initiative to frequently follow up with them.

The next step in the hiring process was setting up an interview at the agency. Most of the agencies' offices were located within a short distance of each other, clustered near the major law firms. Most were rather simply and sparsely furnished, and the employees were generally professional in demeanor. However, there were exceptions. Julie, a single attorney in her early fifties, was disappointed with some agencies that had "crummy little offices where people were not well dressed." Bernice was "shocked at the way some agencies seemed like sorority houses." She added that "some were kind of holes in the wall, with a couple of young attorneys that started their own firm, mom's needlepoint on the wall." I believe this last reference is to an agency that was started by several young attorneys that, when I visited it, seemed to be operating on a shoestring. This agency tried to set itself apart by providing both its own leased space where law firms could conduct document review and its own personnel to oversee much of the review process. Perhaps not coincidentally, it also had the most dismal working space, discussed below.

The screening process did not seem to vary a great deal between agencies and tended to be low-key, even perfunctory. It appeared to me and to the attorneys I interviewed that the agencies were accomplishing just two basic purposes through the interview process: First, they wanted to make sure that the interviewee was reasonably articulate and "presentable." James said he felt that the "interviewer was doing more of a personality check than a check to see if you're qualified to do a certain level of work." Bill recalled his agency interviews as being "sort of silly" because they "had very little to do with figuring out how well I'd fit in as, you know, an attorney practicing law." He went on, laughing: "It wasn't like a normal law firm interview where you're on the hot seat and behind every door there's, like, a pit or a lion or, you know, spikes that come shooting at you."

Thus, most interviews were brief. Maya described one interview as "very, very quick" and just covering "the basics," and Roger said his longest interview lasted fifteen minutes. I had similar experiences. Having survived perhaps a dozen full-day interviews at law firms, I came to the first agency interview very nervous and expecting a thorough going-over. One agency required that I take a "skills test," which required me to edit a legal document, among other things. However, at most agencies, I spent a majority of the time filling out forms and very little time answering substantive questions about my legal experience. At the seven or so agencies I interviewed with, I was always accepted and told I would be considered for work.

The second purpose of the interview was apparently to sell the agency. Most temporary attorneys knew at the outset—or soon learned—that there were more than a dozen agencies operating in D.C. And the agencies were aware that the attorneys knew this—or soon would. Thus, I found that agency recruiters were always upbeat, cheerful, and mostly professional. Typically, they told me they had upcoming projects that they could place me on, and they encouraged me to keep in touch with them.

Some project attorneys I spoke with had the same experience I did— they registered with one agency, sat back, and waited for the work to come to them. However, most of us learned that project attorney work was a "feast or famine" experience, and we could not count on one agency to keep us regularly employed. Julie told me that she initially signed up with a single agency. When I asked her if she subsequently registered with others, she answered:

Well, that's one of the little secrets that I didn't understand. Since the first project was so big, and there were so many agencies working the one project, I didn't understand that agencies bid on different projects around town; that they all didn't go to all projects, so I only registered with one agency. It wasn't until, oh, like, eight months later that somebody finally told me: "Oh, no. You need to register with multiple agencies or you may not get work again."

Julie eventually registered with most of the D.C. placement agencies. Four of the attorneys I interviewed were still only registered with their first agency, but most of them were relatively new to project work. The others reported being registered with anywhere from two to fifteen agencies. Typically, though, project attorneys got most of their work from a small number of these.

In our initial experience with registering, the type of work that was most plentiful—document review—typically was not explained to us. Most of us had no idea what we would be doing as temporary attorneys unless we had a friend or acquaintance who had previously told us about the work. Mitch said he "had no clue" what he would be doing, and Maya "had no expectations whatsoever." Even those who were specifically told they would be doing document review did not have the actual nature of the work explained to them. I asked Julie what she expected the work to be like. She recalled:

J: Well, they definitely told me the hours. You know, there's a lot of
    lingo that you don't really understand until you get into this, so
    they say: "Okay, we've got a project, and it's a Second Request,"
    and blah, blah, blah. I didn't know what that was—

RB: "Review of documents"—

J: Right—"Review of documents"—

RB: You don't know what it means.

J: Right.

RB: Did you have a picture of it at all, do you know?

J: I had no picture of it at all, no idea what it would be like.

Others assumed that they would be doing substantive work. Bernice
thought that she would be brought in as a "wringer, someone of—not necessarily prestige—but, you know, someone of value." She thought that she
would be asked to do work similar to what she had done as an associate at a
prior law firm, but that it would be "just for a shorter duration." Ben said
that he expected he would be "just writing memos or something, you know,
doing like, slightly responsible legal work but not heavily responsible," and
added: "I thought I'd have my nose in law books." Before he was licensed,
Evan had done some temporary paralegal work that required him to do research and to help write motions, so he assumed that all temporary legal
work was going to be similar. Vince knew he would be doing "document
review," but assumed that "we'd be reviewing important documents in support of, you know, research," and added: "I thought they'd want my legal
opinion."

For those attorneys who had imagined important, substantive work,
their actual experience was very disappointing, even disorienting. Ben's first
project as a temporary "attorney" was sitting at a computer and doing basic
data entry. I asked Vince to tell me about his experience on his first agency
project, which involved document review:

RB: So, what happened when you found out things were different?

V: Well, I felt—I go: "These are documents?" You look at them, and
    they're just pages and pages of e-mail, presentations, and crap.

RB: So, what did you think about the work?

V: I thought it was the most boring, horrible thing I've ever had to
    do in my career.

The details of this "most boring, horrible thing" are the subject of the remainder of this chapter.

Doing Document Review

As discussed in Chapter 1, temporary work is typically more fragmented and intensified, and also less skilled than, permanent work. While fragmentation, intensification, and deskilling have been observed in temporary clerical work, there is limited insight into whether the same processes are occurring for temporary professional workers. In one study involving contract attorneys—who typically worked for small- or medium-sized firms doing appearance or overflow work—Jackie Krasas Rogers (2000, 136) found some evidence of fragmentation and deskilling, "with temporary attorneys concentrated in the lower-skilled tasks within the profession" doing the type of "boilerplate" activities or "worker bee" assignments normally reserved for beginning attorneys. However others studying high-skilled technical workers (e.g., Smith 1998) have found that temporary work afforded wide use of skills and opportunities for further training.

Fragmentation through Unbundling

Legal consultants suggest that firms unbundle their legal tasks in order to increase efficiency and reduce costs. Peter Zeughauser (1996) recommends that firms set up separate entities for high-volume, commoditized work; Richard Susskind (2008) advises firms to regularly unbundle and multisource their legal projects. This corporate-style vision certainly has been implemented in the case of large document review projects, where firms have unbundled this work and shifted it from their associates to temporary attorneys. This meets the economic and staffing needs of the firm, alleviates associates from tedious and unfulfilling work, and still provides the firm with work of sufficient quality, given the task. This leaves the firm's partners and associates with handling the more complex and creative tasks of managing massive litigation cases or Second Request responses, which may require work by dozens of a firm's permanent attorneys and paralegals. These cases involve detailed legal strategizing, constant communication, and countless meetings with the client, as well as the drafting and filing of numerous legal documents with the court or the regulatory agency. Litigation can drag out for years, while the timeline for a Second Request is usually measured in several (very intensive) months.

Reviewing documents in such a complex case may require a substantial commitment of time and energy. However, regardless of its size and relative complexity, I frequently observed that law firms appeared to minimize the importance of document review, seeing it merely as the "necessary evil" to obtain merger approval or otherwise comply with legal requirements. The review was always separate from what many saw as the "real work" in the case, which was devising strategy and arguing the case. In most cases, this strategy had been crafted well before document review began; thus, the purpose of looking at documents was to find the ones that supported the legal position already laid out by the law firm (and to minimize those documents that seemed contrary to it). The job of crafting strategy was never something that project attorneys would be involved in, even though we were usually the people most familiar with the documents. Rather, we and our jobs were split off from the rest of the case and the firm. Only rarely were we provided information about the larger case, and a visit from a law firm partner or the firm's client was uncommon.

Spatial Fragmentation

The physical conditions, organization, and size of document review projects I worked on varied a great deal. Some work locations and conditions were comparable to those found in typical office buildings in most cities; others were close to abysmal. Consistent in almost every case was a physical separation of the project attorneys from the permanent law firm employees. Some firms housed the project attorneys on-site if they could physically accommodate them. I worked on several small projects involving from four to ten attorneys where we worked for the duration of the project in conference rooms. This was generally the best type of assignment because the conditions were not unacceptably overcrowded and the offices were comfortable; for example, they were air-conditioned and some of the conference rooms had windows. Some firms were able to conduct substantially larger projects, either at their main offices or in close-by office space that they controlled. I worked on several of these projects at different law firms that involved more than fifty attorneys. Sometimes, the firm set aside dedicated space to perform document review; other times, the project attorneys were split up into various locations within the firm wherever space was available. One firm had an area on a particular floor of its building that was dedicated solely to project work. I spent a year at that firm, being "rolled over" to a second and then to a third project. Other project attorneys I worked with in 2004 remained there as of mid-2007, working on other projects.

At one large firm, I worked on a document review project involving a large computer merger. Because I was part of the second group of attorneys to be added to the project, the "prime" space was already taken, so the firm put the twenty or so of us into a converted storage room in the interior of the building. The room had concrete floors, poor ventilation, and no windows, and was "decorated" only with office chairs and long tables. Melinda worked on that project and found that it was always "freezing in there." She also found it difficult to work sixteen-hour days in very close quarters (there were four of us to a table, two pairs facing across from each other), with no other visual distraction. She told me that "it was hard not looking at anything— basically, we looked at each other . . . so I had to look at [Jane] because she was sitting across from me." She continued: "Not that that's so bad, but at the same time, I think that even pictures, something to break up—I felt like: 'Nothing to look at.'"

Many firms—even the largest ones—did not have sufficient facilities to house potentially hundreds of project attorneys performing document review. Following the tenet of "flexibility," it did not make sense for firms to create permanent document review space on-site that might not be needed continuously. Thus, these firms had to find places to house their project attorneys. One large D.C. firm rented warehouse space in the suburbs and one placement agency leased space in a crumbling office tower in Virginia. Both facilities were to earn a notorious place in temporary attorney lore, and I was unlucky enough to have worked at both. In three of the projects I worked on (including my first project), which together lasted six months, I worked with dozens or hundreds of other contract attorneys in a condemned office building in Rosslyn, Virginia, just across the Key Bridge from Georgetown. This building was nicknamed "Nike Town" by some project attorneys for its alleged sweatshop-like conditions. In 2001, there were plans to raze this building and those that adjoined it to construct a new office and hotel complex. Thus, the buildings were mostly empty. However, an enterprising placement agency (the shoestring operation referred to earlier) leased the space to law firms for document review and also oversaw the work that was done there.

The building had serious flaws. It was not air-conditioned in the summer and had water leaks that created huge mold "blooms" in the carpeting. Some of us developed persistent sinus problems every time we had to work there. The building had wires hanging from the ceiling, and one of the elevators had a hole in the floor covered only by some carpeting. Commenting on the conditions and the oppressive heat there in the summertime, Vince said: "It was quite literally a sweatshop. The only thing missing were the sewing machines." At the start of one project in Nike Town, a newly assigned temporary attorney telephoned the city inspection agency, which promptly came out to the building and ordered the elevator shut down. This attorney was fired several days later, allegedly as a result of her work quality. On this same project, another temporary attorney brought in a wall thermometer from home that regularly showed temperatures in the nineties. One day, six of us walked across to an office supply store in Georgetown to buy desk fans. We billed for the hour we were gone, figuring that the trip was work related.

Betsy told me that she had also worked on projects in Nike Town. She said that among many other problems, the building had "nests of spiders by the window" near her worktable. One of the other attorneys kept a log of how many spiders she killed in one week—Betsy thought the number was twenty-eight. She told me that another project attorney was actually bitten by a spider. When I asked what happened to her, Betsy replied: "She had to go to the hospital, and she was hospitalized for two days and had some procedure where they drained her knee. . . . And the hospital she went to said it was probably from a brown recluse spider, and the venom was eating at her flesh from the inside. So I don't think she was too happy about that." Betsy said everybody on the project was "kind of freaked out." She added that she has a phobia about spiders and after this incident she "had to suck it up to sit there without screaming."

I also worked at a warehouse facility in a D.C. suburb. In a large room at the front, hundreds of contract attorneys were seated at dozens of cafeteria-style folding tables; there was a much larger room in the back that was filled from floor to ceiling (about forty feet high) with boxes of documents from various cases. Forklifts were employed to move pallets of boxes from one place to another within the building. This building was also beset by various problems. In August 2001, I was to begin a project on a Saturday. On Friday afternoon, I received a telephone call from my agency telling me that the project would not begin until Monday because there had been a plumbing problem at the facility. After starting the project, I learned from other project attorneys that the "plumbing problem" was caused by a project attorney putting chicken bones in the only urinal in the only men's room, which served well over one hundred project attorneys. I also learned that the project had been shut down earlier because of a flea infestation—attorneys were getting bitten on their feet and ankles, and an exterminator had to be called in to spray the carpeting. The firm later admitted the flea problem, but claimed the plumbing issue was caused when a "pipe burst" (Triedman 2006a). A partner in the firm called it a "near disaster" when three thousand boxes with twenty million pages of documents "suddenly turned up" and the firm had to bring in extra attorneys, bringing the total to 350. The legal press later reported that the firm "reimagined" the whole document review process, creating a dedicated space holding up to five hundred project lawyers, with up to forty staff attorneys providing intensive supervision. A law firm partner claimed that each project had a 35 to 40 percent carryover in personnel from the prior one, and that the firm paid its temporary attorneys a minimum of $35 per hour (Triedman 2006a).

I heard about another unpleasant location from several attorneys I interviewed. This facility was in the sub-basement of an office building occupied by a large law firm. I was never on assignment with this firm because it required membership in the D.C. bar (I was actively licensed only in California). However, Larry worked there more than twelve hours per day on a six-week document review project. He said that there was only one men's bathroom for the project attorneys, and the firm stationed a security guard right next to it. Larry said that in the attorneys' workroom, "it started smelling like bathroom from a very early point in the day. . . . It was really heinous. It was just tough. People had fans. People drank coffee. People sprayed bathroom sprays in the air. It was just noxious." Larry added that it must have been even worse for the security guard. The basement location is not unique; a law firm manager at a different firm was quoted as saying that the firm regularly places its temporary attorneys on the "concourse level"—the building's basement (Triedman 2006b).

In most document review situations, crowdedness was a major complaint of the project attorneys. James commented that "space definitely can be an issue." Julie said that on one project she had her own office and "felt like a pig in slop"; then she was moved to a conference table with eight other attorneys and was miserable. When asked how she felt about the project she was currently assigned to, Julie said: "I'm fine." Then she paused and said: "That's a one-person office, and there are four of us. And I'm saying I'm fine. How sad is that? But it could be a lot worse." And it certainly had been, as Julie recounted to me her experiences on the "flea infestation" project. Reflecting her resignation over working conditions, Julie said: "I have really not been in any terribly bad setting. . . . You know, there's only so much you can expect from an employer when you're a temporary employee."

Task Fragmentation

Once documents have been "pulled" from client locations, they are assembled and made ready for review by the project attorneys. At the beginning of a project, the law firm provides some sort of information and training for the project attorneys. Typically, reviewers are provided with a three-ring binder that contains the request for documents and information about the client and the relevant business sector. Firm attorneys—usually the associates who are going to run the document review—review the items in the binder with the project attorneys, emphasizing the type of documents that are being requested, and describing (usually only in broad terms) the legal claims and issues involved. This training was brief in the cases I worked on, lasting from one hour to half a day. The real learning about the case came later, while plowing through the documents.

The job of document review is relatively simple and straightforward—to read each client document and "code" (assign) it to one or more of several predetermined categories. Document review can involve paper documents, electronic documents, or a combination of both. Imagine that half of the contents of your work computer's hard drive has been downloaded or printed out and provided to your employer's law firm. Document review attorneys would be tasked with reading through those documents to see if they are relevant to the case at hand. Sometimes there is a prescreening process that occurs. For example, in the case of electronic documents, the parties may agree to conduct a search using specified search terms, and only "pull" and review the documents that contain those terms. At other times—particularly in the case of paper documents or where an agreement to use search terms is not reached—it is not as easy to prescreen documents; thus, a large number of documents must be reviewed even though many may not be responsive to the request. While doing document review, I frequently encountered employees' recipe files, joke e-mails, and birthday party invitations. In one case, a project attorney came across a series of e-mails clearly showing that an employee of the law firm's client was selling illegal drugs.

While a relatively simple process, there are still several levels of "cuts" that must be made in document review. First, a document must be coded as either "responsive" or "nonresponsive." If it is nonresponsive, it gets labeled as such and is placed aside in a separate pile (or is flagged in the case of electronic review). If the document is responsive, the project attorney must determine what category or categories the document relates to. Depending on the case, there may be half a dozen to several dozen different categories. Most of the time, these categories are taken directly from the request for documents, but the producing party also may want the documents further categorized. The next step after coding the categories is to decide how important the document is. Remember, in many cases, there are hundreds of thousands or millions of document pages to review. Thus, the firm's attorneys only want to see those documents that may make a difference in the case—those that provide strong support for, or strongly refute, their legal arguments. This will better prepare them to defend or prosecute their claims. Therefore, important documents are coded with an additional category labeled "hot" or "key," so they may be closely reviewed by law firm attorneys at a later date.

The last step in document review is to determine whether the document is "privileged." A document is privileged if it reflects attorney-client communications or is a document created either by a lawyer or by someone else at the lawyer's direction. Documents that are privileged may be withheld from production—that is, not turned over to the other side. However, the general nature of the document must be disclosed. Labeling documents as privileged is a crucial part of this process and is the main justification for the requirement by many firms that attorneys conduct the document review. If a document that is privileged is inadvertently produced to the opposing party, a court can conclude that the producing party has "waived" its claim of privilege—and not just in relation to that document, but also with regard to the entire legal matter that the document discusses. Law firms would provide project attorneys with a list of all known attorneys who have been employed by the client, as well as those attorneys who worked for the client in-house. Sometimes there would be hundreds of attorneys listed. Project attorneys were tasked with making sure to check the senders and recipients of e-mail and other documents to make sure that all privileged documents were flagged and retained. Given the importance of this task, I always found it surprising to see the way that law firms could be careless in the creation or dissemination of the attorney list. Oftentimes we would be informed halfway through a project that the client or law firm had just "discovered" another attorney or law firm that had worked for them. I would then sit for a minute, wondering if I had let through documents with that attorney's name on them, but of course there was no way to know.

The process of document coding can be illustrated by providing examples from two projects on which I was employed. All identifying information about the companies—their names, industries, the date of the review, and other facts—has been altered. The first document review involved a very simple and stable coding process; the second was quite complex and sometimes shifted. The first review occurred in 1999 and involved a Second Request from the FTC for documents directed to Koolit Corporation, a manufacturer of refrigeration equipment. Koolit had notified the FTC that it had entered into an agreement to acquire a smaller rival company. The FTC issued a Second Request to Koolit that first described the relevant products that were the subject of the request and then went on to request documents related to eleven "specifications" covering a three-year period prior to the date of the request. Most of these specifications were similar to other antitrust Second Requests and included broad categories such as bids, plans, competition, prices, advertising, and research and development. Each specification was further explained in the Second Request. For example, the "plans" specification requested "[a]ll documents relating to your or any other company's plans relating to any relevant product, such as business plans, strategies, goals, objectives, expansion or reduction plans, research and development efforts, retrenchment projects, and presentations to management."

The Koolit case was an electronic review. The firm had rented a dozen computers that were placed at tables in what appeared to be a former storage area. We spent a half day being trained how to use the coding software. Then we were assigned electronic folders, each containing one hundred documents. On our screens were two windows: In the right window, the document itself appeared; in the left window was the coding form. At the top, we could click on boxes marked "responsive" or "nonresponsive." If nonresponsive, we continued on to the next document. If responsive, we clicked one or more of the eleven specifications to which the document was responsive. There was also a category marked "hot document" and a section at the bottom to record whether the document was privileged. Once we had coded our one hundred documents, we were to return to the home page and start on another batch of documents. We did this for twelve hours a day, six days a week.

The second case was much more complex; it involved a request for documents by a state's attorney general against a medical devices company, BodyMed, for marketing its products in excess of Food and Drug Administration (FDA) approval. The case itself was highly confidential because the existence of the inquiry was not publicly known. In this case, there were thirty-five specifications of documents. Some specifications were very broad (for example, asking for all documents related to marketing, sales, and training) and some were highly specific (relating to compensation of the sales force and correspondence with government agencies). Besides being numerous, the specifications were written by the attorney general of a small state and were not terribly well drafted. Thus, during the first couple of months working on the case, there was tremendous disagreement among the project attorneys, and between some of the project attorneys and the firm's attorneys, about which types of documents fell into which of the thirty-five categories. Eventually, over weeks and months, a consensus among the attorneys began to develop and the firm finally produced a ten-page memorandum explaining each of the specifications.

However, this was not the only complexity. The firm added more coding categories for its internal use, including ten categories of "hot" documents. These categories included documents showing BodyMed's concern about particular doctors, reports of adverse reactions to the product, and improper marketing. In addition to checking any of these subcategories, we also had to note whether the document was "hot good" (appearing to help BodyMed) or "hot bad" (appearing to hurt BodyMed). At the same time, of course, we also had to watch for privileged documents, and fill out an additional "pink sheet" for them. Another set of complex rules involved how to code e-mails. There was a different rule for "nonresponsive e-mail with responsive attachments," "responsive e-mail with nonresponsive attachments," "nonresponsive e-mail with missing attachments," and "privileged nonresponsive e-mail with missing attachments."

About six months into the process, a new issue arose. Apparently, a former employee of BodyMed contacted the attorney general with information about BodyMed's product. While BodyMed felt the employee was wrong about the product's safety, it felt it had to respond to potential questions from the attorney general. Thus, we got another coding sheet that added eight new issues to be reviewed. If we saw the employee's name in the document, we checked a box. If there was discussion of a particular biochemical theory (which was fairly obtuse and, frankly, never well understood among the project attorneys), we checked another box. We also were required to go back and recode several dozen boxes of documents that were thought to contain documents involving this former employee.

This was a paper review project, so all this box checking was done manually, and a new coding sheet needed to be filled out for every document in every box. This was particularly cumbersome in the case of e-mail. Each box contained thousands of sheets of paper. If the box was filled with mostly short e-mails, we knew we would be working on that box for quite some time. (At other firms, we were sometimes allowed to "batch code" documents by bundling similar ones under a single coding sheet. This saved time and effort and made the project significantly less tedious.)

On top of keeping all these categories straight, there were substantive complexities, too. The BodyMed product itself was highly technical and had a long research and development history. Many of the documents contained medical terms and discussed scientific research that few of the attorneys initially understood. Thus, there was a long substantive learning curve, as well as a necessary adaptation to the coding process. When I joined the project, other attorneys had already been there for six months. I ended up staying on the project for eight months, until the firm, citing costs, brought more of the review work in-house.

Regardless of the particularities of each document review project—the different corporate industries, legal issues, and law firms—the broad process of document review remained quite similar. We were performing the very limited task of coding documents into categories. While we were occasionally asked to perform other (even simpler) tasks, we were almost never pulled into more substantive aspects of the case. Our job was to read documents and check boxes.

Deskilling

Document review obviously requires certain skills. To properly perform the work, a project attorney must learn about the substantive aspects of the case, including the client's products, markets, and competition. The project attorney also must internalize the request for documents so that he or she can determine if a document is responsive, and if so, into what category it should be coded. Ideally, the reviewer should also understand what is at stake in the case, and therefore be able to recognize a "hot" or important document when it arises. Finally, the attorney needs to understand the basic rules of privilege and must properly identify documents involving attorney-client communication or attorney work product.

Thus, document review work does require some learning and the exercise of good judgment. However, most of the matters I worked on were more similar to the Koolit case than the BodyMed one. And, of course, the fact that document review requires *some* skills does not imply that the work was not deskilled *relative to* other types of work performed by attorneys. Indeed, the work did not require a great deal in the way of *legal* skills. Despite this, most firms required that document reviewers be licensed attorneys, and there seemed to be at least two reasons given for this requirement. First, there is the issue of privileged documents; privilege is a legal concept, ostensibly requiring legal judgment. Second, attorneys at the law firm must indicate to the opposing party—whether it is the government or a private party—that it has used "due diligence" in responding to the party's document request. Many firms appeared to believe that they could not in good faith claim due diligence unless attorneys had been employed to screen and code the documents.

I asked the attorneys I interviewed to rank the skill level required for document review on a scale of 1 to 10, where 1 represented the simplest legal work, typically assigned to law clerks, and 10 the most complex work handled by attorneys. Nearly everyone answered 3. Some project attorneys believed that at least a portion of the work involved in document review should be performed by lawyers, citing the need to recognize privileged documents. When I asked Vince this question, he paused a moment, then answered: "I think it requires attorneys' eyes in the sense that we're supposed to legally find whether something's relevant to a document request by the government and we have to determine whether it's privileged or not. But—having said that, I think anyone could do this stuff. I just say that maybe attorneys have to do this because we have to make the privilege calls."

A couple of others thought that attorneys could better spot legal issues in the documents. Frances said: "I don't think it *needs* to be [done by attorneys], but I think overall it helps catch things. Just from my experience, I've seen document review done by paralegals and done by attorneys. Attorneys catch more, have more of an eye on what the issues are—what would be important, what to use, and how to use those documents later on—whereas a paralegal sees it 'in the box,' so to speak." Debby also felt that attorneys should be used because they could keep their mind on the "big picture," and therefore determine how individual documents could help or hurt the overall strategy.

Melinda disagreed about the privilege issue. She pointed out that one does not need to be an attorney to recognize an attorney's name or spot the difference between a legal document and a business document. Some of the attorneys thought that firms used lawyers only because of their higher billing rates. Kathy said she worked on a project where both attorneys and nonattorneys were reviewing documents, and she did not see any difference in quality between the two groups. Most of the attorneys I interviewed believed that nonattorneys could perform document review adequately if they were well trained and closely supervised. Larry said that "anybody off the street" could do the work. He added: "It's not coloring book easy, but after you've been doing it for a couple of days, you could do it blindfolded." Bernice said that "we're really not contract attorneys. We're clerks. They don't want attorneys. They just need someone to follow the rules." Similarly, Kathy told me: "I think literally, like, all we have to know is how to read, and that is it, and that seems suspect sometimes." Evan succinctly concluded: "It's a real waste of educated people."

Many law firms instituted a guideline about spotting privileged documents that was referred to as "dummy priv" by the project attorneys and even by some of the law firms. Dummy priv required that the project attorney code a document as potentially privileged if there was the slightest indication that it might be privileged, such as if an attorney's name appeared anywhere in the document. (Even though some documents may contain communications to or from attorneys, or even might be written by attorneys, they are nevertheless not privileged. This is because they might be sent to the attorney solely for informational purposes, or were created by an in-house attorney while wearing his "business hat" as opposed to his "legal hat.") The institution of dummy priv seemed to partially undercut the argument that document review must be performed by attorneys—first, the law firms claimed that document review required professional legal judgment, and then they prohibited the use of that judgment.

When I was on a project, I often witnessed "gallows humor," employed to denigrate the skill level of the work. For example, there was an often-repeated joke that "trained monkeys" could do document review. One day, I was sitting next to Randy on a computer-based project, and we were both running through hundreds of documents that were just digital photographs that were all nonresponsive and could be easily—mindlessly—coded. Randy said: "You could train a pigeon to do this—to look at a picture and mark it 'N/R' [nonresponsive]." I told him about a famous study that I had read where researchers trained pigeons to be able to distinguish between paintings by Monet and Picasso. Randy and I spent the next hour listing the ways that pigeons would actually be superior to attorneys in doing document review. Pigeons would be willing to work for food, they would not complain about being bored, and they would not take as many bathroom breaks. We laughed as we pictured rows of pigeons bobbing up and down at computer terminals, coding documents through rote conditioning. Maya also invoked an animal metaphor during our interview—she said she sometimes pictured herself as a hamster in a cage who keeps hitting the little lever over and over to get food.

Most attorneys recognized that these jokes were exaggerated and were largely a response to the mind-numbing repetitiveness of the work. Bill began by telling me that document review "was completely mindless work," saying "it required no brainpower whatsoever other than, like, getting to work safely." He quickly pulled back, acknowledging: "Well, I guess you have to read the documents and think about them." Rick called the work "mundane and pedestrian," but admitted that it "couldn't be done on autopilot." Indeed, it sometimes took me a couple of weeks to really begin to feel comfortable with these coding tasks, even in a relatively straightforward case, although the learning curve became shorter with each project I did. Every day brought new questions and new "wrinkles" to the coding process. This learning occurred over time, and therefore it was not always obvious to the reviewers how much we had come to understand about the case through document review. This was always brought home to us in those instances when a law firm would require some of its associate attorneys to do document review. These requests often were met with groans from the associates, many of whom seemed to feel the work was beneath them. However, when the work always turned out to be more complex than the associates had first thought, the project attorneys would find some perverse, albeit temporary, pride in the associates' struggling over document coding.

Nevertheless, the project attorneys were sometimes called upon to do truly unskilled work. I once performed data entry in a case for twelve hours overnight, after reviewing documents during the day. Other attorneys had been employed to do data entry full-time. Evan began temporary work as a paralegal on data entry projects, earning $12 to $15 per hour. Larry told me of a project he worked on for several weeks that he labeled "sub–data entry work." He was amazed that the law firm had actually hired more than a hundred attorneys and was paying them $25 per hour to "look up a particular Web site, take the catalog number of a particular album, and put it on a piece of paper." He told me: "I mean, it was unthinkably ridiculous, even by project attorney standards."

Mitch told me about one project where he was asked to "unitize" documents for eight hours. He explained that "unitize" was a euphemism the law firm used in its client billing—to the rest of the world it meant "stapling." Mitch said after stapling documents for six hours with a manual stapler, he asked the firm if he could have an electric one. The firm refused. An hour later, the project supervisor told the attorneys they would need to work over the weekend, and asked everyone "to wear your grungiest clothes because we'll need to go out to the warehouse and schlep boxes out to the truck, and then meet the truck back at the office." Mitch left the project, telling the firm: "I'm not a moving man, I'm not a stapler." When I asked Mitch how the firm and his placement agency responded to his quitting the assignment, he told me: "Well, the firm was pretty pissed off. The agency backed me. I mean, there were other attorneys there who were tickled pink to be getting paid $25 or $27 an hour to staple. You know, if I'm going to whore myself out, I choose my johns carefully. Just because you pay me money doesn't mean I'm going to do what you ask me to do. I'm just not going to schlep boxes and staple paper. I didn't need the money that bad."

Evan had a similar experience. He got a call one day requesting him to help a law firm's client move some furniture for four hours. Evan had already felt that he was being underemployed doing data entry projects. He told me: "It's bad enough to have to enter document information for some big old litigation case, but it's something completely different to become, you know, a laborer."

Interestingly, Kevin Henson (1996) found similar evidence of "unskilling" in his study of clerical temporary workers. Many of the clerical temporaries he interviewed already felt underutilized doing regular temporary work. Sometimes they would be called upon to do work that was even less suited to their abilities and training. Henson wrote: "Other temporaries hired for clerical or secretarial work were, on arrival in white-collar attire, asked to distribute flyers on windy Chicago street corners, stock supply rooms, and clean offices and bathrooms. Temporary workers insulate core workers not only from the vicissitudes of the economy but also from tedium, hard physical labor, and disgust" (p. 89). It appears that once a worker is labeled a temporary, any work that does not fit permanent workers' job descriptions can become "fair game" and be shunted off onto the temporary worker.

Management Control

Document review work can require a substantial commitment of personnel, resources, and time. However, in conceptual terms, it is one narrow piece of the larger case and, as demonstrated above, the required tasks are very narrowly circumscribed. Project attorneys read documents and code them into various categories. When all the documents have been coded, the project is finished. Thus, there would appear to be the potential for a high degree of management control over the work process in document review. Comparatively, other tasks required in the same case that are performed by permanent employees—such as legal research, drafting of documents, and planning strategy—are more complex, more difficult to quantify, and therefore more difficult to monitor and control.

In practice, the amount of control that firms were able to exercise over the document review process varied a great deal. Firms employed a number of direct and indirect methods to attempt to monitor output. Direct controls included counting the number of documents (if an electronic review) or the number of boxes (if a paper review) that were completed in a day. Firms also required project attorneys to work a minimum number of hours per day. They sometimes placed paralegals or staff attorneys in the reviewing room with the temporary attorneys to minimize Internet surfing or chitchat. Indirect controls included (rarely) appeals to professionalism or (more commonly) promises to be "rolled over" onto a subsequent project. One agency allowed its temporary attorneys to receive a 6 percent bonus if the firm's partner in charge of the project approved it.

However, these controls frequently met with limited success for a variety of technological, managerial, and economic reasons. Control techniques—and project attorneys' resistance to them—are discussed in detail in the following three chapters. Chapter 4 looks at struggles over the work process, Chapter 5 at struggles over the use of time, and Chapter 6 at struggles over identity.

4

Box Shopping in "Nike Town"

Struggles over Work

Conflicts between employer and employee can be conceptualized in four different realms: product, work output, time, and identity (Ackroyd and Thompson 1999). Within each of these spheres, employers and workers act out a mutually dependent struggle. Struggles over product typically take the form of employee pilfering or embezzlement. Because my research involved the provision of services, pilfering only occasionally arose in the context of "extras," like food. For example, I was assigned to a document review project at the Washington, D.C., office of a large New York firm that had a very nice cafeteria on-site. Project attorneys were permitted to enjoy dinner free of charge, but were required to pay for their lunches. The lunches were partially subsidized by the law firm, so they cost perhaps five dollars. I witnessed project attorneys who would finish their free dinner and then line up at the sandwich station and make a sandwich to eat for lunch the next day. On another project, I saw project attorneys filling Tupperware containers in the buffet line; because we were being fed lunch and dinner on the project, I assumed that these attorneys were taking food home for family members. Bernice told me that she was once subjected to a lecture directed to all the project attorneys—at a different firm—about stealing food from conference rooms and packing lunches from free dinners.[1]

---

[1] The press has reported a few cases of much more serious pilfering by temporary legal employees. Temporary paralegals and word processors have been charged with stealing damaging client documents and leaking them to the media. However, I never witnessed anything so dramatic.

The other types of conflicts were readily and frequently observed in my research. Struggling over work output is the subject of this chapter.

Theorizing Control and Resistance among Project Attorneys

Most studies to date involving control and resistance in temporary work have involved low-skilled work, such as that involved in most temporary clerical assigments (e.g., Henson 1996; Rogers 2000). These have generally found that aspects of the *temporary* nature of the work (such as the duality of control and stigmatization of the work) have significant effects on the patterns of control and resistance in the workplace. The few studies involving high-skilled technical and professional workers suggest that such patterns do not seem to be much affected by the temporary status of the employment. For example, Jackie Krasas Rogers (2000) finds that among the contract attorneys she interviewed, "responsible autonomy" (see Friedman 1977) operated as a sufficient control over their work, rendering direct controls unnecessary.[2] The contact attorneys "spoke of their allegiance to the profession, the practice of law, the intellectual challenge of law, or the values of law. Temporary attorneys cite these reasons for performing well on their jobs" (Rogers 2000, 139). Rogers finds "very little indication . . . that temporary lawyers engaged in acts of resistance except for their resistance to the stigmatized label of 'temporary.' In fact, temporary employment was itself framed as a means of resistance to factors outside of the temporary employment relationship" (p. 154).

It is not apparent that Rogers's conclusions about responsible autonomy are generalizable to other attorneys working in contingent arrangements,

---

[2] Direct controls would not have been effective for this group in any event, because traditional law firm controls involving rewards and sanctions cannot be employed against contract attorneys. For example, the "partnership carrot" could not be used to encourage compliance. In addition, because contract attorneys performed much of their work off-site, the law firm lacked direct surveillance controls. The firm also could not effectively use social control factors such as "demands for masculinized emotional labor" (Rogers 2000, 139). In emotional labor, management requires that certain employees who interact with the public present an emotional state to the public that is consistent with organizational goals, regardless of the employees' actual emotional state (Hochschild 1983). Arlie Hochschild (1983) proposes that the occupations most commonly requiring emotional labor (such as nursing) are disproportionately female. However, researchers have since written about emotional labor in broader settings. For example, Rogers (2000) seems to suggest that in masculinized emotional labor, attorneys might be expected to be aggressive and committed to the client's cause regardless of their personal feelings about the client or their own personality tendencies.

particularly document review. Rogers (2000) acknowledges that her sample of contract attorneys was small and limited to a single geographic area. She also notes that law firms had been downsizing their staffs, and one survey had shown that 70 percent of temporary attorney placement agency applicants would have preferred full-time work (p. 129). Thus, like many clerical temporaries, many attorneys not included in her sample did not seem to be freely choosing temporary work. In addition, there are significant differences in the structure and organization of various types of temporary attorney work. For example, document review differs from the type of work Rogers's contract attorneys were performing, along several dimensions: location, hours, supervision, skills required, opportunity for interaction, and interest level.

In fact, several factors appear to pose significant obstacles for control over document review projects. As suggested already and detailed more below, the work is perceived as tedious and boring; most attorneys are not freely choosing to do project work; and the reviewing attorneys are paid by the hour, providing an apparent incentive to prolong the work and restrict output. Thus, we might ask two related questions: First, does an internalized sense of "responsible autonomy" provide sufficient control over the work of project attorneys? Second, if it does not, what control measures are employed over the work process, and do project attorneys show signs of resistance to these methods?[3]

Law Firm Controls over Work

Attorneys I interviewed described document review using such terms as "obviously boring," "mindless," "grunt work," and "a real waste of educated people." They also complained about lack of autonomy, long hours, insecurity,

---

[3] There are three important considerations in discussing control and resistance here. One of these is theoretical and the other two are methodological. First, because of the unique nature of contract work, work conflicts could arise in several forms—between project attorneys on the one hand and agencies, law firms, and law firm clients on the other. I focus on conflicts between project attorneys and law firms, in part because such conflicts were the most observable. Second, control and resistance are actually joined as two sides to an ongoing struggle, and it is usually not practically possible to find a starting point in this mutually reinforcing conflict process. However, control and resistance must be theoretically disentangled for the purpose of analysis (Ackroyd and Thompson 1999). Third, it is oftentimes difficult to clearly distinguish between resistance, coping, and just having fun. However, the methods chosen here—participant observation and semistructured interviews—do help to resolve some ambiguities. In addition, I have chosen what I think are relatively clear examples of control and resistance.

lack of benefits, poor supervision, and minimal feedback. Most attorneys were doing the work as a last resort, and their attachment to the project was ephemeral. In addition, they were permitted or required to work very long hours—sometimes up to one hundred hours per week. Attorneys were paid time and a half for hours over forty per week, and they frequently did not know when the next project would start after the current one ended. Thus, they had powerful financial incentives to resist the work flow in order to extend projects.

Needless to say, I did not find that "responsible autonomy" was a sufficient control mechanism in document review projects. Thus, I saw law firms utilizing many control techniques, both direct and indirect. Direct controls included an extreme routinization of process and a very dramatic division of labor. The project attorneys performed a very specific task that is a small (but time-consuming) part of the overall project. The greater the division of labor, the greater potential there is for management control (Braverman 1974). In paper review projects, monitoring of output needed to be done manually by checking box sign-out records. In computer review, software allowed nearly instantaneous computing of individual and group output. Firms created coding sheets that left little room for creativity, and they sometimes dictated daily or weekly output requirements. On many projects, I saw that firms showed an extreme unwillingness to modify work requirements, even when it was obvious to the project attorneys that a process was highly inefficient or was even resulting in inaccuracies.

Other techniques included threats, promises, and "babysitting." Direct threats were used relatively sparingly, perhaps because of the professional work environment. Most of the direct threats I witnessed originated from paralegals. I worked at a particularly unpleasant law firm (Kerry and Merson) for several weeks, and was placed there by Harry, a notoriously dishonest placement agency director. Harry had the project attorneys meet at his office before heading over to the law firm. He spent about ten minutes prepping us for working there. Among other things, he told us that Kerry and Merson had a particularly extreme form of "dummy priv." Harry told us: "If a kindergartner with five minutes of training might think a document is privileged, mark it as potentially privileged." He added: "They treat you like you're a kindergartner who doesn't know anything and you have to prove them wrong."

My experiences certainly confirmed Harry's warnings. On the first day of a computer-based document review project there, a paralegal told the assembled project attorneys that if we used the firm's computers for any purpose other than to review documents, "[you] *will* be fired." On a project at a different firm, a paralegal once asked me why I was not going to dinner with the rest of the project attorneys. I told her that I thought I would work through dinner because I had to leave a little bit early. She said that attorneys were not allowed to stay behind in the room unmonitored, and that she would call my agency if I tried to do it.

"Babysitting" was a technique used by only a few law firms, including Kerry and Merson. On one project there, a paralegal was assigned to sit in the same room with the six project attorneys who were reviewing documents. For most of the two weeks he sat in a chair reading a novel, apparently to make sure we did not talk to each other. It was clear that the firm believed the cost of his salary was exceeded by the savings in attorney time that babysitting would create. Kerry and Merson was also extremely security conscious. Harry, the agency director, told me that this was because the firm had "line of sight to the White House." When he said this, I thought of at least one other firm with similar proximity to the White House that was nowhere near as preoccupied with security. At Kerry and Merson, project attorneys were treated like any other temporary visitor. We lined up at the security desk, showed identification, signed in, and then waited for a paralegal to arrive to escort us to our assignment. (At many other large firms, project attorneys were provided electronic badges, like those given to permanent employees. At the end of the project, the badges were deactivated.) This heightened concern about security continued once we were admitted into the building. On the first day of one project, we were told to walk directly from the front door to the project room, and that we were not allowed in other areas of the firm's offices. A project attorney asked if we could use the kitchen, which was not within this direct path. Two days later the paralegal let us know that the partner in charge of the case had granted us permission to use the kitchen to store our lunches and make coffee. On another project, we were required to ask a paralegal for a key card so that we would be able to return to the office after using the bathroom. At the beginning of one review, the document room was locked during our collective, mandatory one-hour lunch, but this was later relaxed.

The use of promises was a more common control technique. The most appealing promise was for further work because project work tended to be very irregular; these promises came in two varieties. First, there was the possibility that some project attorneys could be retained beyond the end of the document review for "special projects." For example, I worked with more than one hundred other attorneys on a project involving the beverage industry. The document review had been completed; however, the federal government had several weeks to review the documents before deciding whether to ask for more. Thus, all the project attorneys were paid to come to work for eight hours a day for more than two weeks, but no work was required of us. (At a rate of $25 per hour paid to the attorneys, plus mark-ups, this two weeks of nonwork likely cost the client at least $1 million.) Toward the end of the two weeks, one of the firm's associates asked for volunteers to move some boxes. Most of the project attorneys kept their noses buried in their newspapers or continued talking to their neighbors. A few days later, the few who had volunteered to move boxes were kept on and the others were let go. After that experience, I learned to be more eager.

The other type of promise of further work was to be "rolled over." As a project was beginning to wind down, law firms and placement agencies would suggest that there was another major project right around the corner. Sometimes these promises were made honestly—my last three projects involved working for the same law firm with barely a day off in between jobs. At other times, the promises were more nefarious. On one project, while passing by the elevator lobby, I overheard an agency manager tell his associate that as a project winds down, he must always be sure to tell the project attorneys that there is another project to which they could be rolled over. Otherwise, he said, "you'll never get them to finish the documents." (As discussed below, he was describing a risk that was quite real.)

Another set of controls was more indirect. It appeared that firms occasionally attempted to invoke the project attorneys' responsible autonomy by increasing their discretion somewhat or by actively soliciting their feedback. Less commonly, firms attempted to derive "emotional labor" from project attorneys, for example, by emphasizing the moral rightness of their client's legal position. One firm that was being investigated by the federal government assembled all of the project attorneys for a rare collective lunch. We were shown a video of an interview with a television personality who had been abusing the firm's product, and the firm's associates used the video as a launching pad to berate the government's claims. However, this type of appeal was very rare—perhaps firms recognized that project attorneys could not be made to care too much about whether or not one massive corporation swallowed another one.

Another indirect control involved insecurity. Theoretically, the relatively short tenure of document review projects should engender neither allegiance to the law firm nor much investment in the matter's outcome. However, insecurity frequently—and yet paradoxically—has worked in the favor of the law firms and placement agencies. Because of the "feast or famine" nature of the work, project attorneys needed to show the firm and the agency that they were good workers so they would be asked to stay on for further work, rolled over to a new project, or invited back later for another job. Some firms developed a core group of project attorneys that they would repeatedly call back.

Firms also closely controlled information. This was perhaps due in part to practical reasons, such as client confidentiality. However, the effect was also greater control over the project attorneys. Details about exactly when a project was scheduled to end or how much work was left were rarely provided, and the process of quality control over project attorneys' work appeared to be intentionally and repeatedly mystified. Project attorney Roger's complaint captured both insecurity and the knowledge vacuum when he said: "Tomorrow the firm could come to me, or the agency could call me and say, you know: 'The matter's settled,' or, you know, 'The firm has changed its focus,' or you know, 'They're downsizing,' and you're just stuck." Bereft of information, many project attorneys seemed to be in a constant "fog" about the project.

More positively, some firms attempted to provide decent working conditions for their project attorneys, including offices with windows. Windows and other conditions were always a major topic of interest for project attorneys, who highly valued the firms that provided better physical environments. Project attorneys traded "war stories" about working in terrible environments, whether the "concourse level" of a prominent law firm or the condemned building known as "Nike Town." Many firms provided on-site meals for the project attorneys, although many of us recognized this (probably correctly) for what it was: a means of keeping the attorneys on-site and therefore billing more hours.

Resisting Controls

Clearly, there were limits to the amount of control law firms could or would exert over work output. One major obstacle to control was access to information. While, as noted previously, law firms maintained control over high-level project knowledge, I saw the project attorneys develop deep expertise—one researcher (Kusterer 1978) terms this "hidden knowledge"—in both the techniques of document review and in the subject matter of the particular case. After all, our only task involved total immersion in the client's documents. This knowledge base could be exploited because it was difficult for managers to determine how quickly the work should be going.

Another obstacle to law firm control was that, while document review work is indeed repetitive and tedious, at the same time, the actual documents appeared rather randomly and were of an enormous variety; thus, the time it "should" take to review a box (or an electronic folder) could not be easily predicted. For example, a box could contain dozens of high-level, dense management reports (to be intensely scrutinized), hundreds of pages of spreadsheets (to be easily disposed of), or some combination of the two. Even if a box could somehow be identified and labeled as "easy" or "difficult," such a determination would have to be made by a law firm employee, requiring a preview of the documents, which would probably be considered poor use of the employee's time. Effective use of such a system also would require careful logging of the time each project attorney spent on each box or folder, and then a close comparison of time spent to time estimated. Law firm employees were frequently too busy for such detailed management tasks. Thus, the ability of law firms to set hard quotas for work output was compromised.

This last point suggests another control obstacle. Most law firm attorneys are not trained to be managers—either of people or of large projects—and many of those supervising document review were junior associates. A visit from the partner associated with the case or from the client was extremely rare and sometimes accompanied by a great deal of notice and an expressed or implied message to "look busy." In addition, many law firm attorneys were overburdened and would have had trouble finding the time to properly manage a project, even if they had possessed the skills.

One last obstacle to control originated in the complex relationship between the project attorney, the agency, the law firm, and the law firm's client. The client generally should be interested in minimizing hours, while the rest of the parties should have an interest in maximizing work (although the law firm, of course, has ethical and practical limits on how much it is willing to bill the client). In this vein, I repeatedly witnessed examples of law firm managers ignoring or even participating in billing abuses, including extended horseplay and overlooking widespread computer game use. On one document review project, a law firm associate sometimes spent several hours a week telling the project attorneys stories about his pedigreed dog, which he took to various regional shows. This associate rarely visited to talk about work, and the attorneys he supervised seemed to spend more time talking among themselves than doing billable work. On a later project at the same firm, the firm's staff attorneys regularly walked into the room where I was working, sometimes finding most of the project attorneys playing Text Twist on their computers. No one ever told us to "knock it off" and get back to work. Generally, this alignment of interests between the law firm and the project attorney changes the "frontier" of control and "creates a space for agency" and therefore for resistance (Gottfried 1994, 117). Project attorneys used this space for agency to engage in a variety of methods to resist the work limitations placed on them.

Work Limitation: "Soldiering On"

The work limitation known as "soldiering" (see Taylor 1911) appeared to me as one of the most widespread acts of resistance. It involved working slower (sometimes much slower) than necessary, while at the same time appearing to be concentrating on the work. Project attorneys were able to exploit the factors laid out previously—the knowledge gap, the typical lack of direct oversight, and the weakness of project management—to control the work flow. All of the attorneys I interviewed who had worked on more than one or two document review projects had witnessed (or had partaken in) soldiering. It could happen at any point in the review process, but was particularly apparent and widespread toward the perceived end of a project. Soldiering occurred in various ways—it could happen spontaneously or be planned, and it could occur on an individual or a group basis. Sometimes, group soldiering began without anyone clearly articulating an impending end of work; rather, the attorneys (most of whom had worked on prior document review projects) appeared to develop a sense that work was ending soon. (One only needed to notice that the stack of boxes was dwindling to "read the writing on the wall.") At other times, one or more of the project attorneys directly pointed out the diminishing number of boxes or files and suggested that the reviewers ought to work more slowly.

I had worked on a small-scale document review project with Susan and three other attorneys for two months and then left that project for another one. Although it was very rare for me to leave a project before its completion, I felt it was ethically appropriate in this case because there appeared to be very little work left. The six of us had worked in a windowless room on the opposite side of the building from the office of the partner who was supervising the project. After the partner had given us a brief overview of the case on the first day, he came by perhaps once a week to briefly check in with us. The following exchange with Susan—repeatedly interrupted by one or both of us laughing—brought me up to date on the project after I had left:

RB: Have you seen the phenomenon of the "slowdown" at the end of a project, where the—

S: Oh, I have *been* that phenomenon.

RB: What do you mean?

S: Where I—at [the law firm] where we worked together—

RB: Yes—

S: Well, there were two of us left. We were still there for a few weeks after you left. It was just me and another colleague—and, uh—it just took us a while to do the last box, and finally they just came in and told us it was our last day, and we should just let them know how far we'd gotten, 'cause I think they realized that we would never finish the box.

RB: Okay. How long do you think they—

S: I think my colleague had one box, I had one box. There was one box remaining, but they knew I think at that point that we were never going to finish.

RB: Okay. And how long would you say you worked on those three boxes together?

S: I'd say we may have worked about a week.

Working at my average pace, I had been reviewing documents in that case at a rate of at least a box per day.

Kathy recalled a similar process happening on a project, while being careful to point out that the attorneys did not overdo it: "So we, among ourselves, not that we were, you know, consciously trying to, you know, take five days to go through one box, but we kind of like . . . 'okay, well, there are only, like, five boxes out there and there are six of us in here, so we may want to not, you know, race through this, and just kind of make it last as long as we can without it seeming ridiculous.'"

In other cases, project attorneys *individually* slowed their work in order to prolong the document review; this could occur at any point in the process. I worked for a few months on a project in the oil and gas industry that involved about fifty project attorneys. We were reviewing documents electronically; for several days, many of us encountered hundreds of files that each contained fifty digital photos of gasoline service stations. It was patently obvious to everyone that the documents were nonresponsive and that each one should (and could) be eliminated from the review in an instant. In fact, I instituted a game among the project attorneys to see how quickly we could get through the files. The process involved a series of mouse clicks and keystrokes—as I later dictated in a note: "zero, enter, control, T; zero, enter, control, T; like, you know, three thousand times." After we had engaged in this game for some time, an attorney who was not "playing" turned to the rest of us and said we were "shooting ourselves in the foot" because our behavior was only going to make the project end more quickly. For the rest of the day, I would occasionally look over at this attorney as she clicked slowly through the photos of the gas stations, spending perhaps thirty to sixty seconds savoring each one.

I witnessed an even more blatant "slowdown speech" during a one-week document review project involving approximately fifteen project attorneys.

We were employed at a "remote" site in suburban Maryland, about a thirty-minute drive from the law firm. The weekend was approaching, the work was dwindling, and the partner on the case was to call in and check on the progress of our work. Even though it was apparent to all of us that the work would not last until the weekend, one of the project attorneys told the rest of us that we should stay through to Monday, "working" over the weekend. He said that he had not had work in a while, and he was going to "get as much overtime as I can." In this case, perhaps because this attorney was being so calculatedly overt, none of the other attorneys in the room supported him, and most did not stay past Friday. (Arguably, claiming to work when there is no work to be done at all belongs in a category separate from "soldiering.")

Another time, I was assigned to a paper review project involving an antitrust case in the electronics field. I was sitting next to another project attorney, Devon, who I noticed was working on a box that had the name of the client's chief financial officer on it. The box was full of mostly spreadsheets that each appeared to be fifty to one hundred pages long. On most projects, spreadsheets might fall into a responsive category; however, they required very little attention and were extremely simple to code. As I worked on my own documents, I occasionally glanced over at Devon. He was moving very slowly through the spreadsheets, examining each page for several seconds, even though they were just columns of numbers. As I said in my notes that day: "I just can't understand people like Devon. It's not worth extending the project if it means sacrificing my sanity. The only way I can get through this is if I keep really focused and really busy." No one managing the project ever questioned Devon's speed and he finished out the project with the rest of us.

Soldiering is a particularly difficult resistance tactic to counter because it is often hidden. Attorneys in slowdown mode *appear* to be working—they have documents and coding sheets in front of them, and they look like they are reading them. Indeed, perhaps they actually *are* reading them, but of course at a much slower pace than they need to. However, some firms did become aware of the slowing pace, particularly when it was toward the end of a project, a point where they likely expected it. When soldiering was identified, the firms sometimes invoked special measures to maintain output. For example, on some projects, most attorneys were let go when there was a small amount of work left, and the "A-list" attorneys were kept behind to do mop-up work.

At other times, law firm managers' efforts to finish a project took amusing, exaggerated forms. On one document review project that involved several hundred project attorneys working ninety-four-hour workweeks in a warehouse location, the project's end was in sight. A staff attorney I deemed "the Closer" was called from the firm's main office to make sure the last of the documents was finished. The Closer's first step was to remove from sight the remaining boxes of documents to be reviewed. He then personally parceled out the boxes to the project attorneys. For several nights in a row, the Closer announced that we should share with our fellow attorneys any documents remaining in our boxes, and that if we finished all the documents by 9:00 P.M., we could leave at that time, but bill two extra hours. This approach largely seemed to work, although Lynn, who also worked on that project, noted that even with these announcements, "people were still holding onto their little pile, because it gave them some sense of job security for some reason."

Of course, the problem with telling people to work at a faster pace is that it can be counterproductive. Reviewing documents resembles assembly-line work in many ways, but the final product is not truly standardizable and thus cannot be checked as easily for quality. When faced with requests to increase the pace, some attorneys said they responded by sacrificing quality for speed. When I asked Bill whether he was a fast worker, he responded: "Yeah, I mean, I definitely, when they say 'Crank up the documents' I crank it up, and that's—to be honest—at whatever expense. I mean, don't get me wrong—I'm not just letting crap go through, but if they say 'get out the documents' . . . I assume that they're smart enough to know that, you know, with increased pace there's going to be increased margin for error."

I also sometimes witnessed attorneys more or less randomly coding documents, perhaps figuring that no one was going to closely check their work. This was particularly true about coding documents as "nonresponsive." Many firms had their own staff attorneys or select project attorneys do a quality check on the document coding. However, most firms only did the quality check on responsive documents. Thus, some project attorneys seemed to feel that putting lots of documents in the "nonresponsive" pile meant that they could get their boxes done faster and would never have their decision making questioned.

This constant "dance" over work flow was part of my experience on nearly every document review project I worked on. However, the particular steps and the pace of the dance varied. It appeared that work output moved most appropriately when the document review project was small- to medium-sized, was relatively closely supervised, and where the physical location was in the law firm's office. Large projects, remote sites, and looser supervision led to greater levels of "hanky-panky," as Julie put it.

Work Avoidance: Box Shopping

"Box shopping" provided individual attorneys with another way to gain some control over their work flow. On most projects involving the review of paper documents, law firms did not dictate in what order boxes of documents were to be selected. Usually, the boxes were lined up against a wall, and attorneys were supposed to pick up a box and sign it out by its number. (There was only one project where we were required to take the next consecutively numbered box.) Some boxes were more desirable than others, and I observed a phenomenon that project attorneys termed "box shopping." Box shopping involved either eyeing the information on the outside of the box or looking at its contents (or both) to determine if the documents in the box would be more interesting to review, or more frequently, easier to code. All the attorneys I interviewed had heard of the phenomenon, and almost all of them had witnessed it. Many of them acknowledged participating in the practice, while a few expressed their disdain for it.

One way to measure the relative difficulty or interest of a box was to check the name of the "custodian" on the box; that is, the person from whom the documents were originally obtained. If the project attorney had recently completed a review of a different box of that custodian's documents, the attorney could determine whether he or she wanted to review more documents from that custodian. If the documents had been easy to code, if the attorney had gained some knowledge of the custodian's files that would speed the review process, or if the custodian merely had more interesting documents, then a box from the same custodian would be desirable. However, if the custodian's box proved to be difficult or uninteresting, then further boxes from that custodian would be avoided. Michael and Betsy told me that they chose boxes from the same custodian "to be more efficient." However, Melinda was more self-serving in her reasons for cherry-picking boxes. She said she sometimes picked a box because she "liked the kind of stuff they did," and she also "might specifically avoid them because I didn't like what they had." Betsy thought that some people box shopped simply to see more interesting documents. She told me, laughing, that she had "seen people box shop for the ones with the dirty e-mails and the more interesting little [office] soap operas going on, between all their responsive stuff."

The other way to get an idea of what was in the box was to open it. Typically, the documents were printed on white photocopy paper, and a piece of colored paper was placed in between each document to separate them. Thus, by eyeing the relative ratio of colored paper to white paper, one could get a quick feel for how many documents were in the box. Normally, more documents meant more work because on most projects a separate coding sheet needed to be filled out for each document. Also, shorter documents frequently meant e-mail, which was denser in form than, say, a spreadsheet or a PowerPoint presentation, and also needed to be read more closely. Melinda told me she had been stuck with boxes that were full of one-page e-mails that "took forever" to code. On her current project, she said she looks for a box that "doesn't have too many green pages." I continued:

RB: Okay. And so, do you open the box?
M: Yeah, I do.
RB: Okay.
M: I do.
RB: And so how many would you say you open before you take a box?
M: Probably two.
RB: Two.
M: [*laughing*] I'm being honest.

Opening the box also could tell you how full it was. (Not all boxes were completely full; in addition, on some projects, boxes came in different sizes, with the smaller boxes being more desirable.) Picking up the box also could indicate how full it was, but this was more conspicuous. Lynn and I talked about how she selected a box:

RB: When you said you pick a lighter box, so you pick some up—
L: Oh— [*laughing*]
RB: —when you're doing that?
L: Oh, yeah.
RB: Yeah? And how many typically before you pick one?
L: Oh, just a couple. Like the first three that are on top of the pile. I don't go digging through the whole pile for 'em. [*laughing*]

However, Lynn said that she stopped short of actually opening the boxes, adding: "That's probably why I always get the crappy ones."

Some attorneys, sensing that the practice was not entirely equitable, told me that they box shopped only at certain times. Larry told me he would box shop only "if I'm having difficulty meeting my limit for the day, for the week, if for whatever reason things are going slowly. Then I'll do that. I'll try and help myself out." Evan told me he would pick a "shorter box" toward the end of the day because he did not like leaving unfinished boxes for the next day.

A few attorneys I spoke with expressed some annoyance at the practice. Frances told me she never would "cherry-pick" a box. She said she had spoken up when she had seen other attorneys do it. She told me: "I mean, I can understand why they do it, but you know, it's a team effort—should be, anyway. It's just a pet peeve." Bill was working on his first project. He said he had never seen anyone box shop, but if he did, he said: "I'd kick 'em in their ass. I'd be like: 'Just take a box.'" Debby said that box shopping is "tremendously selfish to try to increase your numbers and look good," and that "when you're working in a really small, close environment, maybe you should try not to piss off the people surrounding you."

Several attorneys expressed the pointlessness of box shopping. Evan said that we are all being paid by the hour, not by the box, so finishing a box just means that you need to go start another one. Kathy expressed the sentiment of many attorneys—even those who did box shop—when she questioned whether appearing to work faster is beneficial:

> I think [box shopping] is really sad because I think that, you know, we're all contract attorneys. None of us—unless you're really lucky and, like, a miracle happens—are going to be hired [permanently]. I've definitely come into contact with people who seem to think that if they kiss a lot of ass and ask a lot of questions and flip through the documents like they're not really reviewing them, but just so they can get through their boxes faster, that they're going to be seen as special. I think it's really sad.

Box shopping is a behavior that is open to multiple interpretations because it appears to have multiple motivations. For some, it was a way to more easily meet a real or perceived production quota. For others, it was a means to be more efficient by choosing recognizable custodians. Some seemed to just enjoy the sense of having completed more boxes of documents, even though they must have realized that doing more boxes meant neither less overall work nor greater potential for advancement. Box shopping may not appear to be an act of resistance because it does not affect the overall work process. However, it seemed to provide a small way to exert some control over a process that offered the attorneys very little autonomy. It was one way to control the flow of documents, which otherwise could feel endless and oppressive.

Laughing It Off

Humor is an understudied aspect of the workplace, even though by most accounts joking is endemic in organizations (Ackroyd and Thompson 1999).

Some have seen humor as a way of either dealing with threats and adversity or introducing meaning and pleasure into the workplace. Others see humor in the context of control and resistance, where humor serves as a "safety valve" that diffuses tension and thus makes employees easier to control (Rodrigues and Collinson 1995).

Ackroyd and Thompson (1999) see three types of humor operating in the workplace: clowning, teasing, and satire. Each of these can serve to further define and delimit the employees' subculture, and can be seen in the context of control and resistance, but each in different ways. In clowning, people make fools of themselves for the amusement of others. Clowning is extremely common at work, but is the most frowned upon by management because it is highly subversive of order. Teasing is a very common practice in the workplace. While teasing is not resistance *per se*, since it is not directed against management, some see it as strengthening employee bonds and therefore "far from being manageable or supportive of management" (p. 108). Satire has perhaps the most potential for subversion. Satire has been described as involving "a systematic cynicism. Satire engages in mimicry and mockery (from irony, through sarcasm and distortion, to insult) which is used to expose the foolishness, partisanship and/or hypocrisy of its target" (p. 111). As management strives ever harder to control the values of an organization, resistance may grow stronger, and some of this resistance will take the form of satire, which particularly can carry the message that employees reject management's priorities.[4]

Among project attorneys, I saw all three types of workplace humor employed. There were certainly "clowns" among us who kept us all laughing, sometimes by poking fun at themselves and other times by gently mocking the working conditions. Teasing was also a common occurrence. With both clowning and teasing, the main ostensible purpose seemed to be to alleviate boredom. Other times, prolonged joking seemed to be a symptom of fatigue. Joking revolved around the typical workplace topics, as well as those particular to document review. Most of it was lighthearted and did not appear to have an agenda. However, sometimes the joking served as an expression and reinforcement of the project attorney subculture. For example, project

---

[4] Some question the power of humor in the workplace, seeing it as a relatively impotent vehicle for resistance and subversion (Mulkay 1988). Most of the time, humor does not lead to changes in the conditions that employees are poking fun at. And in some cases, management has co-opted employee satire by encouraging it, thus taking away its potential "sting." Nevertheless, some believe that "humorous and satirical utterances may be the only way of expressing an alternative point of view. . . . At the very least, satire keeps dissent alive and sustains the independence of those disposed to be critical" (Ackroyd and Thompson 1999, 114–15).

attorneys would sometimes "joke" about other attorneys working too quickly. I was on the receiving end of such comments, as were some of the attorneys I interviewed. Some claimed that the teasing—"you're going to work us out of a job"—was innocent fun, while others saw these comments as serious attempts to slow down the pace of work ("enforced soldiering"). Other researchers have reported similar situations among temporary workers. One found that temporary employees reported being told by others to slow down, but at the same time they could not work too slowly or they would be fired (Henson 1996).

The clowning and teasing frequently involved "forbidden topics" such as sex and politics. Most of it was well tolerated, but sometimes conflicts developed. I was once assigned to a project that was already in its sixth month. Most of the attorneys had developed a certain degree of comfort with each other, and they joked about many "taboo" topics. About a month after I joined the project, we all received a memo from our placement agency that read in part:

> Please remember to keep the topics of any conversations appropriate for the workplace. For example, discussions touching on issues of politics, race, gender, nationality, religion, or sex are best left outside the office. Additionally, please remember that you are working in close proximity to others who are trying to focus. For the benefit of your co-workers, please avoid conducting loud conversations in the common work areas. If you are calling across the room about something unrelated to work, you are probably disturbing someone.

The memo did not have its desired effect. Rather, the attorneys spent time trying to figure out who had tipped off the agency to our inappropriate conversations; most of us assumed it was "one of us" rather than a law firm employee. Most of the attorneys did not change their behavior, but many prefaced their comments by warning that what they were about to say was "off-memo." Here, I saw resistance to an attempt to regulate our "free space" (Collinson 1988)—represented by our choice of conversation topic—and a real desire to maintain the informal but entrenched project attorney subculture that had arisen.

Satire also was commonly employed by project attorneys as a way of alleviating our frustration. Here, the "safety valve" theory of humor seemed to be at work. A special language developed that frequently mimicked that of the firm's attorneys or the agencies' staffs. For example, the inconsistencies in instructions about coding documents served as a constant source of amusement. We would first receive particular instructions about a type of document, such as: "All health plan brochures are 'responsive' and should be coded as 'plans' on the coding sheet." Two weeks (or two hours) later, a firm attorney might tell us: "We've decided that health plan brochures are now 'nonresponsive' and should be excluded from production." It was obviously impractical to go back and check the already-reviewed boxes to remove all the health plan documents. Thus, the firm attorney would always add that the policy applied "going forward."

"Going forward" became a mantra among project attorneys. When one of us would discover we had been coding a type of document incorrectly for some period of time, we would say: "Okay, I'll start doing it the other way—but 'going forward.'" In this way, the project attorney was expressing his or her disdain for a coding process that seemed fairly arbitrary and subject to constant change: "If the firm can't get it right, why should I?" Satire thus appeared to be resistance in one sense—that is, the intentions, ideals, or instructions from project managers were poked fun at or inverted. However, satire never served to bring about significant change; rather, it alleviated our frustration and provided a collective bonding experience. We were able to recognize the overarching absurdity of much of what we were being asked to do, and at the same time appreciate that all of us saw it, too.

Bitching

In my own experience on projects, I did not encounter a great deal of "gossip" (Tucker 1993); that is, project attorneys had relatively few significant complaints about the way a law firm or agency had treated them specifically. Most of the time, project attorneys felt that the downsides of the work (whether articulated as lack of respect, low pay, or poor working conditions) were rather similar, regardless of which agency had placed us.

However, there were some exceptions. One agency in particular was the subject of complaints by many project attorneys who had worked with it. The head of the agency, Harry, was regularly accused of lying to attorneys by falsely promising them overtime, rollover, and other benefits. I registered with this agency after hearing about it, to find out for myself whether these stories were true. On the first project I was assigned to, Harry told me that it would require "lots of overtime." I accepted the project on that basis. When I arrived at the law firm on the first day, the attorney in charge of the project told the eight project attorneys that we would be working regular forty-hour weeks for the duration of the project. This largely turned out to be true. With the exception of Harry's agency, most of the attorneys I interviewed—as well as the ones I spoke to more informally—did not have many serious problems with individual treatment by their agencies or law firms.

Much more common than gossip was generalized complaining—what I call "bitching"⁵—about a number of aspects of project attorney work, work-places, working conditions, and financial arrangements. One of the most common things to bitch about was the food. Firms had different policies on providing food. Some had full-fledged cafeterias in their buildings. Others reimbursed us for our meals if we had to work through the dinner hour, typically past 8:00 P.M. Sometimes the work site was in a remote warehouse and was not close to reasonable restaurant options, and thus food would be brought in from restaurants or caterers. Because I saw that food was such a constant topic of conversation, I asked the attorneys about their feelings concerning the food that was provided and why it was such a dominant topic of conversation. Many of the attorneys I interviewed told me that they were thankful for the food that was provided to them, and that the quality of the food was "fine." Several commented that they really did not have a right to complain about the food because it was free. Melinda was pleasantly surprised about the food. She told me that it was much better than at the small firm where she had been an associate, where the staff was just offered "sodas in the refrigerator" and was taken out twice a year to a nice restaurant.

Others took the opportunity to dramatically air their gastronomic complaints. Firms that brought in meals from outside vendors caught the most flack from the project attorneys. Bill recalled a recent catered meal that he had despised. He told me: "The sandwiches here are *horrible*. The day that they had that Mediterranean *sand*, I was not very happy about that. The *sand* with *bread*?! That was horrible." However, he quickly backtracked, saying: "You know, it's food. I'm not going to bitch any more than I need to." However, Evan didn't bother to hold back. He told me:

> E: Come on, you know they wouldn't be feeding that [food] to their
> clients or to the partners and it's certainly not the food that they
> were serving on Fridays to all the associates, either. I know that
> they tried, but at some point they relinquished control of it even
> from the paralegals, and gave it to whoever happened to be driving

---

⁵ Researchers have studied employee complaining, and have variously labeled it "bitching," "venting," "outbursts," or merely "disclosing." Here, I use the term "bitching" because so much of the complaining is directed to aspects of the work that could not realistically change very much. The word "bitching" is also chosen because it suggests a harder edge than mere "venting" would imply. I also employ it here because many of the attorneys I interviewed used the term themselves, without prompting from me. By using the term, I do not mean to imply that all the complaints were insignificant, and I certainly do not imply a gendered aspect to the process (see Sotirin 2000; Sotirin and Gottfried 1999).

the van. And I'm like, you know, these are supposed to be brilliant people: Hello, you do that, the taxi service is the one that's going to select it based on their convenience, you know?

RB: Mm-hmm.

E: So we ended up getting sandwiches all the time. Why? Well, because they keep better, you know?

RB: Mm-hmm.

E: Have you ever noticed all the cheese was melted all the time? That's because they were, like, going and getting it way in advance. I mean, it's not brain surgery here.

Vince found the food on some projects to be acceptable, but said that "normally it's crap." He said that the quality "depends on how nice the firm is. They'll bring some caterer in. The food is crummy, it's cold, it's very fattening. It's just like eating in an army cafeteria."

All the attorneys I interviewed noticed that food seemed to be a common thing to bitch about. When I interviewed Debby on her first project, she told me: "We've been so pushy when it comes to food. And I don't know if this is normal on other projects, but it's been insane. If people are bringing you free food, my theory is: 'Shut up and eat it.'" I asked the attorneys why we were so obsessed with the food. Larry responded: "Everybody talks, everybody shares. You sort of get a gang mentality about whether or not you're going to approve the food service that's provided. Rather than being thankful or appreciative, it's one of the few things apart from the documents themselves that people can readily bitch and moan about, with raw data in front of them at twelve and six." Frances said: "I think people bitch because they have nothing else to bitch about . . . or because they feel entitled: 'We're here, and we deserve, you know, to be treated like kings and queens.'" Vince said that people complained for two reasons: "First of all, because it *is* bad. The second thing I think is it gives us something to talk about." James thought that complaining about the food was part of our larger obsession with it. In a fourteen-hour day, food breaks provided an opportunity to get away from the documents. James told me: "I think it breaks the tedium for people." Rick also thought that food was a way of compensating for the boredom, and that obsession naturally led to complaining.

Food was hardly the only thing to bitch about. Project attorneys complained about the lack of windows in some facilities, the boring sameness of the documents, inconveniently located bathrooms, and firms that did not allow us to use headphones and listen to music or the radio. Bitching, like joking and satire, seemed to provide a "safety valve" to express frustration. It resulted in the release of anxiety, but not a change in conditions, because attorneys rarely moved from bitching to actually complaining to project managers. Most of the bitching had a "gallows humor" edge to it and was thus similar to humor in that it reinforced a sense of solidarity, bolstering the project attorney subculture's qualities of cynicism, powerlessness, and hopelessness.

Rationalizing Resistance

The attorneys I interviewed, as well as the ones I observed and interacted with, seemed to know on some level that several of the resistant behaviors described above could be seen as "wrong." For example, intentionally slowing down one's work so that it takes more time than necessary would appear to be a violation of the attorney's code of ethics. On a less-serious plane, rifling through a box would provide an unfair advantage and would "stick" someone else—who chose not to box shop—with the more difficult box.

Because acting unethically is inconsistent with professionals' self-perception, the attorneys I spoke with and observed employed a number of linguistic games to reduce their cognitive dissonance. The "accounts" that attorneys provided were not unlike those observed among white-collar criminal offenders. Researchers have long shown that white-collar offenders have a particular need to "neutralize" their offenses because they do not see themselves as "criminals." Various techniques have been observed, including: (1) denying responsibility (for example, claiming another party made the decision or the outcome was an "accident"), (2) rationalizing that the activity was actually beneficial, (3) denying the existence of a victim (claiming that no one was really harmed), (4) condemning the condemners (the rule itself is the harmful thing), and (5) appealing to higher authorities (i.e., stockholders or the person's family should take precedence over the law) (Sykes and Matza 1957).

Attorneys commonly told me that end-of-project soldiering was inevitable and relatively harmless, although some, like Michael, objected to it. When I asked Lynn about the phenomenon, she said she was aware of it. I asked her to describe it, and she laughed and responded: "A collective effort to get paid longer." It appeared to me that most attorneys rationalized soldiering using one of two accounts: First, they denied responsibility by claiming, like Lynn, that it was a collective effort, thus diffusing responsibility among all the attorneys. Second, they seemed to deny or minimize the existence of a real victim. Many attorneys told me—in this and other contexts— that the clients were multibillion-dollar corporations that could easily afford to pay millions of dollars to make sure their mergers went through. Thus, there appeared to be a sense among some project attorneys—usually somewhat obliquely expressed—that putting extra money in the pockets of the project attorneys was not going to really harm anyone. The indirect nature of the billing—the client paid the law firm and the law firm paid the placement agency—hid the client's actual costs from the project attorneys and likely made rationalization that much easier. In addition, there seemed to be a sense among many that the work was so tedious and unrewarding that we were entitled to any extra money we could wring out of the client.

Most attorneys who admitted that they sometimes *individually* slowed their work down also appeared to understand that this behavior was "deviant" and had to be accounted for. Some attorneys reported that they sometimes slowed their pace as a coping mechanism because of the tedium and the amount of hours worked. The most common rationalization was that the slowdown was actually necessary given the number of hours involved or the tedium of the work (justification 2, discussed earlier). Larry simultaneously minimized the existence of the practice and legitimized it:

> There are always going to be a number of people who joke about slowing down, but as—whether people actually do it, I'd like to think that a majority of them don't. I'd like to think that when people are taking breaks or screwing around, it's because they're tired, because they need to catch their second wind, because they're sitting in an office for twelve hours a day, because it's potentially tiring and antisocial. But as far as not doing a single sheet for eight hours—I know people have done that, I know people do it. I don't go near it. I do my work.

Project attorneys also rationalized their box shopping. As mentioned previously, some attorneys claimed this tactic increased their efficiency—that by choosing a custodian they knew, they could actually increase their work flow. A couple of attorneys I interviewed said they chose lighter boxes because they had back problems or otherwise had trouble lifting heavy boxes.

Irresponsible Autonomy

Some project attorneys professed high professional and ethical standards, took stands against wasting time, and claimed to take document review work seriously. At the same time, I often found evidence of "irresponsible autonomy" (Ackroyd and Thompson 1999) among the attorneys I observed and interviewed. Many project attorneys took part in blatantly unethical practices. I witnessed myriad acts of resistance in document review projects—only a handful of which are documented above—sometimes engaged in by the same attorneys who professed high standards during interviews. What explains, then, the marked difference between Rogers's (2000) findings and those of the current research?

First, explanations may reside in Rogers's methodology. Her conclusions about resistance among contract attorneys were based solely on interviews. However, the interview may not have been the best method to get at everyday acts of resistance, which are frequently well hidden (Prasad and Prasad 2000). Second, the attorneys she interviewed may not have been willing to acknowledge some behaviors that they knew to be unethical, and it is also possible that the attorneys themselves—like the project attorneys I interviewed—had adopted "accounts" to describe their resistance in more palatable terms, and thus to obscure it. In addition, it is not clear what Rogers's definition of "resistance" would have been among her contract attorney sample. For example, given my own experience in a wide variety of law firms, I find it highly unlikely that none of Rogers's contract attorneys had ever intentionally overbilled a client. If this type of behavior was found, it could be experienced or interpreted as "unethical" rather than "resistant"—however, we can only understand what the behavior "really" was through examining the attorneys' subjective accounts, which are necessarily lacking.

However, it may be that Rogers's attorneys truly did not engage in resistance, or did so minimally. If so, this lack of resistance could be explained by personal and organizational factors surrounding the type of contract work that the attorneys did. Rogers's attorneys likely had a more intimate relationship with the attorneys they worked for, because they were performing overflow and appearance work for small- and medium-sized firms. Also, Rogers's attorneys reported that they enjoyed the work they did, and they claimed to possess the power to turn down assignments. Many compared contract work favorably against working for a law firm. If a person experiences very high autonomy, then by definition there is little to resist, except as Rogers (2000) notes, the stigma associated with the label "temporary attorney."

Document review work stands in stark contrast in many respects. First, the work does not allow much professional autonomy—the law firm sets the working hours, as well as rigid conditions about how to perform the work. Second, most of the project attorneys I interviewed were working solely for a paycheck because they could not find work elsewhere. Many accepted work on a project even when they would rather not (for example, if they wanted to avoid working for a particular law firm) because they feared their agency would stop trying to place them. Third, document review is always performed at a law firm or at a site under its direct control. Rogers (2000) acknowledges that the intensity of employer control (and thus theoretically, I would add, the likelihood of resistance) may be enhanced when the contract attorney works in the firm's office. Fourth, the work itself is not enjoyable—it is highly tedious and repetitive—and it provides no room for advancement and no useful skills. Finally, the work is highly stigmatized. Many of the project attorneys I interviewed did not identify with their roles as project attorneys, and adopted highly instrumental approaches to their work.

Therefore, if the qualities of the work—its content and organization—determine the frontier of conflict, then it is not surprising that document review work would have a vastly different matrix of control and resistance than that involving Rogers's contract attorneys. Indeed, the frontier of conflict in document review work shares more characteristics with the findings of those who have studied clerical temporary workers (Gottfried 1994; Henson 1996; Rogers 2000).

However, a critical difference is that document review work is less fragmented than typical temporary work. One might expect that placing workers in collective physical proximity might heighten management control over work output. However, I observed that such proximity also opened spaces for resistance (see Gottfried 1994). Project attorneys were able to share information and thus collude in forms of resistance such as soldiering. (Proximity also allowed other forms of behavior antithetical to work, such as lengthy and distracting conversations.) Attorneys were also able to draw upon their "hidden knowledge" (Kusterer 1978) to resist managers' efforts to regulate the flow of work.

5

"Keeping Count of Every Freakin' Minute"

Struggles over Time

Under industrialization, working time rather than task time (work output) became the primary method of organizing work. Working time was made increasingly regular, defined by a specific number of hours in the day and days in the week. Employers were thus constrained because they could only assign tasks that could be completed during work hours and they had to compensate employees for work performed in excess of the allotted hours (Rubery, Ward, and Grimshaw 2005). Therefore, control over time became a central component of the working relationship (Epstein and Kalleberg 2001). Many researchers (e.g., Rubery, Ward, and Grimshaw 2005) have noted that the organization and control of working time in industrial democracies has changed in profound ways over the last generation. Work has become both more intensified (workers are being asked to do more during work time) and "extensified" (work is spilling out into nonwork time). In addition, there has been an increase in nonstandard work arrangements and a decline in collective regulation of working time.

Both hourly and professional/managerial workers are measured and constrained by time—for example, the factory worker punches a clock, while the lawyer's output is measured in billable hours. Nevertheless, professionals and managers have typically enjoyed much more autonomy than hourly workers in their *use* of time: "Experts are not usually asked to punch time cards, they take their coffee breaks when they like, they arrange their work schedules and vacations with relative freedom, [and] they have free access to telephones" (Larson 1977, 235). Even though professionals lose ideological autonomy as they are absorbed into bureaucratic organizations, they still have substantial control over their working time. There are further differences between hourly and salaried workers. With the hourly worker, the value of a unit of labor is relatively clear, as is the demarcation between working and nonworking life. The value of a unit of labor for those earning a salary is more ambiguous; also, work time is more likely to "bleed" into private time.

With temporary work (regardless of its type), the time-money exchange is explicit. Typically, the work is paid by the hour, the required hours are relatively fixed, and there is a finite beginning and ending to the employment relationship. In addition, temporary workers have little technical autonomy over the work; thus, their *use* of time is also constrained as the timing of work procedures and work output is strictly dictated and regulated. Widespread employment of temporary professionals is relatively new, so the extent that professionals will exercise autonomy over either structuring their hours or their use of those hours is unclear. Certainly in the case of project attorneys, autonomy over setting hours was strictly constrained; and because essentially one task was assigned, there was little autonomy in the use of those hours as well.

Nonetheless, project attorneys had a complex and paradoxical relationship to time. When they got a call from an agency, the first question for many—whether externally expressed or internally felt—was: "Is there overtime?" Time over forty hours per week paid time and a half. At $25 per hour, a forty-hour workweek would pay $1,000, while an eighty-hour workweek would pay $2,500. Because they rarely knew when the next project would come along, most attorneys jumped at the chance to work overtime. However, they also knew that working overtime bore substantial costs—the level of boredom and tedium would rise, their intimate relationships would suffer, and looking for permanent work would take a backseat to the demands of the current project. Then, in between projects, attorneys would anxiously phone or e-mail their agencies and colleagues, looking for the next project. However, once actually placed on a project, attorneys would wrestle with ways to manage the tedium of the work and look forward to its end, although they knew the next assignment probably would not be much different. The project would end, there would be a short sigh of relief, and the cycle of anxiety and tedium would begin again.

These struggles over time could occur "externally"; that is, among project attorneys, law firms, and agencies. Law firms sought control over time by dictating the number of hours and days to be worked, as well as minimum break times. Attorneys resisted these controls by accepting projects with the most overtime, by being less than scrupulous in their billing, and by attempting to control the speed and flow of work (as described in Chapter 4). Struggles over time also occurred "internally"; that is, project attorneys engaged in various strategies to manage the tedium of the work, and would try to strike a balance between outside demands and their need to maximize income in the face of uncertainty.

External Struggles

Life as a project attorney was a "feast or famine" existence. Most attorneys told me they had been out of work between projects longer than they had wanted, and also that they had worked more hours than they wanted to once they were assigned to a project. As detailed in Chapter 2, the idea of temporary attorneys working six months and then spending six months skiing or yachting was a complete fiction for this group. In fact, as Julie told me, it was very difficult to plan a vacation because she knew neither when the current project would end nor when the next one would begin.

Assignments were short (typically lasting a few weeks to a few months); however, some attorneys "lucked into" much longer projects. Susan was employed on a document review project in Chicago that lasted a year. She said that this had been the first project for most of the attorneys there, and so they had not known of the "temp circuit." As the project finally came to an end, they had not yet learned that they should be scrambling to find the next one. Other attorneys, including me, ended up working for law firms that had projects lined up, so we could easily be "rolled over" to a new project as soon as the current one ended. Some project attorneys had worked for several years for the same law firm on different projects, with little time off in between. While long-term projects or continuous rollover were not unusual, they certainly were not the norm, either.

The Agency Dance

Maximizing work while maintaining a positive relationship with our agencies was sometimes challenging. Most attorneys preferred to take on projects with significant overtime, but they were also hesitant to turn down less-intensive work for fear they would not be asked again. Several attorneys told me that they had never turned down an offer from an agency. Another difficult situation was when attorneys were faced with the "feast" of having an agency call them to start a project while they were working on a different project for another agency. Attorneys understood that it was a very bad idea to leave a project early, even though it was sometimes tempting. We would risk alienating our agency and the law firm, and we knew that maintaining positive relationships with our agencies was the key to finding more work. Larry particularly prided himself on his good relationship with agency personnel, saying: "I try and be more friend and colleague rather than just a flatline objective business relationship. There are standards and decorum to observe, but frankly I could end up going out to a bar with several of the people that work at these agencies because I've developed such a strange little rapport with them." However, no matter the quality of their relationships, most attorneys recognized that the agencies were "in the driver's seat." As Lynn put it, the agencies "have no allegiance to us, they're in it for themselves."

Most attorneys told me that they were in touch with all of their agencies at least once a week while they were looking for work, although Mitch told me he would phone in daily. The respect attorneys generally showed their agencies was sometimes not reciprocated. One agency, run by Harry, had a particularly poor reputation. Larry had been burned in the past by Harry, and told me: "I only take a certain sadistic pleasure out of hearing that he's acted the same way [with other people], because hopefully he'll work himself out of a job. He's honestly one of the worst people I've ever had the displeasure of knowing in a professional capacity." Mitch, who had also worked for Harry, nicknamed him "slicky-boy" and said he is "basically slime." Mitch said that after Harry had lied to him repeatedly, he pulled him aside and told him: "Look, I've met your type before. I have no problem working with you as long as you deal straight with me. I'm not responsible for how you deal with other people, but as far as your dealing with me, or dealing with your client regarding me, as long as you're straight with me, I'll make you a lot of money, you'll make me a lot of money, and everybody will be happy. But if you screw with me, you don't get to profit from the relationship." Mitch said after that, Harry stopped "screwing with" him.

This level of active animosity was rare; however, many attorneys felt they had been misled by their agencies. This was most typically related to the strange process by which document review projects were bid out. When law firms decide to use temporary attorneys on a large project, they typically solicit bids from several agencies and then select the one with the best bid. (Sometimes, for large projects, more than one agency is used.) However, the agencies do not wait until they receive word that their bid has been accepted, because typically the law firm wants project attorneys on the job almost immediately. Thus, agencies call their project attorneys before they have been awarded the contract and ask them if they are available for a project starting "very soon" or "next Monday," but do not acknowledge that they are merely bidding on the project. As a new project attorney, I did not understand this process, so I assumed the promised project was a sure thing. Sometimes I would turn down work from other agencies, believing I was starting on a project "next Monday."

Other attorneys reported similar experiences. Lynn was told of an upcoming project in October that did not actually materialize until December. (She had no way of knowing if the December project was even the same one she had been promised in October.) Bill told me that when he was close to finishing up his first document review project, he cleared his schedule when he got a call from his agency about a project. He mentioned the call to another project attorney who told him not to count on the project until he was actually there. Bill was surprised, and remembers asking himself: "Who is this disgruntled fool?" He learned the lesson shortly afterward. As his first project was ending, a staffer at his agency made the rounds of the project, telling everyone that they would be rolled over onto another project the following Monday. He said that several attorneys had registered with other agencies and had other offers, so they "really questioned, they really grilled her." One attorney said: "So wait. So you're basically saying that there's a definite job and we can assume we're all on, and we should clear our plans and not accept anything else." The staffer responded that "it's a closed deal. It's done. Monday is the start date." Bill said that she came back to them on Sunday night and told them that the project had been pushed back. He told me: "Really what I found out that means is they just didn't—that they lost the bid, they never really had it." After that experience, Bill took the advice of the "disgruntled fool" and did not assume he had the work until he actually arrived at the law firm.

Managing Uncertainty

Typically, attorneys were asked to start a project with very little notice. They sometimes received calls in the afternoon to start a project the next morning, although a one- to two-day time lag was more common. More than once, I missed out on a project because I took several hours to return the agency's call; I eventually learned to always carry my cell phone with me. Once a project actually started, firms and agencies sometimes appeared to deliberately obfuscate the timing involved, and a project would sometimes come to a halt with even less notice than it began. There was a story about a particular D.C. law firm that was oft-repeated to the point of legend. The firm, Kerry and Merson (discussed in Chapter 4), did not have much respect for its project attorneys. Several attorneys told me they had heard that during a project there, a firm lawyer told the project attorneys that there was a fire drill and they were to gather all of their personal belongings and leave the building. Once the attorneys were out of the building for a few minutes, the same lawyer told them to just go home for the day because the firm did not know how long the drill would last. When the attorneys arrived home, they found messages on their answering machines telling them the project was finished and they need not return. While I never was able to verify the story, it appeared to fit with the firm's reputation and my own experiences working there.

If this event actually occurred, it was unusual. More typically, we would get a strong sense that the project was coming to a close; for example, we would notice that new boxes of documents were not coming in. However, the precise end of a project was almost impossible to guess. Several times, I was part of a smaller group that was kept on to finish up the review. In each case, the law firm told us late one afternoon that we should not come back to work the next day. At other times, firms would dismiss the project attorneys in groups, saying that our agency would call us if they wanted us back. Two other times, I was called back several weeks after the projects were finished. Once it was because more documents had come in, and the other time it was to help the firm prepare for trial because I was the one most familiar with the documents. Sometimes, however, we were kept on well past the time when we thought the review was over. In one case—noted in Chapter 4—more than one hundred of us were retained for two weeks, though no work remained, because the firm was waiting for the regulatory agency to decide whether it was going to request additional documents.

As a project was ending, there was always a great deal of conversation about other projects that were coming up. Lynn told me she had been working on a large document review project at a warehouse in suburban Maryland when the project appeared to be winding down. She said that word of another pending project "spread like wildfire" and she was "flipped over to [another project] the very next day." When I asked Julie if she had ever noticed this "mad scramble" toward the end of a project, or partaken in it, she told me:

> Yeah. But I'd say I'm kind of a middle-of-the-roader. There are some people who are extraordinarily aggressive. Before the end of a project, when they even get a sense there's going to be an end of the project, they will be, like, 'Charley Hustle,' calling everybody, scoping out what's going on; they're very aggressive about it. There are other people who do nothing. I'd say I'm in the middle, so I will make

some phone calls, but I will be a little more passive in terms of at least waiting to see what the agency I've been working for is going to do for me.

Sometimes we lucked out and, like Lynn, were immediately rolled over to a new project. Other times, it appeared there was no work to be had.

This haphazard nature of the work was something that had to be managed, and the attorneys I interviewed took a number of approaches. Several attorneys said they were not bothered by feelings of insecurity. Lynn was one of the few I interviewed who said she liked the flexibility that temporary work afforded her, and that even after she could not find work in the fall of 2001, "the idea of flexibility still outweighs the fear of job insecurity." Mitch had worked as a solo practitioner for several years and then closed his practice and began taking on temporary work. I interviewed him during the final week of a project—the one where we were all being paid to sit around and do nothing. He told me that "there are other people who are chewing their fingernails down to the nub because they just don't know," but he had "no doubt that next week I will be working." Mitch saw his temporary work as an extension of his prior solo practice, telling me that he sees the agencies and law firms as his clients, and that he constantly "lays the groundwork" for future work by performing well and keeping in close touch with his agencies.

James also was unfazed by job insecurity. When I interviewed him, he was in the sixth month of a project that was to last more than a year. He had previously worked on other projects for this same firm. I asked him how he felt about the lack of security, and he answered:

> Well, sometimes it's a problem. It was a problem twice, but the job came along. But you know, I don't perceive much of a lack of it coming up. I think probably we've found a good group at [this firm] and I say if you were sticking around you could probably work [here] for the next fifty years if you wanted to. Maybe I'm overconfident, but I'm pretty confident that I'd be able to—if there was a project at [this firm] that they'd put me on it, and if I'm not already on one, they'll call me up. And I'd be happy doing that for the next several years. I'll need a couple of weeks off, eventually.

As it turned out, all of us *were* rolled over to first one project and then another. There are project attorneys who have worked there on a temporary basis almost continuously for several years.

Other project attorneys were concerned about insecurity, but felt that they were able to manage it. Maya's husband earned a good salary; thus, her family did not rely on her income from temping to pay the bills. Michael also felt that his professional spouse's income would be sufficient to tide them over if he was unable to find work readily. Ben was single, but was able to put away money he was earning on the current project. He said: "I feel confident enough that I'll have work when I need it, so when I get cut I just look at it as an early vacation."

However, the insecurity made others anxious. Kathy was most concerned about the lack of benefits. She said: "Oh, I hate it. It makes me nuts. . . . I'm scared to death of, like, getting run over by a train and then, like, being in a lot of trouble." Betsy was married to a graduate student who was not earning a great deal. She laughed nervously when I asked her about how she manages the uncertainty of project work. She said: "Once I actually get a project, I try to keep at least a $2,000 cushion, just for another month's bills . . . to keep down the stress level so that I know that at least if I don't find another project within the next month or so I still won't be going bankrupt or anything."

Julie, who had a substantial investment cushion, also tried to take the lack of security in stride. She told me that "it's a little nerve-racking," but "you have to accept these as the realities. If you don't like it, then you need to find a permanent job and have the security that you want. Nothing is ideal in life. You have to suck it up and make some choices." Rick, a married attorney in his sixties, told me that he coped by "trying to improvise wherever possible." He would attempt to keep several income streams going at the same time, for example, by taking on private clients, writing, or trying to find consulting work. He was philosophical about it when he told me: "Basically, insecurity is a fact of life, not just for temporary attorneys but for everybody, so, you know, I basically accept it and try to deal with it."

Putting in the Hours

Projects differed regarding the amount of hours that were required. Some firms strictly limited the workweek to forty hours; others required overtime and also strictly set the hours. One of the projects required us to work from 8:00 A.M. until 9:00 P.M. on the weekdays and 9:00 A.M. to 6:00 P.M. on Saturdays. On other projects, we were given a minimum number of hours to work and also a "window" within which to work them. One project involving a merger in the computer industry required us to bill at least twelve hours per day on the weekdays anytime between 7:00 A.M. and 11:00 P.M., in addition to weekend hours. Some attorneys took full advantage, working sixteen hours every weekday for several weeks, even though some of them commuted up to an hour each away.

All of the attorneys I interviewed who had worked on more than one project had been required to work more than twelve hours per day, and more than five days per week. They reported billing up to seventeen hours per day, sometimes for weeks on end. For many weeks, Lynn had billed for hours "in the mid-eighties," Frances and Larry had topped out at ninety-five, and Vince said he once billed ninety-seven hours in a week. I maxed out at ninety-one hours in each of three consecutive weeks. Each of these projects involved seven-day workweeks. Both Vince and Evan had worked overnight on projects. I too was once asked to stay on and do data entry all night in a final push to get documents produced to the Federal Trade Commission (FTC). I billed from 8:00 A.M. on a Thursday until the project ended at 3:00 P.M. on Friday. Working extreme hours sometimes became a badge of pride for the hardy who could handle the hours. Bill told me that on his second project he was taking advantage of all the overtime and had billed eighty-six hours the prior week. Laughing, he said: "I'm proud of that, by the way."

An axiom of the project attorney subculture was that it was a bad idea "to leave money on the table." Harry, the agency director, in particular made this his favorite phrase. Some attorneys took this advice to heart and squeezed every available hour of overtime out of a project. Ben said he worked ninety-six-hour weeks on one project. I asked him how he kept it up, and he said: "I kept it up at first 'cause I had no money." Then, he said, he just got used to it. Bill was young and single. He said he was working the maximum hours on the current project—7:00 A.M. to 10:00 P.M.—because he could. He said: "I don't have any strings attached. I don't have anyone at home other than my fish who need to get fed. And I can do it, so I work as many [hours]— and they love me, and they let me work, so I work." Betsy also was trying to maximize overtime by working up to thirteen hours a day. I asked her how that compared to the last project she had worked on. She told me that on the last project "it was closer to twelve on average, because I was sick most of the time." I asked whether it sounded funny to her that she had worked "only" twelve hours a day because she had been sick. She laughed and said that twelve hours was not much compared to the sixteen she had wanted to do. Similarly, Lynn told me that she had "only" put in ten to twelve hours a day on one project because she had nearly a two-hour commute each way.

However, some did not aspire to work the absolute maximum number of hours available when given a choice to work less. Larry said: "I've never been someone who, you know, wanted to get one hundred hours [in a week]." Bernice told me something similar. Both Larry and Bernice had maxed out at "only" about eighty hours per week. Larry said he wanted to have some semblance of a home life, and Bernice said she just did not feel it was ethical to bill more than ten hours a day (if she had the choice), because her concentration would decline so much. Maya told me that she was not billing more than forty-two hours per week, though she was allowed to bill up to fifty. When I asked her why, she told me the work was feeling increasingly tedious and she said: "I just can't find the mental strength to stay here beyond a certain amount of hours during the day." Julie also did not feel the need to max out her hours. She told me that "a lot of the weeks, I just have something else I want to do. . . . Money is not the end-all, be-all." Of course, both Maya and Julie told me they were not feeling financially stressed.

Sometimes it seemed to me that project attorneys chose not to work all the hours available to them as a way to exert some control over their work lives. The thinking seemed to be: "You can make me do this tedious work, and tell me how to do it, but *I'll* say when I come and go."

Padding the Hours

On every project, we were instructed to bill only the amount of hours we actually worked; on most projects, we were instructed to "write off" at least half an hour per day. Sometimes we were not given a minimum time to deduct; thus, some attorneys did not write off any breaks at all. Debby told me about a situation that had arisen with an attorney, Chester, prior to my arrival on the project. For several months, Chester billed every hour he was at work (ten each day), explaining that he brought his lunch to work, ate it at his desk, and worked straight through the day. Debby told me that the law firm sent out a memo requesting that all attorneys "take breaks just for your productivity level." According to Debby, Chester's response to the memo was: " 'A,' I'm not a [law firm] employee, and 'B,' they're only suggesting it. When it becomes mandatory, I'll do it." This tug-of-war went on for several weeks until his agency insisted he write off a half-hour break every day.

Many attorneys used the half-hour minimum for their maximum as well. For most attorneys, this amount did not go up if they worked more hours in the day, so they took a half-hour break (at least on paper) whether they were working eight hours or sixteen hours per day. By the time I conducted the first interview, I had worked on several projects and thus had become quite used to seeing questionable billing practices. I therefore asked the attorneys how closely their billing reflected their actual hours worked, on a scale of

1 to 10, where 1 represented complete inaccuracy and 10 represented total meticulousness. From the sixteen attorneys who gave me a number, only three (Betsy, Frances, and Evan) gave themselves a perfect score; the median response was 8. Bill gave himself an 8, telling me that he does not overbill because "I don't want to screw myself. It's not that important." Only three attorneys gave themselves less than a 7. Melinda said her accuracy deserved a 5 and Lynn said "between 4 and 5." Maya told me that in the beginning of the project she would have rated herself a 9, but that after several months she merited only a 5.

These self-ratings meant different things to different attorneys. Mitch gave himself an 8, saying he was about average, while Debby said she rated a "7 or 8" and that she was "trying to be very careful." Mitch was probably closer to the truth. If we take an 8 out of 10 to mean that the attorney actually billed 80 percent of the hours he or she claimed to be working (perhaps a fair inference), then the attorney ought to be writing off 2.4 hours of every twelve-hour day. As already noted, almost all the attorneys were writing off only a half hour.

However, only a few attorneys acknowledged intentionally padding their hours. Roger was one of them; when I asked how accurate he was, he responded:

> Here's going to be a typical lawyer answer for you: It depends. And it really depends on—probably more on the nature of the firm. If I feel that I'm being treated with respect, I'm more likely to play it straight. You know, the firm where I'm working right now, I would say probably between 6-½ and 7, as far as being real careful with my hours. There was one firm that seemed to think that we were all idiots, although necessary idiots or monkeys or whatever, and you know, without—without hurting myself, I took every advantage that I thought I could.

Maya also openly acknowledged billing more hours than she actually worked. When I asked why, she said because the work had gotten more boring and she got tired of "keeping count of every freakin' minute." She added that she felt she was not being watched as closely as she had been at the beginning of the project and so she did not "feel that outside pressure, and my own internal pressure's just not loud enough right now."

More typically, attorneys admitted that they worked fewer hours than they billed, but they used a variety of deflecting techniques to rationalize the disjunction, seemingly struggling with guilt about their billing habits. Even after Larry suggested he ought to be billing fewer hours because of all the talking that went on, he said that "socializing is one of the few benefits" of project attorney work. When I asked Michael to rate himself, he told me: "Given the level of conversation that sometimes takes place, that sometimes I get dragged into, I'd say as far as hours actually staring [at] and flipping pages, probably 8." Some attorneys engaged in highly legalistic rationalizations of their billing practices. When I asked Rick about his accuracy, he laughed and responded: "Ah, all these definitional problems here. I had an attorney one time say: 'If you go to the bathroom, you're working on the project,' you know?" Similarly, Lynn, who gave herself a 4 or 5 on accuracy, responded to questions about her billing in this way:

L: You know, being the typical lawyer, you really need to define the accounting, because you are allowed to take—if you compare it to—you can tell I'm totally justifying myself.

RB: That's okay.

L: If you could compare it to what a normal salaried employee—the amount of work that person actually does in a day, then my accounting is probably pretty close to right on. If you say: "Am I working every single minute of those fourteen hours?" No! [*laughing*]

RB: Of course not.

L: [*laughing*] So—define those things.

Bernice also became legalistic in her defense, telling me: "Well, I've always gone by the fact that I think the law allows a fifteen-minute break for every four hours you work, so I've always figured half an hour . . . of break times— going to the bathroom, getting a cup of coffee—is legitimate."

Evan took a different approach to rationalizing his billing: "You know, I've always believed that if you work hard you should be rewarded for it, so I reward myself." I asked him to explain what he meant, and if he thought that all the hours he billed were truly "billable." He answered, in terms that were in turn legalistic, evasive, and rationalizing:

E: Oh, well, that's—that's a very subjective thing. I can't really answer that question. I mean, because what you may define as unbillable time—

RB: Well, it's how *you* define it.

E: Oh, well, I think what I bill is accurate. Well, I don't—[*laughing*] I think there are guidelines for these things, and, like, I shouldn't be charging to go to the bathroom, but I'm not going to mark all that time off.

RB: Okay.

E: But I would charge them anyway, so all of it, I guess. I'm entitled to at least two fifteen-minute breaks by law—

RB: Mm-hmm.

E: —and, you know. [*sighing*] I'm going to make an analogy. See, when I stocked merchandise in the hardware store, I would work really, really fast so I had more breaks, so I could do whatever. But I still was charging them for the time I was taking those breaks; otherwise I'd just be going slower.

RB: Okay.

E: So I'm entitled to everything I write down.

Of course, Evan does not recognize that the two situations are not really similar. In the hardware store, when all the merchandise had been stocked, there was no more work to be done. On a project, however, we almost never ran out of documents to code.

Several of the attorneys used a "self-preservation" explanation in telling me why they billed more hours than they actually worked. Bernice said that she pauses every once in a while to play some computer games, adding: "I used to feel guilty about it—I don't anymore. I've found twelve hours in front of a computer I—I can't do and be really that seriously productive. So I just take what I think doesn't bother other people—little breaks." Melinda told me: "Look, I will slow down my pace sometimes if I feel like I need to because I'm going crazy." Immediately, she added that she felt "guilty because I've sat there, probably not reading that many documents," so she quickly shifted to another account—"group norms." She said: "I think that I'm doing—I think that everyone does that—that everyone has to take their little break by—you know, just talking, and, you know, and not thinking about work, looking at documents. Everyone needs that little break."

Ben said something similar when I asked him how he was able to work sixteen-hour days: "Actually, and again this being confidential, all the hours you bill you don't necessarily—you kind of work, but you kind of don't. You kind of look at the papers and relax, you talk with other people." He paused, then continued: "You know, that makes it sound shady, but I think that everyone understands that if they want a certain amount of work, and the upper-level people who are supervising know that you have to allow that sort of leeway. . . . I think it's kind of like an unspoken deal, so to speak." James also felt it was understood that only "in a perfect world would they want you to be glued to your chair for the entire time." He said he did not know if it was ethical to bill for all the little breaks that are taken, but added, half-jokingly, that while you are on a break "you're thinking about that [coding] specification." He continued: "Plenty of people bill for sleeping on things."

A majority of the attorneys I interviewed believed that most other project attorneys had billing practices similar to them—that is, they were not perfect, but they were pretty good. Debby told me: "I would say, on average, people are about the same as me. Like, we're not going to be, like: 'I'm going to look at my watch, and I have to pee, and I'm going to be back in exactly two minutes and thirty seconds, and I can go to the bathroom so many times a day.'" However, everyone told me that there were always a few attorneys who really stood out for their abusive billing. Some attorneys would take two-hour lunch breaks, make numerous telephone calls, surf the Internet, read the newspaper, or engage in constant talking. Some attorneys took this behavior in stride; for example, Bill noticed that some people spent much of the day surfing the Web, but told me: "You know, I'm not their boss. They're grown adults. Whatever comes to them, comes to them. I mean, it's not my job to police them."

However, most of the others were openly resentful of the liberties taken by those who overbilled. Betsy, who claimed she wrote off every minute she was not working, told me that sometimes she "felt cheated" because other people "would disappear for two or three hours a day" or "be in the building, but just walking around on another floor talking to their friends . . . and not mark that down for time." The older group of attorneys I interviewed— Bernice, Julie, and Rick—became the most incensed about this behavior. Each of them had worked on projects where it seemed that most of the attorneys were barely working. Rick talked about his first project, where "there were just one or two other dedicated attorneys in the room." The rest of them "just seemed to be barely there." He said that one project attorney "took from 8:00 A.M. to 2:00 P.M. every day to actually start the work. He would spend the entire day reading instructions and talking about people he'd seen on the way to the men's room and so forth. It made my blood boil." Bernice told me of a project that was very poorly managed, where she saw "wasted time, wasted people, shocking behavior" by other attorneys. I asked her what she meant by that, and she responded: "There was no work ethic. They didn't work. They just wanted to know when the next meal was coming in. . . . They weren't even looking at the [documents]. They were turning pages as they carried on conversations at the table. . . . So it was just a shock, you know, a shock. And I just—I was stunned. And I was ashamed."

On a different project, Bernice described "a lot of hanky-panky going on—guys and girls flirting, not working at all. Talking, constant talking."

She said she was happy to be on the current project (where I was interviewing her) because she felt that we were all "serious about being lawyers." Julie told me she had been "horrified" at some behaviors and said "it's something that continues to horrify me most days that I do this work—people who absolutely lie about their hours." She told me that on her first project there was a sign-in sheet at the door. She said that she would be right behind another attorney signing in who would write down a time that was forty-five minutes earlier than what it was. She concluded: "We're all supposed to have a duty to the client, and I don't understand how lying and cheating can be a part of being a lawyer."

While many were bothered by this behavior, only Evan told me that he actually did something about it. He said that on one electronic review project he sat next to an attorney, Charlie, who spent nearly all of his time either talking on his cell phone or surfing the Web for pornography. Evan admitted to me, while laughing nervously, that he "sort of ratted Charlie out" to the agency. Evan was concerned that his agency would resent him for it, but he did not suffer any negative consequences. I asked if Charlie was fired, and Evan said: "Much to my chagrin," Charlie was merely moved to a different location where he could be more easily monitored by the associates.

Like the attorneys I interviewed, I witnessed a wide variety of work habits. Some project attorneys seemed to be quite meticulous in their billing. Others were frequently "missing in action" for extended periods. Some attorneys spent hours out of each day playing computer games or doing job searches on the Internet. One attorney had "instant message" conversations with her boyfriend and then regaled the attorneys around her with stories of her sexual practices. On some projects, the noise from the talking was so loud that I had trouble concentrating. On most of those, it was the other project attorneys talking, but on one of them, it was the firm's own associates who could not seem to work. Other times, attorneys were absent *from* work—at the gym or at long lunches—and continued to bill time. Opportunities for not billing were highest on computer review projects because they gave us the chance to check e-mail, look for job opportunities, or play endless games of Text Twist.

Law firms rarely intervened in project attorneys' poor work habits, whether on an individual or group basis. As discussed in Chapter 4, sometimes law firm associates and staff attorneys themselves would instigate or encourage excessive talking. Other times, it seemed that law firm attorneys were overwhelmed and preoccupied with their other tasks, or tolerated some "hanky panky" as an inevitable cost of very long days. I sometimes noticed individual attorneys around me who were doing very little work, day after day, and wondered why the law firm kept them on. It seemed likely that the firm was more concerned about whether the group as a whole was meeting the firm's output expectations because these were more concrete and readily measurable than the performance of any one individual.

And—full disclosure here—there were certainly times when I departed from ideal billing practices. Like the attorneys I interviewed, I also would rationalize my talking, game playing, or occasional gym trips. I would think to myself: "I'm so much faster than most other project attorneys, while also being careful and attentive, that even if I take some personal breaks and don't bill for them, I'm still doing much more work in less time." This rationalization is similar to Evan's and is equally insupportable.

Internal Struggles

There were occasionally things of interest to break up our boredom. Some attorneys claimed to find interest in the documents, at least on occasion. Debby was on her first project, involving a pharmaceutical liability case, when she told me: "I love learning new stuff, and you know, what that stuff is. So while this stuff may never again come up in my life and may have nothing to do with anything, ever, I now have stuff in my head that I didn't have there before." Debby may have meant what she said, but she also told me that she listened to game shows and talk shows on the TV band of her radio for most of the day. And after she was switched from paper to electronic review, I saw her spending much of her day playing computer games.

Most of us learned shortly into our first project that we needed to find ways to cope with the tedium of document review. Maya told me that she found the work to be "intellectually easy" and that sometimes some of the documents would be interesting. However, she said that the "difficult part of the job is being able to do it for ten hours, and having the mental endurance to do the same type of work for ten hours, five days a week for fourteen months." Kathy said that the "one thing that I probably complain about the most [is] the fact that it's so repetitive and, I think, so mundane." Susan told me that she found the work to be a "2 out of 10" on the "interesting scale." When I asked her whether her rating varied from project to project, she responded: "I mean—by maybe—a point or so. Not that much."

Others felt that the projects *were* different from each other. Several attorneys I worked with complained about working on an antitrust case involving rock-crushing machines. To them, this was the most boring industry they had ever dealt with. Michael initially told me that document review "is not stimulating in any way." However, he added that his boredom level did decline somewhat if the project involved subject matter that he had an interest in, like digital technology. Similarly, James said: "Every document review project is probably a 10 on the tedium scale, but that's ratcheted down if the interesting variable is high, comparatively."

Sometimes the environment conspired with the documents to make the work even more tedious and grueling. Working in a warehouse, an interior storage room, or a basement with no windows would slowly lull us into a fugue state. Most attorneys strongly preferred working in locations that had natural light; however, there was also a downside to having windows. Michael told me that "it's nice to have the natural light from the window, but at times it makes time drag a little bit more. You feel the daylight hours and you see the night coming." He referred to the location of the last project that he and I had both worked on for six weeks—an interior storage room at a large law firm—and said: "We sort of had the benefit of sensory deprivation as far as the outside world, kind of like with casinos, where you just go in and be there for hours and hours and hours and not really feel the time pass as much, because it didn't matter what time of day it was outside—it was the same fluorescent-lit closet." Frances had worked in a firm's basement review room and said it was the worst physical location she had been asked to work in. Working there meant "you have no idea what's going on in the outside world." I mentioned that I had heard the space referred to as "the casino room." She responded: "Yes, the casino room. Or it's like a jury room. No concept of time. It's like you're frozen." I laughed, and said: "It serves their interests, doesn't it?" and Frances responded: "Well, that's it. If I was on their end, I'd probably have done the same thing."

Notwithstanding the numbing sameness of the work and the physical environment—in fact *because* of it—project attorneys found ways to "mark time."

Marking Time

It was always apparent to me that project attorneys felt the passing of time differently compared to the law firm's permanent associates and partners. While we both shared the practice of billing our work by the hour, we nonetheless each experienced a unique temporal reality. In his study of shop floor workers in a large bakery, Jason Ditton (1972) illustrates the differences between shop floor workers and their managers. He notes that managers see time in a linear way, and as upward movement. This outlook "helps to structure life into a recognised pattern." For managers, this structure "turns time into a scarce resource rather than an empty residue." However, shop floor workers do not have a linear sense of time: "For them, work means a lifetime of waiting at machines where attendance is necessary, but full attention is not; a non-career situation with little control of personal time and physical movement" (Ditton 1972, 679). Similarly, law firm associates—the law firm employees we worked most closely with—perceive an upward arc of their career over time. They perceive the project they currently are assigned to in the context of their careers and the law firm's business. They view the conclusion of the case as a "success" that puts another feather in their cap on their march to partnership. (Law firms often hosted large parties at the conclusion of a major case, to which the project attorneys were almost never invited.) In their day-to-day work, law firm associates generally have a variety of tasks to attend to, even though supervising document review may be more mundane than other potential assignments.[1]

Project attorneys, however, experienced time very differently. Our day-to-day tasks—reading and coding documents—were mind-numbingly repetitive. Our chances for extra rewards and advancement were negligible. Even the "plum" assignments like quality check and privilege review (at times, I was assigned to each) developed a dulling sameness. At the project's end, we did not experience the thrill of victory; we only felt that we had worked ourselves out of a job. As Bill told me, document review is a "funny field" because "if you do your work faster than they expected, I mean, they're not going to keep you on for any particular reason, they're going to let you go." So time was perceived in "clumps"—as projects that were bookended by (mostly involuntary) time off looking for other projects—rather than in some sort of linear career arc. Attorneys often felt stultified and "stuck," even if they knew they were doing the work only as a means to some other end.

The workers described by Ditton (1972) worked in twelve-hour shifts and their tasks were extremely repetitive and monotonous, requiring some mental attention but not immersion. According to Ditton: "It was this sort of underemployment that was the most difficult to endure" (p. 679). Because the work itself did not contain any relief from the monotony, the men

---

[1] While I did not interview law firm associates for this book, I was myself an associate at three different law firms, so I believe I can say something about the differences between associates and project attorneys in marking time. However, I do note that for some associates, being extensively involved in supervising document review projects for a long period might stymie their own advancement in the firm because the work carries some stigma and may be perceived as less challenging. In addition, this discussion does not include the feelings of staff attorneys—lawyers not on a partner track—who supervise document review. It is possible that they share some of the project attorneys' sense of nonmovement, but in most cases, they have more job security than project attorneys and also earn considerable benefits.

"managed to spend a lifetime delicately engineering a compromise between surviving monotony and yet not completely becoming a machine." One way they did this was by creating structure to their workday, using teatime and lunch breaks as a "cyclical scaffolding within which more cycles proliferate" (p. 680).

Document coding shared some of these qualities. Because the work was so repetitive, there was very little built-in structure in our day. Thus, we— like Ditton's workers—created daily structure for ourselves.[2] There was very little to look forward to, and little else happening, so a lot of interest revolved around meals. Several attorneys told me that they were very aware of the role of meals in marking time. James told me that a meal "breaks the tedium for people. It's a routine. People like routines and they expect it." Bernice worked on projects "where they literally feed you to death." One firm "brought breakfast to get you in early. They brought the cookies in at four to make sure you didn't slow down." When I asked Rick if he noticed our inordinate focus on food, he began laughing and replied:

> R: I think it's kind of funny—sometimes it's good and sometimes it isn't. I guess, I forget from time to time that food is such a—such a major factor in the lives of so many people who work on these projects. I mean, it's just sort of humorous. Everybody starts talking about what's for dinner, and when, and that sort of thing, and as soon as dinner's announced, they rush up and leave the room in order to fill up their plates.
>
> RB: Why do you think that is?
>
> R: I don't know. It's probably some sort of compensation for nervous anxiety or boredom or tedium or something.

I worked on one assignment that involved three hundred project attorneys working in a large warehouse. As the weeks wore on, the attorneys

---

[2] By citing Ditton (1972), I do not mean to say that the working experiences of shop floor bakery workers and project attorneys are perfectly analogous. As members of a profession, project attorneys earn more for their work and have superior long-term career prospects. We also (as outlined in Chapter 4) seem to have more control over the work flow, and work in less isolation. We also could at least look forward to a change in environment every so often, even if the type of tasks did not change much. However, the experience *while* working—because the qualities of the work were similar—seemed to engender similar experiences and group practices. We shared a common need to shape the day—to fill in the structure that was otherwise missing.

began lining up increasingly early for lunch and dinner. Eventually, a line began to form as soon as they noticed the caterer had arrived, even though it was at least another fifteen minutes before anyone could take a plate. The project managers saw this as a waste of billable hours, so they instituted a formal system of calling tables one by one, like at a wedding buffet, rotating the order each day so that every section of the room would have the opportunity to go first.

Others attempted to create structure by marking their progress through the documents. When I asked Evan how he organized his day, he said that he usually had "a system to when I take breaks or whatever. So I set goals of where I want to be at a certain time, or I want to get this far before I get up and do something else." Similarly, Rick told me: "I set short-term goals for myself; I like to measure how rapidly I'm getting through databases." On a long project, I would do the same thing. I wrote in my notes that I had once promised myself: "After I do these next one hundred documents, I can get up and get a can of Diet Coke." In hindsight, this seems rather pathetic, but in the moment it was a rational way to structure the seemingly unending, unvarying onslaught of documents.

We also made attempts to structure our lives beyond the day. All of us appreciated the fact that we were paid weekly on projects. One particular agency would deliver their paychecks to the job site each Friday, along with a box of some very large gourmet cookies. This ritual at times assumed comic dimensions, as attorneys would wonder aloud what time the cookies were coming. After delivery, they would buzz around the cookie boxes looking for their favorites. Some weeks, the cookies never arrived because of scheduling problems and there would be cries of disappointment. Julie found the whole thing rather ridiculous: "I've never heard so much complaining about free cookies in my life. 'There are too many chocolate chip. There aren't enough chocolate chip. They're too big. They're too hard. They're too soft. They're too this, they're too that.' Get over it, people! It's a freakin' cookie!" What Julie failed to appreciate was that all this attention was not about the baked goods; rather, the attorneys looked forward to and savored this weekly ritual as a way of organizing their experience.

Many projects also allowed us to have Saturday or Sunday off, which made the week more bearable. However, the projects with a seven-day work-week were much more difficult. The days would bleed one into the other, and I would lose track of which day it was. Eventually, I would focus on looking forward to the "short day" on Sunday, when we might have to put in only eight hours.

Managing the Tedium

Ditton (1972) describes how new bakery workers would constantly watch the clock, but at some point would switch to doing "easy" time rather than "hard" time (referring to the pattern of acculturation of prison inmates). He cites another author who describes this process as going "benuttered here . . . then they become sane again" (p. 680). For project attorneys, too, paying close attention to the clock was usually out of the question. Thus, project attorneys engaged in a number of practices to cope with the tedium. I recount these here as conceptually and functionally different from the overbilling practices discussed earlier and the project-extension tactics detailed in Chapter 4. Here, attorneys are employing practices to resist the tedium and drudgery of the work, whereas in overbilling, they knowingly bill for time not spent working, with the goal to inflate their hours for the purpose of being paid more. There is some overlap between all these practices; it is difficult to know where resistance ends and greed begins. When is talking to one's coworkers "goofing off" and when is it "coping with boredom"? Some have noted similar difficulties in distinguishing between coping, resistance, and misbehavior (e.g., Ackroyd and Thompson 1999). This may explain why the project attorneys I interviewed frequently resorted to various rationalizations about their use of time.

The attorneys told me they used a variety of methods to cope with the tedium and long hours. Many of us used caffeine. Roger told me he used "lots of it," and Michael said he needed it for "alertness, almost to the point of nervousness, I guess." On one project, the barista at the nearest Starbucks learned my complicated drink order—half-caf grande nonfat extra hot with whip mocha—in under a week. Bill said he generally avoided drinking coffee; however, there were a few times in the beginning of the project when he was not used to the sixteen-hour days that he had to resort to caffeine: "Even after the walks, even after the bathroom trip, even after the bathroom splash and, like, looking in the mirror, I was like: 'What the hell is wrong with you?'"

Other attorneys told me that they just felt naturally equipped to deal with the work. Michael told me that he had "an above-average tolerance for boredom." He said that he would watch people on projects who would "literally just be jumping out of their seats to move and do something," but that he did not "have that much of a problem sitting for extended periods and focusing on one thing." Bill told me that because he was much younger than his siblings, he became accustomed to keeping himself entertained. He told me if you sat next to him on a project, "you might hear me, like, starting to be silly, talking to the document: 'Oh, you think you're going to get a redaction? No, no redaction for you!' Stuff like that." Melinda said that she thought of herself as being very disciplined: "I was one of those kids, when I was really young, that I could sit down in one place, and not *move*, and not even utter a word to anyone. I've always been the type that if I need to do something, I do it." She added: "That's what keeps me going—finish the project, finish the project." Frances told me: "I guess I've just been doing grunt work for so long. I mean, I felt like law school was very repetitive and very, like, the same routine every day, so this in comparison seems like: 'Okay, well, instead of *paying* to do this, I'm getting *paid* to do this.'"

Some attorneys reported that they adopted an attitude of stoicism about the work. Rick told me that "basically, I guess my attitude is I'm there to work, I'm not there to have a good time. I'm there to accomplish a job for somebody. Even if it seems dull or stultifying, or repetitive, that's my job just to slog through that work." Roger, who had a family to support, also would tell himself when he felt overwhelmed by the tedium: "I've got to do it." He said it did not make the work less boring, but it did remind him that he had no other choices at the moment. Ben told me that on the last project, he had worked sixteen-hour days for six weeks during the end-of-the-year holidays. When I asked him how he dealt with the monotony, he told me he was not sure how he did it: "It was more like desperation—just doing it and doing it. And there was nothing more important to me than making sure I could pay my rent. Um, I generally, I don't know—it's just willpower, I think."

Mitch said that he survived by talking to his coworkers. However, he added that there were some projects "where it's just a bunch of people sitting in a stone-silent room; then it truly is just drudgery." In those situations, he said:

> I just do it because it's my job. And I'm reminded that—I mean, I've worked in factories, I've worked in the food service industry, I've had a lot of menial jobs. And when this starts to feel like a menial job, I look around and I—it's like, well, it's air-conditioned, it's clean, I am being treated with a certain amount of respect, I don't have to worry about whether I'm going to lose a hand in the machinery [*laughing*], um, you know, so I—I mean, I just look around and so I'm—if at this point I'm stuck with doing something that's menial, I've done menial before in a lot worse conditions than this, for a lot less pay.

The pay was something that kept other attorneys going, as well. Melinda told me: "I think about the money. Isn't that horrible? I seriously do. I think: 'I *have* to do this.'" Frances said when she receives her monthly bonus check (one agency would pay us 6 percent of our salary if the law firm approved of our work), "you just want to do cartwheels."

Ditton's (1972) bakery workers had to bear the monotony with the extra burden of solitude. Project attorneys, however—unlike many other temporary workers—have the benefit of proximity to each other. Thus, one of the main coping techniques cited by nearly everyone was talking. Kathy told me that "being able to sit around people that you can talk to and joke with" helps to make the day go by faster, and makes the whole experience a little more bearable." Michael said that he needed the "occasional sanity-saving joke, so you laugh so you don't cry." On most projects, law firm employees tolerated talking among the project attorneys. (Kerry and Merson was an exception, where paralegals were sometimes stationed in the review room to prevent us from talking to each other.) On projects at some firms, conversations were almost constantly going on somewhere in the room. Vince told me: "I try to talk—a lot. And I know I've been to places where the project manager tells you to stop talking, but I like to talk." I can attest to this. When I started the project where I interviewed Vince, I recognized him from a prior assignment, where I would listen to him talking most of the day, clearly understanding his table's conversations from twenty feet away. I wondered how much work the attorneys at that table were actually doing, or how well they were doing it.

Most of the time, these conversations had the qualities one might expect from people trying to concentrate on two things at once. Like Ditton's workers (1972, 679), "the minimal but ever present work demands ruled out sustained and complex thought," and so many conversations were silly, empty, or repetitive. Most attorneys took part in these conversations, in spite of themselves, but some expressed annoyance at the level or quality of conversation. Julie told me: "I can't stand the banal conversations that go on among the other contract attorneys. They will sit and talk forever about nothing of any interest or consequence on this planet. And they'll spend day after day doing that. That is so much more boring than this work could ever be. Sometimes I just want to shout at them: 'You think this document is boring. Listen to *you!*'" When I asked how *she* dealt with the tedium, because she did not like talking to the other attorneys, she replied: "This is going to sound crazy, but I tend to do more work. I find that sitting around and complaining makes the day go longer and so I would rather challenge myself to do more work and to do the work accurately, and just lose myself in the work." She said other people seem to sit around all day doing nothing, and "that makes the day go twice as slow." Similarly, Maya also would sometimes "turn in" to the documents when things were getting tedious, as she said: to try to "psych myself out." She would read the documents with an eye toward how they could be used in the case, asking herself questions like: "How would I use this if I were prosecuting this case?"

Sometimes the documents would be a source of amusement—Betsy told me that she would look forward to running across "the mindless e-mails that are nonresponsive but have jokes or something." She added: "Even though we don't necessarily have to read those, every now and then I'll read one just to break up the monotony and get a chuckle." I remember once on an electronic review project, an attorney found an e-mail with a video attachment. The video showed a pipeline with a small crack in it under several thousand feet of water. A crab was walking on the pipe, and because of the difference in pressure between the pipeline and the water around it, the crab suddenly got sucked through the crack into the pipe. Throughout the day, word of the video spread, and groups of attorneys would gather around, watching it again and again.

It was relatively rare to find much amusement or respite in the documents. More commonly, attorneys would tune out by *retreating* from the documents. One way to tune out is by daydreaming. However, only one attorney told me that she liked to do this. Susan said that when things got really boring, she liked to plan her vacations, to "fantasize what I'm going to do, where I'm going to stay, so that occupies some time." Another way to tune out was to listen to music or the radio, which we were usually allowed to do. However, at the orientation meeting on one project, I asked the staff attorney who was running the document review if we could wear headphones. He said the firm would not allow it because it was too distracting. I must have looked chagrined because he laughed and said: "I guess we've lost one [attorney] already." Most of the attorneys liked listening to National Public Radio (NPR) or talk radio at least a few hours out of the day, and most said that this did not affect their work product. Another way to cope was by taking small breaks from the work, a practice all the attorneys relied on. Rick told me he "spent a fair amount of time" on an electronic review project darting in and out of the *New York Times* Web site, "seeing what's changing in the world." Kathy said that every once in a while she has to stand up and take a break, "even just walking to the window and looking outside."

The Toll of the Hours

Working long hours was not just an exercise in willpower and stamina but also a challenge to maintaining outside relationships. When I asked Bernice how she manages her personal life while on a project, she laughed and responded: "Oh, is there supposed to be one?" Frances told me that she feels like her life stops when she is on a project, and it is difficult for her to get involved in any community activities or even to make plans with friends. She agreed with one of the other attorneys, who referred to his house as being in a "time warp" because "you're never there." Frances said that her husband tries to understand, but "it's still tough on your lives." Melinda was working eighty hours a week when I interviewed her. She said that in order to go out with friends the weekend before, she had driven an hour to where they all worked and it "became a big ordeal." She told me: "I feel like it's easier for me just to tell everyone that my life is on hold—I can't do anything with you, you know: 'Love you, but, you know, but I just don't have the time.'" Similarly, Ben said: "Well, I think relationships that are not very strong start to weaken or break off, and ones that are strong just kind of get put on hold for a while."

Others spoke to me about doing little else than commuting to work, working, and sleeping when they were on a demanding project. Susan said that at the end of the workday: "I just go home and I get in bed. Maybe talk to a couple of friends and watch TV, look at the newspaper if I haven't read it already, check my e-mail, and that's it." Those who had spouses with more normal hours would ask for patience and extra help when working, and then would "pay them back" between projects. Michael told me that his wife understood the demands and would take over tasks like paying bills while he was on a project. Rick said that he makes "brief appearances" at home, usu-ally after his wife and children have gone to bed. The next day, he usually leaves before they are awake. Betsy said that she tries to get in to work as early as possible—7:00 A.M. on some projects—so that she can "get home at least before my husband goes to bed if I can, so I can see him for at least an hour or two during the day." She said her husband "doesn't like it any more than I do, but he doesn't complain because he knows that's what has to be done." She added that what kept them both going was "the hope that even-tually we'll both get jobs with normal, steady hours that are enough to pay our bills."

Those who did have family obligations sometimes took on assignments with shorter hours or chose not to work the maximum number of hours. Larry told me that he had been required to work more than ninety hours in a week before, but added: "I don't think I've ever topped a hundred. I don't aspire to that." Later, he said he had seen people work one hundred hours a week, week in and week out, "who have important other parts of their life that they just neglect." However, he added: "I can't physically work for more than twelve or thirteen hours a day without feeling that I'm neglecting myself, my house, my wife." On the project where I interviewed him, he was working twelve-hour days Monday through Friday and ten hours on Saturday. He told me that even if the firm began to require working on Sundays, "I'm not looking to go that far beyond seventy hours," and he added: "Not that I have the financial security to be so bold, but there are things that are far more important to me than the paycheck." Mitch told me that he was able to split child rearing with his wife because he would take care of their children in the morning and his wife would pick them up after school. He said his agencies knew that he could not be expected to arrive at work early. When his wife occasionally was not able to pick up the children in the afternoon, Mitch said that he would take advantage of one of the few benefits of temporary work, and simply tell the project managers that he needed to leave early that day.

Single attorneys generally found it somewhat easier to work longer hours. Bill told me that he does cut back on going out with friends when he is on a project, but as long as he gets six and a half hours of sleep each night, he is "good to go." Kathy told me she was able to manage her outside life "because right now I really don't have much of one." She continued: "I'm not really dating, I don't have a boyfriend, I don't have a pet, I don't even have plants. So I feel like I'm fortunate in the sense of I don't have a lot of outside things depending upon me that if I work a twelve-hour day I feel guilty." Julie also told me that being single meant she had few outside obligations that could not be worked around.

The toll of the hours also affected attorneys' job searches. Larry told me that when he arrived home between 8:30 and 10:00 at night, he wanted to spend at least a little time with his wife: "I don't want to go immediately to the computer and do—you know—what I consider to be work. Despite the fact that it's something I need to do, I can't physically do it, and I can't mentally do it, and I don't want to do it, and that makes for a horrible job cocktail." He added that it's a vicious cycle because "you need the money so you need to work, but you need to look for another job in order to get it, but when the hell are you going to look for that job?" Michael told me he had been able to send out only two resumes in the past month, when he was working more than ninety hours a week. Betsy also said that "the energy and the hours just aren't there" when she is on a project, and that she does all of her job searching between projects. When I asked Ben, who is single, how he fit in his job search, he told me, laughing: "I just kind of do what I can in the evenings with the half hour I have between getting home and sleeping." When he has a Sunday off, he spends much of the day looking at want ads and sending out e-mails and letters. Larry said that he even has a hard time with the job search after a project ends because "there's a very self-destructive tendency to just relax, not look for that other job until you've had a couple days to relax. And then a couple of days turns into a week, and so on, and in retrospect, I wish I had some time back so that I could have been more aggressive in my job search."

Julie was quite content doing project work for the medium term, so she was not looking for permanent work. She said that other attorneys told her: "It's so hard to find a job when you're working sixty hours a week." Her response to me was: "Bullshit." She referred to a project attorney we worked with who would complain that she could not find permanent work, but "is sitting playing computer games at her desk—hours and hours every day." She said that she had seen other attorneys get a job lead or an introduction and do nothing about it. I also often saw other project attorneys being less than aggressive with their job searches. It seemed to me that part of the reason was the time squeeze these attorneys referred to, but it also seemed that the work we did sapped some of our confidence and motivation. I noticed on projects that there was a rather strange lack of discussion about why the attorneys were doing project work, or what their future plans were. It appeared that we all were perhaps collectively embarrassed to be there, and thus thought it best not to talk about it.

This research underscores the notion that time is socially constructed. Individual project attorneys demonstrated that they were sometimes successful in "shrinking" time by employing various coping methods. In addition, due to the nature and organization of the work, project attorneys appeared to experience time differently compared to attorneys in standard work arrangements. Research shows that repetitious work performed at a constant, steady rate has more negative impacts on workers than work that allows intense performance with some periods of rest (see Epstein and Kalleberg 2001). This may explain why project attorneys sought to impose their own rhythm on the work by taking breaks and alternating hard work with relaxing moments. Research also tends to show that the lack of control over hours—rather than their sheer number—may be more relevant to whether workers experience "time conflict" (see Kalleberg and Epstein 2001). Project attorneys usually had limited control over their work schedules; when they were able to assert control, they reported that they used it to better balance their work/life relationship.

Research also demonstrates that one's perception of work (more than total number of hours worked) determines the amount of time conflict one feels: "When individuals engage in identity-affirming activities, they will tend to perceive less conflict" (Epstein and Kalleberg 2001, 12). If this is true, then for many project attorneys, the work/nonwork conflict could be expected to be intense. As is demonstrated in Chapter 6, many project attorneys felt that document review work seriously conflicted with their prior identities as lawyers.

6

"A Glorified Data Entry Person"

Struggles over Identity

Our work tends to define us. This may be especially true for professional work, which has long periods of socialization and is afforded a high degree of prestige and exclusivity.[1] For lawyers, formation of identity begins in law school, where students are trained to "think like a lawyer" (Mertz 2007). Identity socialization continues through professional interaction and is reinforced through collective action by bar associations, attorney discipline systems, and specialty practice groups, among others. Through this socialization, certain qualities or personality characteristics are emphasized and expectations about behaviors are communicated. For example, the legal profession tends to emphasize autonomy and independence; it also tends to value certain stereotypically male personality characteristics, such as aggressiveness (Schleef 2001). Some researchers thus view the identity of lawyers as forming from a coherent set of values that originate within official pronouncements of bar associations or other bodies, or from the socializing practices of law schools, which are sometimes seen as rather unitary.

However, many challenge this normative approach, which suggests the development of a single "attorney identity." Robert Nelson and David Trubek (1992), for instance, claim that a multitude of attorney *identities* may develop

---

[1] Nonprofessional occupations also may engender a strong sense of identity. For example, Jeffrey Kidder (2006) writes of bike messengers' strong sense of emotional attachment to their work. Those involved in so-called "dirty work" also may develop a strong sense of identity through defense and management of their stigmatized status (see, e.g., Dick 2005).

in response to various situational, social, and economic forces, and that these identities necessarily shift over time as the influences change. The authors also suggest that identity formation is unpredictable because some influences are inherently contradictory. For example, legal training emphasizes dedication to "justice," but also creates cynicism; the value of "serving the client" can result in overzealousness and violation of ethics codes; and ethics codes themselves can appear vague and are sometimes underenforced. Thus, attorney identity is seen as a complex and variable property, not reducible to a series of normative expectations espoused by law schools or bar associations.

Formation of identity is further complicated by multiple types of stratification within the legal profession. Prestige varies according to the types of clients one serves (Heinz et al. 2005). The increasing fragmentation and bureaucratization of law practice are also factors. Even within "elite" law firms, the old associate/partner dichotomy has been replaced with new classifications (discussed in Chapter 2) such as non-equity partners and staff attorneys. It would seem that differential access to rewards such as pay, mobility, client contact, autonomy, and quality of assignments would result in differing self-conceptions. Layered over this fragmentation are patterns of stratification based on social factors such as gender, race, and religious background (see Heinz et al. 2005). While these social factors tend to predict one's place in the hierarchy (for example, significant barriers to partnership in elite law firms continue to exist for women), there are many exceptions that suggest great complexity in identity formation. At the same time, the practice of law is viewed skeptically—or even with hostility—by the public. Surely, some attorneys are relatively immune to negative public perceptions, but others are likely more affected and thus must find ways to resist or incorporate this stigma.

Some suggest that attorneys' identities may be further weakened because of *de*professionalization or *re*professionalization of the law, marked by changes in technology, competition, law firm structure, and increasing accountability and quantification (e.g., Espeland and Vannebo 2007). Attorneys who work in increasingly bureaucratized systems may become more subject to manipulation of identity. Stephen Ackroyd and Paul Thompson (1999, 27) conceptualized this as a battle over "symbolic resources" in which employers attempt to indoctrinate employees into adopting attitudes that serve the organization. This battle would seemingly be much more difficult to win in the case of temporary employees (including professionals) who lack commitment (temporal, emotional, and social) to their temporary employer.

In addition, the stigmatization of the "temporary" label also could potentially affect the formation of professional identity. Researchers suggest that those who work in temporary positions are viewed as unreliable and incompetent, and are thus accorded the deviant "master status" of "temporary" (e.g., Henson 1996). Therefore, given that temporary work is stigmatized, and that most legal work is not, an interesting empirical question arises: Would temporary attorneys be stigmatized because they are *temporary*, or would they be accorded the full status of the profession because they are *attorneys*?

In the only prior study of temporary attorneys, Jackie Krasas Rogers (2000, 149–50) interviewed fifteen contract attorneys and finds that temporary legal work "provides less prestige, less financial remuneration, and even less interesting work compared to traditional legal work." She concludes that temporary legal work is devalued in ways similar to that of other types of (feminized) temporary labor, and that this stigmatization "derive[s] from gender ideologies that characterize women as 'uncommitted' and 'soft' at the same time that they devalue women's domestic labor" (p. 133). Thus, temporary attorneys are perceived to be "defective" in some manner. However, Rogers also finds that temporary attorneys are rarely referred to as "temps" and are "accorded the full status of the profession" (p. 154). Thus, she concludes: "Despite the fluidity of temporary employment, temporary lawyers had little difficulty constructing a stable identity as 'lawyer.'"[2] This is because the contract attorneys she interviewed saw themselves as solo practitioners who were choosing to work temporarily because of the flexibility it afforded, and they saw their relationships with law firms and with placement agencies "as a relationship of equals for the most part" (p. 145). However, Rogers notes that the contract attorneys she interviewed were aware of the "temporary" stigma and showed efforts to resist it.

---

[2] Rogers (2000) acknowledges that many temporary attorneys (outside of her sample) would prefer permanent work, undercutting her claims of flexibility and choice. She also concludes that temporary attorneys are less exploited than clerical temporaries because the attorneys even "working part time could supply a substantial income *relative to* what clerical temporaries can earn full time or part time" (p. 146, emphasis added). This "apples and oranges" comparison appears somewhat strained. Rogers also claims that while the two types of temporaries are stigmatized, clerical temporaries are said not to have a "real job," while temporary attorneys are seen as not being "real lawyers." Rogers says that this difference is significant because the clerical temporaries are not accused of not being "real secretaries," but of not having a "real job." She concludes that she may be "merely splitting hairs" by focusing on these differences, when the important point is that temporary work—for each of these groups—is stigmatized (p. 156).

Identity in the Project Attorney

I asked all the attorneys what it meant for them to say: "I'm a lawyer." The answers were complex and support the assertion that there are many potential attorney identities, even within the same person. Some of them heartily defended the legal profession and were proud of their accomplishments, while others recognized serious flaws in contemporary law practice. Half of the attorneys told me that, if they had the choice to make again, they would not go to law school, and several mentioned that they do not readily reveal their profession to others because of public perceptions.

There were several themes that emerged from these discussions. Some attorneys described their identity in very practical terms involving training or function. Michael described himself as a sort of "navigator," a "servant of the client to do his bidding or her bidding and nothing more." Roger saw himself as having been trained "how to look things up and find things when I need to, how to help people, you know, if they need assistance." Mitch said that he has neither pride nor embarrassment in being an attorney: "It's my job. I mean, it's what I've chosen to do. It's a trade. You know, it's—I went to trade school." Others saw their identity in terms of personal accomplishment. For example, Betsy said she did "a lot of hard work to get there" and "I'm proud of it, and you know, glad that I've made it this far and I can say that I'm a lawyer, 'cause that was always my dream." A few attorneys told me that they also enjoyed the sense of having a high status in the community.

Other responses were more idealistic. Ben told me: "I kind of take it to heart that you should try to be a role model to people, and show them that, you know, lawyers exist to maintain a way of society and a way of life, not just to screw other people over and get their money." Bernice said: "I'm very proud to be a lawyer. To me it is one of the highest callings, to be a lawyer. It's a guardian of the morality of society. And it's—it's about helping people who haven't had the opportunity to understand how to function in society, and what the rules of our society are." Similarly, Evan told me: "I think that I'm part of a large organization that is dedicated to the integrity of our system—I mean, that the country is built on the law." Maya said that she had read an article advocating "the lawyer as healer." She liked this idea, and added: "I think of someone that's not only looking for ways to be adversarial, but someone that is looking to build relationships and use the law in a positive rather than in a negative way."

Interestingly, many of the attorneys responded to questions about their own identity by referring to public perceptions of lawyers, usually without prompting from me. Everyone was aware of negative public attitudes, and some sympathized with them. Kathy said it "felt good" to be a lawyer, "as much as we get totally reamed on, and put in a very bad light for, you know, not always unjustified reasons." James commented that lawyers "get a certain level of respect, as well as a certain amount of negative reaction 'cause lawyers are greedy bastards. Which I disagree with, to a certain extent, but I agree with it to a certain extent." Mitch told me: "I mean, there is a reason why there are so many lawyer jokes. Um, you know, I mean, we're sort of grouped together in—in a lot of the public's eye, we're grouped together with used car salesman as far as trustability." For many of these attorneys, then, identity was complex and also already partly stigmatized because of public opinions of lawyers. Their identity was further complicated by the stigmatizing effect of being a "temporary worker."

Temporary Attorneys and Spoiled Identity

I found that document review was even more strongly stigmatized than the types of temporary legal work that Rogers (2000) studied, such as overflow work or appearance work. Doing document review was perceived to be more similar to performing temporary clerical work than it was to doing "real" legal work. The work was deskilled, autonomy was limited, and tasks were fragmented, both spatially and conceptually. The attorneys told me in many different ways that document review work was undesirable and that they thought they were at the bottom of the law firm hierarchy.

One common complaint was about deskilling. Bernice told me that she was very disappointed to be doing project work because "we weren't being paid to think." (This statement is commonly uttered by manual workers, and it has been echoed by temporary workers in other contexts [see Henson 1996, 100].) Bernice continued: "We're not really contract attorneys, we're clerks. We're doing clerical work, but they want to be able to tell the client: 'We have all these attorneys working' . . . but it's really clerical work. Very little of what I've done can come up to the level of what I'd consider legal work. Very little." Thus, many attorneys felt anonymous and interchangeable. The language of the attorneys I interviewed was replete with degrading terms referring to the work of document review. Many of these involved colorful metaphors. Maya said that when she first saw the project room filled with boxes and tables, she immediately thought of the assembly line. I asked her if that sense continued as she did the work or whether it changed; she laughed and responded:

It continued, but it sort of just became—well, the first day I think also we were all in suits, so you don't expect to be put in an assembly line, factory-type environment, so I think that was a little disconcerting. But then, you know, you come in with more regular clothes, you don't mind as much. I think you start to get desensitized to the fact that you're doing assembly line type of work. 'Cause you're prepared for it. You're dressed for it, so you're physically ready for it, and then you just mentally adjust to the situation.

Both Bernice and Michael told me they felt like "cogs" in the process, and Larry said that doing the work, "you do feel just like an automaton." Betsy told me she frequently feels like "a number on a cost balance sheet or something." Kathy said she felt like she was "actually contributing" in her former job, but now: "I feel like I'm just, like, a number, you know, I'm a glorified data entry person." Others evoked images of trained animals (pigeons, hamsters, and monkeys) to describe the skill level required. Kathy referred to project attorneys as "worker bees" and "warm bodies." Vince went furthest, using the terms "drones" and slaves," and added that he feels "unimportant and miserable." The effects of limiting autonomy seem apparent. Kevin Henson (1996, 95) wrote: "When the risk of error is minimized, so too is the possibility of taking pride in avoiding it."

The physical fragmentation also affected how attorneys perceived their work and their identity. They were separated from other members of the firm and thus had contact with few firm employees other than those who were directly supervising them. They also were alienated from the outcome of their work, as were Rogers's (2000) and Henson's (1996) clerical workers. Attorneys were typically provided little or no context about how their work fit into the larger case or whether their work was even proving useful. Mitch told me that he had worked on many projects, and that usually he would have moved on to a different assignment before the prior project's deal closed or the merger occurred: "So I didn't even know what happened. I don't even know—it's like—'Did the deal go through? Did it not go through?'"

The effects of this disconnection were felt by the project attorneys. Larry told me:

If it's not actively degrading, then it's disappointing in that within a month after a project ends, I can't tell you what the subject matter was. You're that far removed. Um, you see every day the documents that are at the crux, at the heart of the matter. Quite possibly you see some very important documents, but that's fairly rare, all things considered. But, you know, uh, do I brag about work on the tobacco litigation? No. Do I brag about working on paper products, or on tabletop surfaces, or am I enthused about any of it? No.

In addition, some attorneys felt exploited. While some thought the pay was at least adequate—Kathy, who had worked as an attorney in the public sector, and had also resorted to secretarial temping, thought the pay was "awesome"—most felt differently. Bernice told me: "For this work, I honestly think a lot of people are making a lot of money on this. I think we're underpaid." Julie called the pay "appallingly low," and added: "I think most appalling of all is the markup and then the double markup on what we do." Many attorneys also raised complaints about working conditions and hours.

Not surprisingly, project attorneys tended to be perceived as temps first and attorneys second. They were frequently referred to as "temps" or "temp attorneys" by law firm personnel and by each other. Once, while I was working on a project at Kerry and Merson, a law firm associate, Jen, put up a sign instructing the project attorneys where to put completed boxes, which read: "Temporary Attorneys." After she left, a project attorney crossed out "Temporary" and wrote "Contract." For the rest of the project, Jen referred to the group as "contract attorneys," but there was always a slight pause beforehand, as if she were making sure she was using the right term.

Most attorneys who had worked for several firms related some negative experiences involving law firm staff. Roger told me he had been at some law firms that had "a real 'us/them' attitude." Lynn said that on one project, the law firm attorneys "thought that they were too good for us." Vince found such an attitude at most law firms. He told me that "there's a definite hierarchy, a . . . 'better than you are' attitude. The people who are not attorneys—the paralegals, the secretaries, are the worst . . . And you're always reminded that you're 'the temp.'" When I asked Vince how the "just a temp" message is communicated, he said: "When you first start the project, they tell you how to do things, like how to fill out the forms. 'We need you to do this—this is where you sit, this is when you eat, this is how you eat,' you know, 'here's the'—how you go to the bathroom sometimes, it's very demeaning. It's like putting a whole bunch of kindergartners in a big room and telling them: 'These are the rules.'"

In contrast, Julie thought that project attorneys sometimes felt disrespected because they lacked self-respect: "I get very angry when I'm treated poorly, and there's an associate here . . . who one day came into our workplace and started yelling: 'You people in this rat hole!' And I got very angry.

I don't like being called 'you people,' and I don't like being told that I'm working in a rat hole. And I let other [law firm] people know how vehemently I felt about that." Whether or not attorneys felt they had been mistreated (regardless of the perceived reason for it), they were aware of the stigma of doing document review. Bill said: "I can tell you . . . I always joke about this because like, you know, when we see some people act up—acting weird, or you know, sort of abnormal, we say: 'You see, that's what you get when you temp, man. That's why they're temps.' Or, 'that's why we're temps.'"

For most attorneys, then, the "temporary" stigma had an additional impact on identity formation. Sometimes the effect was subtle—for example, some attorneys spent a great deal of our interview time deflecting or neutralizing the temporary label, as discussed below. Other attorneys were acutely aware of the effects of doing temporary work on their self-image. Melinda said that she had felt like she "could really help people" when she got out of law school. After doing project work, she said: "I guess I can, but I really don't feel that way right now." When I asked Frances what it meant to her to be a lawyer, she told me that she feels a sense of pride in accomplishment, but quickly added that she also feels "kind of empty" because "I hadn't really been *employed* at these firms." She continued: "It's the whole stigma, I guess. It's a cloud over my impression of what I've done in my life as a lawyer."

I asked Vince how he felt about being a lawyer; there was a long pause, and then our conversation continued:

v: It doesn't mean anything. I thought *then* that it would be something glamorous—glamorous work—
rb: When you say 'then,' when do you mean?
v: Like, when I was—during law school or just out of law school, I felt—important. Now I just feel like [I work] to make someone more money, or make someone rich. I just feel like we're slaves to—we're drones. [*laughing*]
rb: Drones?
v: Mm-hmm.
rb: Okay. So do you have any pride in the identity?
v: No. Before, yes. Now, no. I'm not proud to say what I do.
rb: And what do you think that change is the result of?
v: I think it's from being a contract attorney. Yup. Definitely.

Larry had similar feelings. He told me that after doing document review for a year: "I don't feel like an attorney. So, it's depressing in the sense that you're not professionally where you want to be, and even though you have 'project attorney' or 'contract attorney' as your job title, you're not doing anything that anybody who was plucked off the street *really* couldn't do with the same, you know, daylong or hour-long training session that we go through at the start of every project."

These attorneys were confronted with a "status incongruity" (Sennett and Cobb 1972). They were highly educated professionals and, in some cases, high-ranking graduates of good schools. However, they were doing work that they recognized (or that they knew others recognized) as low-status. The attorneys adopted a variety of coping measures to manage this incongruity.

Managing Spoiled Identity

In managing stigma, a person has two choices—either internalize it or employ techniques to deny or deflect it. In temporary work, "continual verbal and nonverbal assaults on one's self-concept become increasingly difficult to escape, deny, or deflect" (Henson 1996, 149). All the attorneys I interviewed were aware of the stigma of being a "temporary lawyer," even if they claimed to have been generally treated well and respected. Thus, all of them displayed various techniques of internalizing or neutralizing the stigma. This process is not a resistance to the work itself or to the working conditions (which is described in Chapters 4 and 5), but to the classification and meaning of "temporary." These attorneys fought to resist the assumptions of incompetence, flakiness, and lack of motivation that come with the "temporary" label.

Rationalization and Neutralization of the "Temporary" Label

Lynn was the only attorney I interviewed who made no obvious attempt to destigmatize the work she was doing. She had worked for a law firm and also briefly had her own practice. She said she enjoyed temping because she had burned out on practicing law; she had a short attention span; and she enjoyed the flexibility, the low demands, and what she considered the good pay that project work afforded. She looked with amusement at other project attorneys who were itching to find a permanent job in a law firm: "I've had those 'real jobs.' They're not all they're cracked up to be." She began to laugh, and added: "All of these people that are fresh out of law school on these assignments are, like: 'I'm looking for that firm job.' Oh yeah, I'll see them in a couple of years back on these projects."

The other attorneys used a number of different techniques to rationalize or neutralize their status. Some emphasized that they were only doing the work temporarily or were really self-employed, others asserted their primary identity as "attorney," and some blamed outside forces for their status. These explanations were interrelated, and sometimes attorneys used multiple neutralization tactics in answering a single question.

"I'm Really Self-Employed"

There were two attorneys besides Lynn who told me they would not mind doing project work long-term. Mitch had closed his solo practice and subsequently had been employed on a number of projects, some of them long-term, and was not anxious to start a practice again. James had not been happy with practicing law, but also did not know what else he would rather be doing; he thought he could "do this temping thing indefinitely." Both Mitch and James "reframed" their status from that of temporary employee to self-employed. James said that he might eventually have to "get a job," but that he "prefers this free agent thing." He added that he had briefly owned a small business and found legal temping to be similar: "I like structure, but the way my mind works is not conducive to working for other people. So while I consider this working for other people, it's not *really* working for other people." Mitch similarly likened project work to when he had his own practice: "I approach it that I have two clients. I have an employer but I have two clients, and it's the law firm and the law firm's client." Both James and Mitch also pointed out that they had always obtained work when they wanted it, and had been employed for long stretches of time on a variety of projects. Similarly, Frances told me: "I've been fortunate in being at long-term assignments and so I describe them to others as being 'virtually employed.'"

By calling themselves "self-employed," "virtually employed," or "free agents," and by emphasizing their nearly continual employment, James, Mitch, and Frances neutralized the stigma of "temporary" while also asserting a sense of independence and control over their work life. Henson (1996, 154–55) found a similar pattern, where clerical temporaries would repeatedly seek out work in the same sector or would secure a long-term assignment that "routinizes the presence of the temporary in the workplace to the point that he or she may be mistaken for a permanent employee."

"It's the Economy, Stupid"

When I asked why they were doing project work, or why they thought other attorneys were doing it, many attorneys externalized the cause by referring to economic conditions or discrimination. Melinda told me: "I blame the market" because Washington, D.C., is "saturated with lawyers." She said that a few years ago when conditions were better, recent graduates would have been able to find a job in a firm. Instead, many of them were now project attorneys. Bernice agreed that "the job market in this area for attorneys is very tough." Debby said that "this economy just sucks" and that she was amazed to meet people doing project work "who were partners or junior partners, and then got laid off." Maya added: "I think this is a tough city on lawyers. I mean, there's a lot of lawyers practicing law, there's a lot of lawyers coming from, you know, 'Ivy' or whatever." Rick told me:

> Most of us are doing this I think because there are relatively few op-portunities right now for us. We've been closed out of other avenues in the legal profession, either because we haven't found work as a re-cent graduate, or, you know, we've worked through our eight or nine years of being an associate somewhere and there's nothing much left at this point unless you've got a half million in billings to [bring to a firm]. . . . So most of us do it by default. I hate to be cynical, but that's the case. Few people do it by choice.

The oldest two attorneys—Rick and Bernice—felt that age discrimination was another reason they could not find permanent work.

Several attorneys also felt that the stigma of temporary work itself was to blame for some attorneys not finding permanent positions. Larry said that project work was a good stopgap, but added: "It can also be difficult to get out of the quicksand if you don't move fast enough." Vince also said that there are "people who have been a temp too long, and they get a stigma, and it's hard for them to find any work." By blaming outside forces for their pre-dicament, the attorneys could neutralize the stigma that the temporary em-ployee is somehow unfit for permanent employment.

"It's Only Temporary"
Most of the attorneys I interviewed emphasized that they were doing project work only temporarily—or at least that had been their intent when they began doing it. I asked each of them how long they would continue to do project work if their other plans—such as finding a permanent legal job or making a career change—did not work out. Half of them responded that they would not continue to do project work for more than another year. (I saw many of those attorneys well over a year later on other projects.) Larry told me that he "could probably do it for another year before I absolutely imploded" and he was "amazed that I've stayed with it for as long as I have,

actually." Vince said he would last six months, and "maybe a year . . . I'm not happy. I'm happy otherwise, but in my career, I'm miserable." Several other attorneys told me that they could not see doing anything else that would provide enough income to pay their expenses, so they would keep doing project work until they found a permanent job. Frances, who had done secretarial work, told me: "I'm not going to go back to making $30,000 a year." When I asked Roger how long he could see himself doing project work, he paused for quite a while, let out a long sigh, and responded: "As long as I had obligations to my family."

Most attorneys, then, saw themselves as having little choice other than to do project work. By asserting their lack of options, they were claiming that the status of "temporary" was essentially an involuntary one. At the same time, their emphasis on their plans to do something else allowed them to focus more on their identity as a *lawyer* than as a *temporary* lawyer. These claims also acted to separate these attorneys from the dreaded "permatemps"— those who were voluntarily choosing to do this work long-term. Indeed, even those who were most sympathetic to the plight of their fellow project attorneys—those who viewed them as mostly competent and blamed the market—showed some disdain for the permatemp. I asked Bill whether he could make a career out of temping. He immediately said "no." When I asked him why not, he responded:

> Because, one, I'm proud of my brain, and it would rot doing this, okay? I mean, it would absolutely rot. Um, and you know, the reality is, it's—it doesn't—you have no direction. I mean, no career growth. I mean, you get stuck doing this, and when you come out, I mean, you haven't learned anything new. You can't say that you have some new skill—and, like, you—even if you're a fifth-year temp, you're still going to get paid the same amount. I mean, you know, there are no real perks to it, so no, no.

I asked Ben what he thought of people who wanted to make legal temping their career. He told me: "I can see the appeal, but . . . they don't have a lot of ambition. They're more concerned about just getting the cash to meet their basic needs."

"At Least I'm Still an Attorney"

While the characteristics of document review are quite similar to those of clerical temping, project attorneys have a resource that many clerical temps do not—the ability to make use of their professional status as a means of reducing the stigma of temporary work.[3] Attorneys did this in one of two ways—first, by emphasizing that they were attorneys first and temporaries second, or by comparing temporary attorney work to other, lesser work that they *could* be doing. Evan told me that when he first began project work, he quickly became aware of his secondary status: "I'm not sure what irritated me more, though, the fact that they had a class system like that, or that I was at the bottom because I was a temp, you know? I'm still an attorney, you know what I'm saying?" As described in Chapter 3, both Evan and Mitch declined certain types of work that they felt were beneath them. Evan refused to spend the day moving boxes, telling me he did not want to become "a laborer," and Mitch left a project after spending the day "unitizing" (stapling) documents. Evan also turned down projects that paid him less than he thought he was worth. Once, when he was offered $18 per hour, he thought to himself: "You're treading into the servitude thing here." Conversely, several attorneys pointed to what they felt to be good pay as providing salve to their wounded status. Debby told me: "It may bruise your ego a bit for being treated like a peon, but we're being paid better than one."

Others rationalized their status by considering themselves fortunate that at least they were doing legal work. (Interestingly, many of these attorneys told me in other moments that project work really was not using their legal skills.) Larry told me that project work was disheartening, but that the law is "a wonderful profession to fall back on," and that "many people don't have the opportunity to be depressed at making forty to sixty thousand dollars a year." He added: "You know, despite the uncertainties, you could be unemployed; you could be in a different profession where if you were not in the top of your profession you don't have the fallback you need to. So at least this industry is here as long as the world of antitrust or the world of litigation is still going at the same pace. So, it's here, you know? Deal with it."

Betsy told me that the work is "pretty much mindless," but "at least it's legal work, so in that sense, I'd rather do this than waiting tables or something like that." Kathy also said that when she learned about temping as an attorney, she thought: "Oh, good. 'Cause maybe I can actually do something

---

[3] Henson (1996) finds that the clerical temporaries he interviewed would sometimes tell "cover stories" to neutralize the temporary stigma. They would carry "identity props" or "prestige symbols" such as books, scripts, or backpacks to show they had another status such as student or struggling author. Henson himself would let people know that he was a graduate student. I also told the attorneys I worked with that I was working on my doctorate. Part of the motivation was ethical (disclosure), but I also benefited personally from conveying the message that I was "really" something other than a temporary.

as a lawyer, that I didn't have to go back to, you know, typing eighty words a minute." Each of these attorneys was able to draw on his or her primary status as a lawyer to reduce the "temporary" stigma.

Internalizing the Stigma

In addition to attempting to deflect the stigma, attorneys employed a number of techniques to internalize it. They did this through normalizing project work, negating claims of incompetence, and by sometimes becoming the "supertemp." Attorneys also sometimes "trashed" their fellow project attorneys, thereby elevating their own status.

Normalizing the Work

As discussed previously, many attorneys were aware of the stigmatized status of document review work. In response, they employed several techniques for normalizing the work. Larry called it a "necessary evil." Betsy called the work "mindless but important for [the clients'] purposes." Susan told me: "It's important work. It's got to be done." James said: "Somebody's gotta do it, and it might as well be me." Ben commented: "I feel like we have a bigger importance than it might seem. I mean, there's a limited number of us working this, and we're helping move it along incrementally, maybe, but, you know, our little push adds together to one big push that gets this thing accomplished." Later, he continued the theme, but then seemed to reconsider and retreated to a more instrumental attitude: "I think it has some importance. It is important, um, as far as—in theory, it's important, but in practice it seems to be not quite that important, but you can't screw it up. You know, you have to do—you have to do a decent job, at least. So, you know, it doesn't bother me. I enjoy learning about the industries."

Mitch told me that he tries "to come in taking [the work] very seriously." Julie said: "I don't demean the work—it needs to be done. I have high self-esteem, so I don't demean myself for doing the work," and continued: "Is it boring sometimes? Of course. But I know why I'm doing it, it serves my purpose, and it's an honest living." As our conversation continued, Julie repeated the theme in various ways, telling me she "was fine with" the work, and "didn't have a problem with" it. As our conversation continued, I got the definite sense she was "protesting too much."

Others used a related idea—that even if the work *was* stultifying, the "temps" were not the only ones who had to do tedious legal work. Frances told me that she had worked for a law firm in a position akin to a staff attorney: "I did realize, working at [the firm], that it's not just [the project attorneys] who do the grunt work, either. The partners do it, too. So it's not just us doing it." Ben told me something similar; after talking to partners and associates of law firms, he felt that document review is "close to the work that regular associates have to do."

It is undoubtedly true that some work assigned to beginning associates shares some of the qualities of document review—for example, it may be boring, rote work that is highly fragmented. Indeed, associates (but never partners) were even occasionally assigned to do document review along with the project attorneys. However, even if there are some similarities, the important difference is that associates are not marginalized by having their identity coupled to the task; they are members of the firm, with greater security, benefits, remuneration, chance for mobility, and respect. The work is seen as a rite of passage rather than a dead end; as Evan told me, associates may sometimes have to do similar work, "but the difference is that there's no invested future in working as a contract attorney." Nevertheless, by comparing their work to that of permanent law firm employees, these project attorneys reduced the stigma of doing temporary work.

Circling the Wagons

I found that project attorneys rarely discussed with one another why they were doing the work. Kathy told me she thought this lack of disclosure was particularly true for the "older attorneys"—she referred to a senior attorney who worked for "a major company," but "he never brings up why he does this instead of a regular job." Bill also found that most project attorneys did not volunteer career information. When I asked him why he thought this was, he replied: "I mean because it's really no one's business. I mean, you know, it's like—it's like anything else, you know, like, if you're in a traffic jam, you don't ask someone: 'Why are you in a car? Where are you going?' You just say: 'Hey, stay out of my way, and everything's good.'" This is an interesting metaphor. It seems to suggest that, like those stuck in a traffic jam, project attorneys are all doing temporary legal work for the same reasons—to continue the metaphor, that they are all traveling during rush hour or are stuck because of an accident. However, this does not explain why they were on the road to begin with, nor does it say anything about their destinations. More important, the metaphor fails to recognize that project attorneys have opportunities for social interaction and sharing that are not available to automobile drivers.

Thus, it was interesting to interview these attorneys and to find out why they thought others were doing project work and what they thought of their competence and skills. The majority of them had rather positive opinions of most of the other attorneys doing project work. They viewed the others as mostly "like them"—either just out of school, between jobs, or transitioning to some other career. Roger told me that project attorneys "are no different than what you'd find in the general legal community." Vince thought that while there were a few "bad apples," most of us were "very competent." Bernice told me that "there are a lot of very good people doing contract work." Betsy thought that we were all "pretty competent and knowledgeable about the law," and added: "I guess there's always people who seem to be maybe not as quick at grasping concepts, but I don't think they're any less competent or intelligent." Melinda said that she was surprised to meet people doing project work who had graduated from top schools, and "that if we were given a chance, I think that most of us would do very well." Ben also though most project attorneys were "people who I don't think should be temping, for the most part." Several attorneys told me that most of us were probably just as able as the associates in the law firms we worked for. Larry said: "If we played *Freaky Friday* [a classic children's novel in which a mother and daughter magically switch bodies] and [transposed] all the contract attorneys with all the associates, the difference in work product wouldn't be that great. . . . I think we'd be just as capable."

Asserting their collective skill and intelligence was one way to neutralize the stigma of temporary work; these claims dovetailed with other explanations referred to previously, such as blaming the economy. The message was: "We're as good as anyone; but we're just stuck doing this for now."

Becoming the "Supertemp"

In her research, Rogers (2000, 156) notes that some clerical temporaries became "supertemps," either "motivated by the rejection of stigma or the desire to land a job." Similarly, Henson (1996) found that some clerical temporary employees would pride themselves on doing quality work and some would take on extra tasks in order to obscure their status as "temporary" by negating the assumption of incompetence that came with it. We might expect an even stronger reaction to the "incompetence" stigma from professionals doing temporary work because expertise is a strong component of professional identity and expectations.

Indeed, most attorneys went out of their way to assert their positive work habits and document review abilities. Even those who had denigrated the work were quick to point out that they did the work well. However, some attorneys went beyond assertions of competence and declared their superiority over others.[4] One attorney, Joseph,[5] was a particularly extreme example of the supertemp. When I asked Joseph how he would describe his relationship with his placement agencies, he responded: "Generally superb. I'm an A-list. I'm an A-list project attorney." He told me that the latest agency he'd registered with "has been trying to get me to work with them for most of the last year," but that their timing had not coincided. He said that all the agencies know that he is reliable and that he also brings "fifteen years of litigation and transaction experience and management with me, at only a slight premium." I was surprised by Joseph's reference to a "slight premium"—I had always assumed that the rate the agency set was nonnegotiable—so I asked him what he meant. He told me that on 90 percent of his projects he had negotiated a higher rate than was paid to the other project attorneys: "It's typically not much of a premium, but it depends." On one project, where Joseph had begun by mostly reviewing documents and later ended the project helping to write briefs for the firm, his hourly rate doubled over the course of the project. He told me:

Again, that's my years of experience and my years of being a businessman, and it's like, just because they say: "It's X dollars an hour" doesn't mean that's what it is. Unless you just say: "Okay, thank you." If you say: "Well, I don't work for that rate. I'm going to need X-plus." And any time I've ever asked for it, I've always gotten it. I haven't always asked for it. This project, I did not ask for it, 'cause this project I knew I was going to be one of the—you know, rank

---

[4] There are probably other motivations for a project attorney to assert his or her competence. Rogers (2000, 156) writes that "it is difficult to unravel the extent to which one's 'supertemp' behavior is motivated by the rejection of stigma or the desire to land a job." In the case of project attorneys, there were some tangible benefits for doing a good job (although the relationship between performance and future assignments was often rather mysterious). Many of us believed that if the law firm or agency were impressed with our performance, we would more likely be assigned to further work (as discussed in Chapter 2, the chance of being hired as an associate was close to zero). In addition, such behavior simply may have been a reflection of personality characteristics; some project attorneys would likely be "tooting their own horns" regardless of the status of their employment. However, most often, the behavior seemed to be impression management directed at other project attorneys, thus sending the message: "I'm not an ordinary temp." And there would have appeared to be little tangible benefit for attorneys to assert their abilities in interviews with me, other than to negate the stigma of incompetence attached to the "temporary" label.

[5] Joseph was one of the twenty attorneys I interviewed for this project. I am using a different pseudonym for him here because it is likely that he would be recognized by employees at his placement agencies because of the unique features of his supertemp persona.

and file. It's also my first project for this agency. I had no leverage—it wasn't: "Hey, you know that I will help—I will help secure your position with this client." You know: "Having me on this project will do nothing but help you keep this client."

Joseph said that his agencies think his request for a premium is "an ego thing—that I have to be the highest paid contract attorney there." He added: "I'll let them think that, as long as they keep paying me more." After my interview with Joseph, I asked the remaining project attorneys if they had ever negotiated a higher rate with their agencies. They all told me they had not even known it was possible.

I also directly observed "supertemp" behaviors when working on projects. For example, some attorneys took great care in reading all the documents very slowly and becoming experts on the case. I met an attorney, Otis, on a telecommunications project lawsuit. There were at least fifty other attorneys reviewing documents in two shifts. After about a month on the project, the firm asked twenty of us to stay on, to be hired by the firm directly. (I have never known of another law firm that used this method to screen out the "best" reviewers.)

Otis and I were among the group that was asked to stay. Otis revealed that from the beginning of the project he had been reviewing documents at approximately 10 percent of my own rate. I wondered to myself why he had been asked to stay when he had been working so slowly. (I also wondered whether his work product was truly superior, given that this particular project only required us to check a handful of boxes on a computer screen.) I had noticed too that Otis would always speak up when anyone in the room had a substantive question about the industry. So I asked him why he worked so "carefully." He told me that he spent a great deal of time reading the documents and prided himself on his in-depth knowledge of the case. (However, Otis's extra time did not always lead to greater knowledge; for instance, we once engaged in a somewhat heated argument when he insisted that DSL was faster than cable.) I asked him whether he thought that his presumptively greater knowledge was worth the trade-off in speed: "What if we all worked that slowly? Wouldn't we need to hire ten times more people? Do you think that's what the client wants?" He became irritated and offended, and I dropped it.

I worked with Debby for many months on one project, and noticed that she also took every opportunity to answer others' questions. Debby told me that she prided herself on understanding the substantive aspects of the case. She said she found the work interesting at times, although it also could be quite repetitive when the same documents would repeatedly appear. I asked her: "So you don't usually feel like it's tedious work?" She replied that "some of it can be a little tedious," but added: "I'm actually one of those people that read stuff, that actually read what I'm supposed to scan." Immediately, she began laughing and said: "That sounded really bad. You know why? It sounds like: 'Other people suck.' And they don't. It's just—different styles of document review."

In fact, there were always a few attorneys in any room, like Debby and Otis, who seemed to believe it was important to become experts and to broadcast their expertise. (At times, I may have been one of them.) Sometimes an attorney would get stuck on a document and ask the others in the room for an opinion about how to code it, or would ask a question about the client or the industry. Usually the room "expert" or "experts" would jump in first; sometimes there would be a battle of the experts and minor arguments would ensue. At other times, discussions would occur between the project attorneys and law firm personnel. These moments seemed to be a chance for the project attorneys to assert their autonomy and expertise and sometimes to challenge managerial rules or knowledge. On one project, James, who had some prior experience in tax law, coded documents as "privileged" when they contained a certain type of tax advice. The staff attorney came back to James and told him to stop marking the documents privileged (this would save the priv team some time in having to "de-priv" them). She told James the firm had determined that the documents contained accounting advice rather than legal advice. I listened as James strongly (and ultimately vainly) defended his position to the staff attorney. When the staff attorney left the room, he announced to the rest of us that the law firm was making a big mistake in producing these documents. He seemed to be quite chagrined that the firm was not accepting his legal advice.

Typically, disagreements between law firm staff and project attorneys were short-lived. Usually the law firm employee won the argument, but sometimes law firm staff would agree to incorporate project attorneys' suggestions into future instructions. However, most project attorneys recognized the limits of their influence. Mitch told me that, even though he had a great deal of legal experience: "I am in fact somebody's employee, and I'm not the king, I'm not the one who's making the decisions, and so I will do what I'm told to do. Unless it's egregious, and then I'll say: 'No, I'm not going to do that.'" When I asked him if he ever had been asked to do something "egregious," he told me that in one case, there were documents "that were not good for the client," and when he came across them, he was told to "basically bury them, basically destroy them." He said that he refused and "made quite a stink about it." He added that he did not know ultimately if someone else in the law firm destroyed the documents because the project ended before the documents were turned over to the other party.

Transferring the Stigma

As Debby's "other people suck" comment indicates, there is a fine line between asserting one's competence and denigrating another's. Some attorneys managed just to tout their own abilities; however, several attorneys attempted to neutralize their "temporary" status by transferring the stigma to other project attorneys.[6] Even those attorneys who helped to "circle the wagons" told me that there was some percentage of project attorneys who were incompetent, unmotivated, unintelligent, or unethical, or who had flawed characters. A few of them seemed to think that *most* project attorneys were flawed in some way. And as noted above, many attorneys distinguished themselves from the "permatemps" by emphasizing that they were only doing project work temporarily, and not by choice.[7]

Sometimes these messages were communicated in a subtle way. For example, Larry told me that he is able to work very quickly "and do far more than what's expected of me, and I honestly believe with greater accuracy than most people. I couldn't tell you why." Other attorneys were much more critical of others. Some focused on the project attorneys' intellectual capacity. Michael said that while there were many capable project attorneys, "on the other end of things, there are some people where—not that I'm elitist, but you would question their literacy at times." Evan told me that "some of

---

[6] Henson (1996, 163) finds that clerical temporaries sometimes define themselves "in opposition to the other." For example, they might denigrate permanent employees by thinking: "At least I'm not a secretary." In this way, temporary employees "would minimize the stigma of association and the ever-present, ever-threatening fear that one might really belong." Henson writes: "The fear of fitting in or belonging was far greater than the fear of being seen as other and isolated" (p. 165). Project attorneys rarely denigrated law firm employees, except to sometimes complain about lack of respect; however, a few seemed to evidence a "sour grapes" approach. Larry thought that project attorneys were more "well-rounded" than attorneys at large law firms, who tend to be snobbish and "antisocial" and for whom "salary is more important than other issues." However, this type of comment was rare. Henson finds that temporary employees sometimes also lessen their stigma by thinking "at least I'm not a lifer." One subject told him: "'People who just do this all their lives! I just want to say, "You poor things. Where are you going with your life?" You know?'" (p. 165). I found this type of comment to be much more frequent, as project attorneys also disassociated themselves from the permatemps, as discussed previously.

[7] Rogers (2000, 88) also finds that some clerical temporaries deal with stigma by "disparag[ing] other temporaries as a group." She notes that this practice contributes to their individual isolation because it reduces solidarity.

these people really aren't all that intelligent." When I asked Bernice what she thought about the other project attorneys, she answered:

B: There's the whole panorama of human drama on these projects. You get—you get the losers. I don't really think there are any losers on this particular project that I've observed. Um, you get people who can't—

RB: Let's go back a sec. By 'loser' what do you mean?

B: They're not very bright.

RB: Okay.

B: They're not very sharp.

RB: Mm-hmm.

B: And they probably just couldn't get a job even if there were jobs.

Similarly, Mitch told me: "You know, there's a reason why some people are doing project work. It's because it's the only work they can get. I mean, sometimes the work product is appalling—it can be pretty sketchy."

Some project attorneys also "trashed" the work ethic of the others while emphasizing that they had higher standards. Mitch told me that "there's a lot of shenanigans that go on in this business." He said he had observed the soldiering process (discussed in Chapter 4), where the message was communicated, sometimes unspoken, "but sometimes very loudly spoken: 'You need to slow down. You need to—we need to stretch this out.'" Mitch— who had told me he's "never worried" about finding the next project—said that he might "nod along, and go 'ha-ha-ha' with everybody else," but then "just . . . continue at the same pace I'm going, which is a diligent and careful pace." He said he does not participate in soldiering because: "I have an obligation to my client, and I have a work ethic."

Julie was particularly critical of project attorneys' lack of ambition. She had held a high-paying job as an in-house lawyer for a major national retailer. We got on the subject of ambition when I asked her whether she felt it was important to get to know the other project attorneys. She responded: "I find that to know them is not to like them." I must have reacted visually, so she immediately backpedaled, saying: "Listen, there are a few people that I like. There are more people I like than I respect." She said that the other project attorneys did not seem to be "putting one ounce of effort into finding a job," and added: "There are some people who might as well just tattoo 'loser' across their foreheads. Not because anyone else has made them a loser—they're making *themselves* losers." Julie said that there are two groups of people doing project work. The first consists of those "who are going to find it hard to obtain and retain permanent employment because of their work habits, their personalities, their demeanors, . . . lack of being terribly bright, whatever." She said the other group, which is "appallingly large," consists of "people who are too damn lazy to go out there and do what needs to be done to find a job." Julie continued: "And I'm appalled. I don't understand why someone would go to school for seven years, and be heavily ridden with debt, and then be satisfied to sit in a room day after day, saying that they're bored and not challenged, looking at boxes of documents." Of course, it is interesting that Julie found only "two groups of people doing project work." One would assume from her comments that she thought she fit into neither.

"Passing as Normal"

In his pioneering work on stigma, Goffman (1963) describes a person's status as "discreditable" if the person could choose to reveal or to hide his or her stigma. Goffman uses the term "passing as normal" to describe the process by which people conceal their stigma. One holding a "discreditable" stigma could choose to disclose it to no one or could reveal it to a select number of persons or social groups. For example, researchers in one study found that topless dancers "divided their social worlds" by not revealing their employment to others (Thompson, Harred, and Burks 2003). Temporary attorney stigma was "discreditable" because it did not normally need to be revealed. Thus, I was curious to know whether and how project attorneys disclosed their work to other people with whom they interacted outside the project.

I found that there were three approaches to disclosure. Only a couple of attorneys appeared to have little concern with revealing the details of project work to any audience. More often, attorneys chose to "pass" by mystifying their work, providing just the barest outlines, or obfuscating the work with legalistic language. Most attorneys engaged in selective disclosure, mystifying their work to certain audiences while disclosing more details to other audiences thought to be more sympathetic.

Laying It All Out

Bill appeared to make no effort to hide the kind of work he was doing. When I asked him how he describes project work to other people who are not lawyers, he responded: "Grunt work. That's what I say. I do—'I'm in the mines. I'm in the pits.'" I asked what other peoples' reactions were, and he said they say: "'Oh, well, that's what you'd be doing anyway.' Or they say: 'At least you get paid for it.' You know, stuff like that. They don't really fathom what it's—what it's really about." Bill said he goes into more details if asked. For example, he tells them that he reads and categorizes documents, and even after he explains it, "it still doesn't register. They're like: 'Oh, it's just lawyer stuff.'"

Kathy also told me that she lets people know exactly what she is doing as a temporary attorney. She said that she was recently visiting her family over a holiday weekend and explained to them the document review work she was doing. She was surprised when they said: "Oh, that must be so exciting. You must be learning so much. . . . That's great." She said, laughing, that she told them: "No, it's really not that great. But it's paying the bills." It is interesting that even though Bill and Kathy told me they felt comfortable with full disclosure, the reactions they describe make it clear that their audiences did not understand the work, thus making even full disclosure a low-risk option.

"Just the Facts, Ma'am"

Full disclosure under all circumstances was not the norm, and "passing" was relatively easy for project attorneys, at least if their audience consisted of nonlawyers. The public knows relatively little about what attorneys actually do, so project attorneys could mystify the work either by providing few details or by using special legal language that obfuscated its true nature. Ben told me that he tells people "basically what I put on my resume—which is, I determine if it's relevant to what the government asked for, and if it's privileged." Lynn said she typically tells others only "that I'm doing contract work for D.C. law firms on antitrust litigation. Something like that." Melinda told me "I don't go into specifics. Like, I keep everything very general, very vague." Maya appeared to deliberately use legalese to obscure the nature of the work, telling people "that I am working to produce documents to a grand jury subpoena." Then, she says, "they don't know what else to ask," and so she quickly changes the subject, "'cause I don't like to talk about work."

I never asked the attorneys *why* they chose their particular style of disclosure; many nevertheless explained themselves. For example, Ben told me that "nonlawyers aren't going to understand any more than" the broad outline of what he tells them, so he lets people just think "he's just working long hours—he's a lawyer working long hours, with documents, you know." Roger also said that he does not explain the work because "I know nobody in my family would really understand it. So they know that I work on individual contracts, individual projects that I'm assigned by the agencies, and I just tell 'em it's like, it's litigation support." Debby also said that she is tight-lipped about her work with most others. When I asked her if it is different with friends or family, she said that she tells her family members she reads documents and codes them: "I'll look at every sheet of paper and try and figure out if it fits a bubble on specified terms on another sheet of paper. And if it fits the bubble, then it goes in one pile. If it doesn't fit the bubble, it goes in another pile." I asked her what their reactions were to that explanation and she replied:

> D: I don't think my family actually listens when I talk anymore, so they don't have a reaction. They mostly just pat me on the head and keep going. I could have told them that I tap dance around the office carrying a bright blue chicken and they would have done the same thing, so—
>
> RB: I look forward to the chicken.
>
> D: [*laughing*] Yeah.

Susan said that she never provides any details about the work because, except for one tobacco litigation case she worked on, "nothing's been interesting enough to spend more than one minute talking about." James said that when he tries to explain the work to nonlawyers, they respond: " 'How? What? You're doing what? Huh? Okay, what do you want to drink?' They get bored with it very fast." Frances also told me that "after you say 'I'm a lawyer,' they tend to tune out everything else." Julie said she reveals little about her work because "people really don't want to know the details. They're very happy to know you're a lawyer and you're working someplace. Let's move on."

Other attorneys I spoke with seemed to rationalize their parsimony by citing confidentiality concerns. As project attorneys, we were typically required to sign agreements with law firms and our agencies that prohibited us from disclosing the matter we were working on, as well as any client confidences that we became privy to. (Ethical rules also prohibited us from disclosing confidential information.) Michael said he tells people only that his work "involves a lot of document review." He added that, if pressed, he might tell someone he is working on a merger case, "and that's about that." He told me that limiting himself in this way "makes things much easier as far as client confidences, and so on." Evan's conversation with me showed his attempt to use confidentiality to explain his lack of disclosure, when it was really the stigma of the work that motivated him to "pass as normal":

> RB: How do you describe the work you're doing now to people in your life who are not lawyers?
>
> E: I don't really describe it.

RB: No? What do you tell people that you're doing?

E: Uh, I would just say I was doing contract attorney work. Uh, if they ask specifically, I'd say: "Well, I'm working on an antitrust case." If they want more information, then I will go into the legal jargon of it. I wouldn't tell them I'm sitting there every day looking at thousands of documents. Well, you know, I mean, I don't do that, because I feel like there's a breach of confidentiality there. I mean, I can't tell them who the clients are, and so I don't feel like I can really say what the subject matter is, really, either. And besides, who wants to hear about it? [*laughing*]

RB: Mm-hmm.

E: You know, it's not very exciting. [*laughing*] So, I don't really tell people anything about it.

It seems that these attorneys were rationalizing their lack of disclosure either by projecting their own boredom or lack of interest onto their potential audience, or by exaggerating their confidentiality concerns. This kept the stigma concealed and avoided the potential embarrassment of disclosure. The fact that some of these same attorneys selectively disclosed more to some audiences than others—discussed next—seems to support this conclusion.

Selective Disclosure

Most of the attorneys told me that they would decide how much to reveal based on the particular audience. There seemed to be two different motivations—to garner social esteem from some audiences (by "talking up" the work) and to receive emotional support from others (by telling "the truth" about it). Bernice said that she tells most people: "I'm doing legal support for major law firms in downtown Washington," and added: "That sounds great." When I asked her if there are ever follow-up questions, she replied:

B: Sure. "What are you working on? Oh, Wall Street." I mean, what we do can sound very glamorous. Now if it's an intimate, I will very quickly tell 'em it's dull, tedious work that the law firm attorneys don't want to do, but some attorney has to do.

RB: Uh-huh.

B: But um, you know, I certainly make it sound good—

RB: Mm-hmm. Okay.

B: [*laughing*] —unless you want, you know, me to cry on your shoulder and tell you what it's really like.

I asked Larry how he described project work to other people who are not lawyers. He laughed, saying: "Unfortunately, with thinly veiled contempt." He continued: "If it's a family member, I talk it up. If it's a friend, I talk it down. If it's an acquaintance, I'm neutral or I talk it up. I don't mean to give the legal profession a bad name simply because I haven't been a success at it, but the fact remains that what I do is not—uh, challenging. Like I said, it's a necessary evil."

Betsy also said that she addresses different audiences differently. She said that if she is talking to, say, a potential employer, "I'd obviously not want to make it sound horrible, try to make it sound somewhat respectable, but if it's just a friend or whatever, I just say it's just temp work. I'm just doing this until I get a real job; I don't like it. I don't hold back on that as far as that goes." Mitch said he tells most people that he has closed his practice and now is hired by a law firm for a project "when they don't have enough people to staff it, and then when it's done I'm on to the next law firm." When I asked him if he ever describes the details of the work to anyone, he replied: "Oh yeah, I mean, if you're close to me, I mean everyone knows that, you know, I'm doing mind-numbing, really boring work when I'm doing document review." Frances said that her friends know she is temping, but she only tells other people "kind of on a need-to-know basis," adding: "I guess I am embarrassed to say: 'Well, this is what I do,' 'cause I think that I haven't accepted that I am doing this permanently."

For some of the attorneys, close friends or family members were a sympathetic ear to their complaints and frustrations about the long hours, the tedium, and the working conditions. Roger told me that he kept the substantive details of the client matters to himself, but would talk to his wife, who had become his "sounding board." However, I found one attorney who was worried about disclosure even within his family. Rick said: "I'm going to face [explaining the work to] my daughter, who's old enough now to try to figure out what I do for a living and it's hard to explain. Sometimes I just say I read documents looking for important evidence in cases." He smiled wryly, and then added: "It's a dirty job, but somebody has to do it."

Deprofessionalization Revisited

It should be clear from this and the preceding chapters that project work was nearly thoroughly deprofessionalized. It lacked ideological autonomy because project attorneys had no voice in the way their work was used and also technical autonomy because it was deskilled, routinized, fragmented, intensified, and rigidly controlled. On many projects the one true legal task—determining if a document was legally privileged—was deprofessionalized through "dummy priv" rules. Contrary to depictions in the legal press, temporary work did not offer project attorneys "flexibility" in any sense that the word was used. Project attorneys had little choice in the hours worked, and they always had to work at the client's location, which sometimes was physically uncomfortable or even unsafe. The work was also highly insecure. There was little advance notice of when projects began or ended. Most attorneys lacked health insurance, pension plans, and other benefits. We were loath to plan vacations or turn down work for fear we would not be offered further engagements. Also, the work was not an effective stepping-stone to permanent employment. Project work also had negative subjective effects. For many, a former sense of professional pride and identity was seriously compromised and recast. Others, attempting to cling to their former identities, appeared to expend a great deal of psychic energy defending against the stigmatizing effects of the work.

In this context, responsible autonomy was insufficient to ensure management control over work process and work output. Thus, firms tried a variety of other direct and indirect controls over work process and time. However, project attorneys countered these controls and engaged in a number of resistant behaviors, such as soldiering and "box shopping." They were able to do this by exploiting both their knowledge of the work process and the poor management of document review projects. In addition, project attorneys "leveraged" the commonality of interests that they shared with their agency and the law firm (to maximize billings) to achieve some control over the work process and to extend the length of projects.

These findings involving degradation, insecurity, control/resistance, and stigma/identity in the project attorney sample are similar to those reported in ethnographic studies of low-skilled clerical temporary work (e.g., Henson 1996; Rogers 2000), and are contrary to what has been reported in the few studies of highly skilled temporary technical and professional workers. Temporary or "freelance" status has been found to increase the sense of autonomy among graphic designers (Van Wijk and Leisink 2004) and attorneys (Rogers 2000), without negatively impacting a sense of identity. Temporary work for technical workers frequently requires high skills and can include training similar to that provided to workers in standard work arrangements (see Smith 1998). Some studies have reported little individual or group resistance among professional temporary workers, either because responsible autonomy seemed to be a sufficient control (Rogers 2000) or because it was precluded by the specific qualities of the workers and the work organization (Smith 1998).

In the only prior study involving temporary attorneys, Rogers (2000, 155) finds that the work the attorneys performed was comparatively deskilled, involving rather "boiler plate" or "worker bee" assignments. However, the work was not devalued. Rogers's contract attorneys were rarely referred to as "temps" and they valued their autonomy, maintained their identity as attorneys, and did not feel exploited. Rogers finds that the "deskilling that takes place in temporary law parallels that in clerical work; however, law's system of bestowing credentials and prestige distinguish [sic] it from clerical work, which can be described as truly monotonous" (p. 165). She concludes: "To be a freelance attorney is to be a solo practitioner and to be accorded the full status of the profession" (p. 154).

The description of the work of project attorneys should make it clear that "bestowing credentials and prestige" does not operate as a magic wand that does away with "truly monotonous" work. "Prestige" involves a social process—it is afforded to professional work in part because the work is perceived to be highly skilled and autonomous. When the work loses these qualities, it becomes devalued—to those doing the work and to those observing and evaluating it. Even Rogers (2000) acknowledges that prestige is relative—the contract attorneys she interviewed were afforded less prestige and their work was deskilled *relative to* other lawyers.[8]

However, while Rogers's attorneys felt they retained some autonomy and sense of professional identity, this is best explained by the marked differences in the types of work those attorneys were performing and the conditions under which it was performed, compared to the work of project attorneys in this sample. Rogers's attorneys felt free to turn down assignments, performed much of the work independently, and were provided a variety of assignments. Project attorneys, however, had many more organizational and

---

[8] Rogers (2000, 154) is not always consistent. She first claims that being a temporary attorney accords one the "full status of the profession." Later, she concedes that temporary lawyers are "marginalized vis-à-vis other lawyers" (p. 162) and "have lower pay and prestige" (p. 164). She also writes that "the juxtaposition of *temporary* with *lawyer* is incongruous. To be temporary is not to be a lawyer" (p. 161, emphasis in original). In addition, temporary lawyering is highly feminized, meaning that more women are doing the work, and the work is relatively deskilled and lacks power. In Rogers's view, "men and women temporary attorneys are stigmatized differently" (p. 161). Women lawyers are understood to be "mommies," while men lawyers are viewed as "defective" unless they can reframe their temporary status as entrepreneurialism (p. 162). Rogers's inconsistency—that temporary attorneys simultaneously enjoy both high status and stigmatization—appears to flow from two alternating comparisons. Temporary attorneys are stigmatized when compared to other attorneys; however, "there is no doubt that they still enjoy a privileged position over other workers" (p. 162), such as the clerical temporary workers that Rogers interviewed.

technical constraints. They were grouped together and required to perform the work on-site; had little control over the pace and scheduling of the work; and were doing essentially the same, tedious work day in and day out. The work was deskilled to a much greater extent than the contract work described by Rogers, rendering it "truly monotonous." Thus, the organization and experience of project work was more akin to the temporary clerical work that Rogers (2000) describes than it was to the work of Rogers's contract attorneys.

It appears that efficiency pressures on corporations and law firms combined with advances in digital technology will continue to expand law's "dirty jobs," as Rick put it. Some of these will remain located in the United States, while others will be conducted in offshore locations by attorneys in India or other nations, as described in Chapter 7.

7

"I Would Rather Grow in India"

The Emerging Legal Underclass

The Changing Professional Contract

We expect professional work to be autonomous, collegial, and independent and to involve interesting, challenging, customized, and individualized work that serves a broader public purpose. However, powerful forces are reshaping professional work, making it more like other types of work. Professionals are becoming proletarianized and losing ideological autonomy as they are absorbed into hierarchical organizations. Professional work is becoming more insecure and, in some areas, is also being degraded. Just as craft work was deskilled and brought under management control, digital technologies are now allowing some aspects of professional work to become more routinized, controlled, and intensified. Some professional work is increasingly commoditized—unbundled and sent down the chain to the lowest-paid worker. Contact with clients is becoming attenuated with regard to both time and place; for example, "telemedicine" is no longer an exotic term (see McLean 2006). A variety of professions—law, medicine, university teaching—have been affected by increasing insecurity and a decline in both ideological and technical autonomy.

While such trends are clear, the question is the extent to which they should be resisted. Some authors suggest that the professions neither need nor "deserve" the benefits they have long possessed (relative autonomy, independence, respect, high remuneration, security, self-regulation, and interesting work); rather, these benefits are merely the class-based rewards flowing from the attainment of a monopoly over certain types of services. For such observers, monopoly power is seen as sometimes contrary to the best interests of clients, the general public and even the professions themselves; therefore deprofessionalization would have some beneficial consequences for each of these groups.

Commoditization through Unbundling and Multisourcing

What is the significance of this study of project attorneys? Does their work represent some errant "blip"—an unusual exception in the practice of law—or does it portend further deprofessionalization and deeper stratification of the legal profession? Certainly, the sample is limited to time, place, and type of work. So it is perhaps best viewed in the context of other changes occurring or predicted to occur in the practice of law.

Some see a future where demands for efficiency coupled with the application of information technology will drive a process of commoditization of legal services.[1] Richard Susskind (2008, 31–32) defines a "commoditized" legal service as "an electronic or online legal package or offering that is perceived as commonplace, a raw material that can be sourced from one of various suppliers" and is offered "certainly at highly competitive prices."[2] Under such a system, lawyers become essentially "interchangeable producers of marketable products" (Johnson and Coyle 1990, 396).[3] Attorneys dislike the commoditization of legal services for ideological reasons because it devalues

---

[1] Several British firms appear to be at the forefront of providing packaged legal services. Eversheds provides software to create employment contracts and Linklaters provides a number of products under the "Blue Flag" brand, offering training modules and legal software to its clients (Susskind 2008).

[2] In Marxist discourse and in semiotics, "commoditization"—or more commonly, "commodification"—refers to turning things into goods or services that were not previously thought of as goods or services. Susskind (2008) uses the term as found in business literature, involving the dilution of the distinguishing characteristics of competing goods or services until they are viewed as essentially the same and purchased on consideration of price alone (see Holmes 2008). The term has been applied to various professional services, including medicine (see Borgstede 2008; McLean 2006). I use the term broadly to refer to the unbundling, packaging, and systematizing of legal services, regardless of whether such services are Web-based.

[3] Typically, the transfer of information involves a trade-off between "reach" and "richness" (Evans and Wurster 1999). Reach refers to the number of people sharing information; richness is a composite measure that includes customization, bandwidth, security, reliability, and interactivity. Information technology allows for both reach and richness, obviating the normal trade-off between the two (Evans and Wurster 1999). Thus, some would argue that widespread availability of legal services over the Internet does not necessarily mean a decline in the quality and customizability of the service.

the practice of law. They also fear it because commoditization will drive down the price of legal services. Once investment is made in producing a commodity product, competition drives down the price toward the marginal cost of producing one more product; for services offered through information technology (IT), this price approaches zero (Susskind 2008). The head of a company providing legal document software over the Internet illustrated this notion when he said: "The legal knowledge we've compiled . . . is in a centralized location . . . and it's easily accessible to consumers. It costs us little to create, it costs us virtually nothing to store, and it costs us nothing to deliver" (see Norris 1999, 33).

Susskind (2008) acknowledges that some legal services cannot or should not be commoditized, and that law firms will continue to invent new types of customized services. However, competitive pressures (among law firms, as well as between law firms and potential corporate providers of legal services) will drive services away from customization and toward commoditization. To decide the optimum mix of service type, Susskind (2008) advises law firms to undertake a Taylorist analysis of each case, breaking it down into its component tasks and determining the optimum methods to perform and deliver each task.[4] The firm will discover that some tasks might not need to be performed at all, and the firm should "multisource" the remaining tasks to the most efficient labor possible. Susskind (2008) offers twelve different forms of multisourcing. "In-sourcing" is Susskind's term for the delegating of work to junior associates within the firm. "De-lawyering" refers to handing off tasks to paraprofessionals or laypeople. Some other possibilities include "relocating" (having work performed in another of the firm's offices where rates are lower), offshoring, outsourcing, and leasing of lawyers on a project basis.[5]

Only a few of these practices are currently widely deployed. It is common for firms to "in-source" to junior associates and "de-lawyer" tasks by assigning various aspects of a case to law clerks, paralegals, or legal secretaries.

---

[4] While Susskind does not cite Frederick Taylor, he is essentially suggesting the application of Taylorist methods to legal services: separating out constituent parts of a task, determining the most efficient way to deliver each part, and then assigning each part to the cheapest labor possible.

[5] Susskind's (2008) other types of multisourcing are: subcontracting (to firms with lower rates while retaining the "brand" for the services); cosourcing (law firms either work together or they jointly create offshore servicing centers); home sourcing (using independent contractor lawyers working from home); open sourcing (making legal software available at no cost); computerizing (offering packaged, commoditized services); and nonsourcing (deciding that particular tasks or matters are not worth doing, if not acting carries low risk).

There is also broad acceptance of the use of temporary attorneys for at least some types of work. Some of these other multisourcing options will become much more common in the future, as firms use information technologies to respond to increased competition and to demands from corporate clients.

Application of Information Technology

Law firms have sometimes been reluctant to apply advanced technologies to legal practice because of their inherently conservative nature and their desire to preserve traditional income streams. Large law firms especially tend to see their services as highly customized; thus, they constantly "reinvent the wheel" for every client's problem rather than "recycling" prior work.[6] However, firms have been most open to applying technology in the areas of discovery and document management. Discovery costs represent half of all litigation costs in federal cases (Willging, Stienstra, and Miletich 1998) and such costs are rising. One cause of greater costs is an increase in merger activity, which doubled between 1995 and 2000 (Triedman 2006b); another is the explosion of digital media (Uribarri 2007). There are at least two additional explanations, each rarely acknowledged by attorneys: The first is the use of aggressive "Rambo" litigation tactics (Androgue 2000). Another is the inefficiency involved in the delivery of legal services. Most complex legal work is billed by the hour, creating incentives for inefficiency.

Before the advent of digital tools to manage discovery, paper documents had to be carefully cataloged and maintained by hand. This process was highly inefficient: "The documents for the case were kept in a large room, often called a 'war room.' Each time there was a name or issue that required research, an army of employees and temporary workers was called in to dig through the boxes" (Nieuwenhuizen and Priebe 2000). Now, however, firms must "keep pace with the technology used by their corporate clients" (Pfeiffer 2007); therefore, they employ sophisticated data management software to save costs, increase accuracy, and help with trial preparation (Nieuwenhuizen and Priebe 2000). In addition, electronic databases allow the convenience of worldwide access (Pfeiffer 2007) and around-the-clock availability.

---

[6] Firms such as plaintiffs' personal injury firms that bill on a contingency basis (charging a percentage of damages) rather than charging an hourly fee tend to apply more streamlined, routinized procedures. Small, consumer-oriented firms that bill hourly have been more likely than large corporate firms to embrace efficiencies such as standardization, in part because of the nature of their work and in part due to more direct interfirm competition.

While these systems have increased efficiency, there are still significant costs in developing and maintaining such data archives. The costs only begin with the investment in hardware and software; there is still a great deal of human effort that is required. Documents must be collected for inclusion in the database. This frequently means that attorneys or paralegals must visit client sites to "pull" paper documents, which must then be electronically scanned. Corporate IT employees or outside vendors also must collect electronic documents. Some of these documents, such as stored voice mail, may be difficult to access (Wiggins 2003). Once the documents are collected, scanned, and loaded into the database, in many cases, attorneys or paralegals must still review all the documents, code them, and determine if they contain privileged material.

Corporations and law firms continue to try to reduce the amount of human labor required in the discovery process. For example, parties to litigation may agree to do a "sweep" of their databases using relevant search terms and then review and produce only documents that contain those terms. The remaining documents would automatically be considered "nonresponsive" to the document request and would not need to be reviewed. I was employed on several Second Request projects (requests for document production under federal merger review) where the federal agency and the law firm negotiated a group of search terms to employ. For example, the names of particular products or more generic terms such as "price," "merger," or "plan," could be employed. This technique is, of course, rather crude and would still pull in irrelevant documents; for example, an employee's personal e-mail discussing the *price* of the car she just purchased or a meeting to *plan* a birthday party would be flagged as responsive. It would also likely exclude certain relevant documents that did not happen to use particular terminology, so private litigants may be unlikely to agree to such discovery limitations.

Current software can go beyond searching for keywords. The chief information officer (CIO) at the Boston firm Burns and Levinson was quoted as saying that the firm used to employ teams of paralegals to code documents page by page, but times have changed: "Now we just scan those documents and use algorithms to determine what's important or not" (Pfeiffer 2007). However, such programs are not perfect, and many firms still require each document to be viewed and coded by humans. The development of programs with greater artificial intelligence could make searching, organizing, categorizing, and producing documents even more automated. Even some current retrieval software can "use fuzzy logic to search not just by keyword but by concept" (Bennett 2005), and some studies have shown that automated systems are as good as attorneys at categorizing (coding) documents (e.g., Roitblat, Kershaw, and Oot 2009).

To some commentators, document management software is only the leading edge of an eventual boom in the automation of legal practice. Some such programs are already being used by attorneys, government agencies, and consumers; increased efficiency should lead to lower costs and a need for fewer legal professionals and semiprofessionals. For example, in Australia, a program called SplitUp is used to predict "with impressive accuracy the likely results of divorce proceedings" in order to encourage settlements and avoid litigation costs, and another program called GetAid is used by a government agency to determine whether applicants are qualified to receive legal aid (Bennett 2005). The latter program has reduced the work of attorneys by 80 percent. Online companies like LegalZoom and Standard Legal have automated the process of drafting relatively simple consumer legal documents such as wills and living trusts. Corporations such as General Electric and DuPont have used corporate quality control initiatives to make their legal departments more efficient, and a group called the Open Legal Standards Initiative (OSLI) is working on standardizing routine corporate legal documents, including patent applications and basic contracts (Paonita 2006). Some are using OSLI's recommendations and creating computer software. According to one reviewer, a product for creating contracts is "in a Web form that seemed hardly more complicated that negotiating Amazon.com's checkout" (Paonita 2006). The increasing sophistication of corporate legal departments (and their willingness to share innovations with each other [see Susskind 2008]) has the potential to entirely "disintermediate" law firms from at least some types of legal services.[7]

Offshoring: From Boston to Bangalore

Several attorneys I interviewed told me about their frustrations with the document review process, particularly in Second Request projects. Michael complained about some of the low-tech processes involved, such as the extensive use of paper documents with their concomitant document flags, written notes, and other accoutrements that tended to bog us down. When I asked him how to improve the process, he said: "I would say automate it to the

---

[7] "Disintermediation" refers to the process of "cutting out the middleman" in the delivery of a product or service. The Internet has the potential to disintermediate by bringing buyers and sellers together directly. It also has the potential to reintermediate by creating a new middleman that links buyers and sellers—eBay is one such example.

greatest extent possible." Rick also told me that "there's a lot of waste and inefficiency in these processes. . . . There's just a lot of wasted money." He said that the waste comes in part from "the number of people looking at the number of documents and trying to make fine distinctions when it doesn't really matter," and he suggested that "it should be done much more as a bulk process." He added: "In my view, it should be done in India with lower labor costs, and the same relative skill level on the whole, or else it should be done mechanically, without human involvement." At the time of our interview, I was aware that software was already being used to reduce human labor in the discovery process. However, I thought he was joking about the use of offshore attorneys. As it turns out, he was not.

In fact, cost concerns are driving a booming offshore legal services market. After law firms and corporate legal departments became accustomed to outsourcing certain noncore functions, they broached another frontier—the offshoring of some of these functions. For instance, the insurance company Fireman's Fund laid off all of its legal secretaries after sending the work to a company in India (Ainsworth 2003). Offshoring is most economical for large law firms (Smith 2004), so firms such as Clifford Chance and also Milbank, Tweed, Hadley, and McCloy began to experiment with offshoring their word processing or secretarial work (Friedmann and London 2006; MacEwen 2005). Hildebrandt International, a large legal consulting firm, partnered with an Indian firm to offer back-office functions like human resources, accounting, and marketing research (Knotts 2004).

Next, corporations even began to offshore some of their "core" legal work as well. In 2001, General Electric began sending some work to its affiliate in India, saving $1.7 million in legal costs over two years; the company's senior counsel claimed the move was "a real success story" for the two divisions involved (Reisenger 2003). Microsoft has used an Indian firm to do all of its patent investigations (Coster 2004). Oracle's general counsel noted that India had been "a hot spot for companies looking to find cheaper labor," so why not legal services as well? He said he would "rather grow in India" (Deger 2003).

Some suggest that the widespread acceptance of using temporary attorneys for some types of legal work has paved the way for accepting the next step: the offshore lawyer. One legal consultant said: "In a way, the process is somewhat akin to law firms using lawyer temps, except in this instance, the lawyers are thousands of miles away" (Ainsworth 2003). Similarly, a law firm attorney said: "There's not much difference in hiring a temporary lawyer in New York and a temporary lawyer in India—as long as you control it" (Hechler 2004). One writer compared the reluctance to hiring offshore attorneys to the initial reluctance of firms to hire temporary attorneys, and implied that eventual acceptance of offshore lawyers was inevitable (Coster 2004).

Most offshore work is performed in India, but some work is done in other countries such as New Zealand. Currently, the market is limited to commodity work that "is fairly similar and can be systematized" (Flahardy 2005), the type of "low-level work typically performed by legal assistants, paralegals and possibly even junior lawyers who cut their teeth on rote assignments" (Crawford 2004), including document review and coding (Ramstack 2005). Some commentators believe that there are natural limits to the growth of this market because attorneys are unlikely to send any work overseas that requires advanced skills, creativity, or a high degree of collaboration. However, others predict that "this will eat its way up the food chain" (Ainsworth 2003) and that the market, which was estimated at $146 million in 2006, will increase to as much as $4.7 billion per year by 2012 (Bach 2007).[8] One estimate from 2004 predicted that 8 percent of legal work in the ensuing five years, and eventually up to 75 percent of legal work would migrate offshore (see *Compensation & Benefits* 2004). Other predictions are more conservative; Geanne Rosenberg (2004) suggests that 20–25 percent of legal work will be performed offshore by 2014. According to Forrester Research, 12,000 U.S. jobs had already been lost to offshore legal services as of 2004, and the United States will be losing 79,000 jobs annually by 2015 (Crawford 2004).

While some estimates of future offshoring appear exaggerated, it is also quite possible that ten years from now a significant amount of at least certain kinds of legal work—especially the commoditized work referred to above—may be performed by offshore lawyers.[9] Some of the biggest losers may be those in certain niche areas like patent law prior art research. Other losses will likely occur among the ranks of temporary lawyers, particularly those

---

[8] Some legal process outsourcing companies are already offering more-sophisticated services—one firm, Lexadigm, crafted a brief for a U.S. firm that was filed with the U.S. Supreme Court in a tax case (see Krishnan 2007).

[9] Brian Uzzi of Northwestern University has claimed that significant offshoring is unlikely to take place because "the practice of law is difficult to break down into smaller tasks—unlike, say, the manufacture of a car, where bolts can be made in one place, tires in another and the car put together in still another place" (Myers 2005b). This is contrary to what most commentators (e.g., Johnson and Coyle 1990; Susskind 2008) have noted about the increasing fragmentation and rationalization of legal work. It also seems to contradict Uzzi's statement to the same reporter, quoted in another article that appeared during the same week (Myers 2005a) that temporary attorneys "are good for any kind of work that's boilerplate. They're basically interchangeable in quality or features, no matter what the work." Given the state of digital technology, it is perhaps difficult to see how legal work could be separated out to be performed effectively by domestic temporary attorneys but not by offshore lawyers.

assigned to due diligence and document review projects. Document review work would appear to be well suited to offshoring because it is highly systematized, is not highly collaborative, and—because of digital technologies—can be performed easily at remote sites.

Likely Effects of Reprofessionalization

Competition and cost-cutting demands from clients will continue to drive the commoditization of aspects of legal practice (Susskind 2008). This will likely include a dramatic increase in the use of offshore legal service providers because the benefits clearly outweigh the risks, and government protectionist intervention is unlikely (see Patterson 2008). It also will mean that fewer lawyers will be required (see Susskind 2008), and that tensions between lawyers and paraprofessionals will increase (Crain 2004). Even if the more dramatic predictions regarding commoditization and offshoring are not realized, it appears that legal practice is in the early stages of a profound reprofessionalizing, with potential effects on lawyers' remuneration, status, autonomy, and independence. The public also will feel the effects of these changes.

Effects on Lawyers and Legal Practice

Unbundling, commoditizing, and multisourcing will further deepen the bifurcation of legal practice between the elites and the rank and file (see Freidson 1986). The elites will retain high-level, challenging, interesting, customized tasks that involve a significant exercise of judgment, skill, and discretion, while those in lower positions will take on "lesser" tasks that can be unbundled and routinized.[10] This creates an "underclass" consisting of temporary attorneys, staff attorneys, and more recently, offshore lawyers. Some members of this underclass may be able to move on to positions with greater responsibility and autonomy; indeed, I saw some temporary attorneys attain associate positions at small- or medium-sized firms or within government or nonprofit agencies. However, for others, the qualities of the position—deskilling, fragmentation, and stigma—may render them "untouchable" and they may have

---

[10] Of course, division of labor *per se* in legal work is not new. As a new associate, I quickly became familiar with the expression "shit rolls downhill"; that is, undesirable work is pushed down the organizational hierarchy. The difference is that in recent years, the "shit work" is no longer performed solely by associates (who take on the work with the understanding that they will work their way up the hill), but by persons who may be more or less permanently assigned to those tasks.

few exit options. And even these positions may face threats of reduction or elimination due to advances in automation or the growth of the offshore market.

It is difficult to accurately estimate the current size of this emerging legal underclass. Surveys show that the use of temporary attorneys by large firms more than doubled between 2002 and 2005 (Lewis 2006). The use of temporary attorneys can be quite substantial at some firms, particularly those involved in antitrust and complex litigation. For example, an antitrust partner at Howrey and Simon in Washington, D.C., was quoted in 2005 as saying that the firm was "trying to find the right mix of attorneys" and that it then had 220 temporary attorneys working, compared with 182 the prior year (Jones 2005). Howrey and Simon employed 550 attorneys in 2005 (Perin 2005), which means that nearly 30 percent of the total attorneys at the firm worked there on a temporary basis. The firm also employed forty-four staff attorneys (Jones 2005). Several other firms reported having more than one hundred temporary attorneys on hand (Jones 2005).

Deepening of Existing Stratification Patterns

Significant stratification already exists in legal practice. There is a clear demarcation in status; those serving corporate clients have more prestige than those serving individual clients (Heinz and Laumann 1982; Heinz et al. 2005). There are differences in organizational form; lawyers can practice as solo practitioners, within partnerships that are self-managed, or as part of the "global professional network" megafirm that is professionally managed and international in scope (Brock 2006). Besides private practice, attorneys also can work in-house, in government service, and for nonprofit institutions. Law is also stratified through specialization by practice area, which is mostly informal. Within firms, hierarchy is increasing, with new categories of attorneys that include non-equity partner, staff attorney, and senior attorney. Income and other remunerations also vary widely among practicing attorneys.[11]

---

[11] In 2008, the more than 500,000 attorneys employed within organizations other than law firms (e.g., government, business) had mean income of $124,750 and median income of $110,000. Within this group, attorneys employed in local government earned the lowest mean income ($89,320), while those employed in management of companies earned the highest ($151,820) (United States Department of Labor 2009). The median income of attorneys nine months after graduating from law school was $60,000 in 2005; those in private practice earned nearly twice as much ($80,000) as those in government service ($46,158) (United States Department of Labor 2007). For attorneys in private practice, the size of the law firm significantly impacts starting salary. In 2009, the median salary for a first-year associate

In addition, racial, ethnic, and gender diversity in the bar has increased over the last several decades (Heinz et al. 2005; American Bar Association 2006a). While there is greater diversity, especially among more recent law school graduates, lawyers overall are much more likely to be white (89.3%) and male (71.3%), based on 2000 census data,[12] and there are still significant differences based on gender class, race, and ethnicity. Nonwhite and women lawyers earn less pay, are concentrated in less prestigious types of practice, and are underrepresented in the judiciary and in law firm partnerships. As of 2003, women attorneys earned 76 percent of the amount men attorneys earned, and made up less than 20 percent of the federal judiciary, the partnerships in major law firms, and general counsels in Fortune 500 companies (American Bar Association 2006a).[13] The American Bar Association (2006a) also found that women lawyers suffer from gender stereotypes at work, experience barriers to networking and bringing in business, and must negotiate extra challenges to balancing work and home life. Women of color face a double set of biases (see American Bar Association 2006a, 2006b) and tend to leave law firm practice in disproportionate percentages (American Bar Association 2006b). Socioeconomic class also determines attorneys' career trajectories—the higher a law school graduate's social class, the more likely he or she is to find a job at a large corporate firm (Sterling, Dinovitzer, and Garth 2007).

Increasing commoditization and deprofessionalization will likely lead to further fracturing of the existing fault lines in legal practice. Already, there is a tendency for women lawyers to be disproportionately concentrated in part-time employment. There is a danger that women and people of color will be "ghettoized" into temporary work (Rogers 2000) and into other work settings that involve deskilled, routinized legal work (Johnson and Coyle 1990).[14] As

---

at firms employing from 2 to 25 lawyers was $70,000; at firms employing more than 1,000 lawyers, it was $160,000 (National Association for Law Placement 2009).

[12] As of 2000, 3.9 percent of attorneys were identified as African American, 3.3 percent as Hispanic, and 2.3 percent as Asian (American Bar Association n.d.).

[13] In the past, the low percentage of women partners and judges was explained by the lower percentage of women lawyers generally. However, women have made up 39 to 49 percent of law school graduating classes over the last twenty years, and thus this explanation no longer holds. Many (e.g., DRI n.d.) attribute the underrepresentation of women in partnership and in large firms to difficulties in balancing work and home, negative gender stereotyping of women, and challenges to women lawyers to be "rainmakers" and bring in business to the firm.

[14] Rogers (2000) cites statistics concerning the lower pay and prestige of women lawyers, and their greater tendency to be employed part-time. Given also that women tend to be employed disproportionately in temporary work generally, Rogers claims that "there is good reason to suspect that temporary attorneys may be disproportionately female if temporary employment

such work becomes more institutionalized (for example, law firms are beginning to hire permanent document review teams, a development discussed further below), attorneys from the lower socioeconomic classes, women, and people of color might be "funneled" into dead-end, low-skilled, and relatively poorly remunerated work. Lacking the protections of partnership (and perhaps even the advantages of standard employment contracts), these attorneys would appear to be at the most risk of layoffs and downsizing as markets shift.[15]

However, some attorneys may experience upskilling and an increase in autonomy. Law firms and other legal service providers will require a new position, the attorney-manager, to coordinate work within the firm and between the firm and other service providers. These members of the "professional-managerial class" (see Ehrenreich and Ehrenreich 1977) will represent a further stratification of the practice of law. These managers also will be needed because—if my research regarding project attorneys is any indication—it seems rather clear that firms cannot rely on "responsible autonomy" (Freidson 1977), nor can they "manufacture" consent (Burawoy 1979) when workers are performing regimented and tedious work, especially when they are doing

---

for lawyers represents a sort of occupational ghetto" (p. 129). She found that 52 percent of the lawyers working for the temporary attorney agency involved in her study were women, while women comprised just under 23 percent of U.S. lawyers at the time. Rogers concludes that this is evidence of "ghettoizing" women lawyers into temporary work (p. 129). However, this evidence is probably not as significant as it seems. Most research, including mine, shows that the majority of attorneys doing temporary work are relatively young. Thus, the proper comparison statistic for Rogers is not 23 percent (the percentage of *all* women attorneys), but the percentage of women who have graduated more recently. Use of this figure would result in a less-dramatically disproportionate ratio.

[15] The sample of project attorneys lends some limited support for this idea. Most of the attorneys I interviewed did not graduate from elite schools, most of their parents did not have professional degrees, and none had worked as an associate at a global law firm (see Appendix C). While I did not witness clear evidence of a disproportionate percentage of women and people of color on most projects I worked on in the D.C. temporary attorney market, my observations were rather unscientific. They were necessarily limited to the seventeen projects I was assigned to, and reflected my own estimate of the percentage of women and people of color I expected would be found in the larger Washington, D.C., legal market. In addition, many of the projects on which I was employed demanded a substantial time commitment, which would potentially exclude women attorneys who were looking for temporary work as a way to balance their home-work demands, such as raising small children (see Rogers 2000). Two attorneys of color who I interviewed told me that they believed they saw disproportionately high percentages of attorneys of color doing document review, and two others told me they did not. Unfortunately, such perceptions are impossible to verify. Statistics on the racial and ethnic composition of the temporary attorney market are not available because placement firms apparently do not maintain records on this basis.

so on a temporary basis.[16] Therefore, new supervisory structures will need to be implemented to ensure that the work is performed competently, appropriately, and in a timely manner. However, it would appear that additional costs of more intensive management would reduce some of the efficiencies gained by greater commoditization.

Decline in Satisfaction and Changes in Identity

It should be obvious from the review of Susskind (2008) and from the description of the work of project attorneys in this research that unbundling and multisourcing can result in an increased division of labor, intensification of work, deskilling, and a decline in technical autonomy, at least for those attorneys performing the more routinized, unbundled tasks. Associates at large firms report the least satisfaction with the intellectual challenge of their work (see Sterling, Dinovitzer, and Garth 2007), most likely because they are not afforded a great deal of responsibility and are given very small parts of larger projects. Attorneys who are asked to do work that is even more standardized and rote—like the project attorneys in this sample—would be expected to be even less satisfied.[17] In addition, more commoditized work will reduce the regularity and significance of client contact; the attorney-client relationship will move from a professional one based on trust to an "encounter relationship" tied to efficiency (Gutek 1995b). One also might expect a decline in collegiality among attorneys doing more routinized work (see Wallace and Kay 2008) because collaboration is not an important component of such work.

As legal practice is further stratified, changes in lawyers' identities also should be expected. Attorney identity is already a complicated phenomenon, composed of multiple identities that shift over time (see Nelson and Trubek 1992). Some argue that attorney identity has been eroded by bureaucratization and rationalization of the law (Espeland and Vannebo 2007). Working

---

[16] Susskind (2008) predicts even greater stratification. Some attorneys will continue to offer customized services, but four other "types" of attorneys will emerge. The "enhanced practitioner" will offer mostly standardized services and be expected to make use of third-party providers of legal services. The "legal knowledge engineer" will design standardized and packaged services and will direct the unbundling and multisourcing of projects. The "legal risk manager" will help clients avoid potential legal problems, tapping the unmet need for preventive law. Finally, the "legal hybrid" will be an attorney expert in one or more other disciplines who will be able to give value-added services in addition to legal advice.

[17] However, as expectations about "attorney" work changes, there may be a decreasing effect of commoditization and routinization on work satisfaction, as attorneys come to expect to be doing certain kinds of work that have been deskilled or reskilled (see Derber 1983).

on deskilled, intensified, and tedious tasks will further erode the professional identities of attorneys, as the results from this research indicate.

Changes in Organizational Form

Law firms already have become more bureaucratic and hierarchical. Some authors (e.g., Patton 1996) suggest that law firms should move away from the Cravath "triangle" or "pyramid" pattern (associates at the bottom supporting equity partners at the top) to a "diamond" shape (junior associates at the bottom and equity partners at the top, with "laterals"—junior and senior associates, non-equity partners, and contract attorneys—leveraging the firm from the middle). As legal services become more systematized, packaged, and commoditized, organizational forms will continue to evolve. One legal consultant suggests that once firms begin to unbundle various services, they will "shed themselves of their least-expert and most management-intensive employees— the factory workers, so to speak" (Zeughauser 1996). Firms will then create "separate entities for delivering high-volume, production-oriented work or identify capable, strategic alliances with providers they can outsource to." These separate entities will likely take some sort of corporate form because the delivery of commoditized services does not require the collegiality and collaboration that the partnership form encourages (see Greenwood and Empson 2003). In fact, some analysts suggest that commoditization of legal services also will lead to eventual public ownership of law firms (e.g., Susskind 2008). This may result in a decline in attorney self-regulation.

Greater Border Erosion

Laws in nearly every state prohibit a person from the unauthorized practice of law (UPL). UPL statutes are vaguely worded and vary between jurisdictions, but they generally prohibit three activities: (1) representing someone else in a legal proceeding, (2) giving legal advice, and (3) preparing legal documents (Rothman 1984).[18] Determining whether a person has violated

---

[18] This lack of specificity can be traced to the legal profession's failure to clearly delineate in its own professional codes exactly what the *authorized* practice of law entails (see Lanctot 2002). For example, the American Bar Association's 1969 Model Code of Professional Responsibility provides the following: "Functionally the practice of law relates to the rendition of services for others that call for the professional judgment of a lawyer. The essence of the professional judgment of the lawyer is his educated ability to relate the general body and philosophy of law to a specific legal problem of a client" (Lanctot 2002, 811). Many state definitions are similarly tautological, essentially stating that the "practice of law is what lawyers do" (Rhode 1981, 45). One author recently noted: "Resting a fundamental regulatory principle of the legal profession on such a formless concept creates its own set of problems when lawyers seek to prevent lay people from encroaching on their professional territory" (Lanctot 2002, 812–13).

the first prohibition appears rather straightforward; however, determining what constitutes the provision of "legal advice" and the preparation of "legal documents" can be quite difficult.

The ostensible purpose of such laws is to protect the public from receiving poor, or fraudulent, "legal" advice.[19] However, UPL statutes also serve to protect lawyers' professional monopoly against encroachment by other groups (Rhode 2004). The first bar association committees on unauthorized practices were formed during the Great Depression, suggesting that lawyers were attempting to protect their economic interests (Rhode 1981). The focus of most UPL charges in the ensuing years was against other professional groups such as bankers, real estate brokers, and title companies; in the 1970s, the focus turned to lay providers of legal services, as "divorce kits" and preprinted legal forms began to be provided by nonlawyers (Rhode 1981).

In recent years, UPL disputes involving other professional groups in addition to lay providers have increased. For example, in the tax arena, the distinction between accounting advice and legal advice had been largely settled in the 1950s through an agreement between the American Bar Association (ABA) and the American Institute of Certified Public Accountants. However, certified public accountants (CPAs) "now engage in the most complex areas of tax planning, estate planning, and entity formation," and determining to what extent these areas involve the unauthorized practice of law is presenting vexing problems for courts (Black and Black 2004, 4). Conflicts between credit counseling services and the bankruptcy bar also have increased (see Mund 1994). The ABA recently proposed a Model Rule that defines both the practice of law and its unauthorized practice. The U.S. Justice Department and Federal Trade Commission found that the proposed rule was "overly broad because it would prohibit nonlawyers from offering a number of services that they currently provide in competition with lawyers to the benefit of consumers" (United States Federal Trade Commission 2002).

As some legal services have become more commoditized, a new frontier of conflict has opened up involving publishers of software that provide legal documents delivered over the Internet.[20] Such documents can be either blank

---

[19] See *Sperry v. Florida ex rel. Fla. Bar*, 373 U.S. 379 (1963).

[20] Commoditization of such services is not new; self-help law books have existed for more than three hundred years (see Brown 1999). What is different now is the high "latent demand" among the middle class for legal services, as well as mass distribution through print editions or via the Internet.

forms or customized documents that are created using data inputted by the client. The latter is more controversial.[21] In the United Kingdom, a product called "Desktop Lawyer" has been introduced that uses Rapidocs software to assemble "personalized legal documents in a wide array of areas, including divorce, wills, powers of attorney, and sales of goods" (Lanctot 2002, 815). A U.S. company, LegalZoom, was founded by Robert Shapiro, among others. It offers similar services to those of Desktop Lawyer, including preparation of documents in connection with incorporations, wills, trademarks, patents, and leases. Its Web site proclaims: "Created by top attorneys, LegalZoom helps you make reliable legal documents from your home or office. Simply answer a few questions online and your documents will be created within 48 hours" (LegalZoom n.d.). Online document preparation is one type of commoditization; it has the potential to disintermediate lawyers entirely from certain types of consumer legal services.[22]

Effects for Consumers of Legal Services

Legal services are expensive because of the law's monopoly. Some legal aid is available for the poor, but services are limited in scope (for example, involving most criminal cases and certain narrow civil matters such as landlord-tenant disputes) and are sometimes deficient and subject to budget cuts (Rhode 2005). Middle-class consumers must pay out of pocket and thus tend to avoid legal assistance unless severely pressed. The notion of "preventive law" for most segments of the population is nearly completely unrealized. Those who support

---

[21] Most courts have held that the publication, distribution, and filling out of blank forms—so-called "scrivener" services—does not violate UPL statutes; however, a nonlawyer giving advice to a person as to which form to use, or how to fill out the form, *would* violate such statutes. See, for example, *State Bar v. Gilchrist*, 538 P.2d 913 (Or. 1975). Some courts have held that providing generalized written instructions also does not violate UPL statutes. For example, the New York high court found that distribution of a book designed to help people avoid probate did not constitute the unauthorized practice of law; see *N.Y. County Lawyers' Association v. Dacey*, 234 N.E.2d 459 (N.Y. 1967). However, other state courts have found such books to violate UPL statutes; see *Fadia v. Unauthorized Practice of Law Committee*, 830 S.W.2d 162 (Tex. App. 1992).

[22] Both LegalZoom and Desktop Lawyer provide disclaimers on their Web sites that they are not law firms, are not providing legal advice, and are not entering into an attorney-client relationship with the purchasers of their services. (Whether courts will agree remains to be seen [see Lanctot 2002].) Both companies recommend that their customers obtain legal advice regarding the proper use of the documents their Web sites help create. If this advice is followed, then attorneys will not be disintermediated; however, it appears that the attraction to consumers and small businesses of commoditized services is to entirely avoid the expense of legal advice.

the efficiencies of deprofessionalization and commoditization (e.g., Susskind 2008) see mostly benefits for consumers of legal services, who will receive greater access and pay less for it. Some commoditized services will fill the large "latent need" for consumer legal service. Organizational clients also will benefit, as even complex legal matters become increasingly unbundled and multisourced.

However, there are risks inherent in deprofessionalization and commoditization. Corporate clients likely will be sophisticated enough to avoid most such risks because the majority of them possess at least some in-house legal expertise, have access to legal knowledge that is increasingly shared (see Susskind 2008), and likely will continue to rely on law firms as a primary source for the coordination of the delivery of legal services. Individual consumers face potentially greater risks. There is a danger that they will receive incompetent advice from fly-by-night providers. They also may make use of some services they do not really need, and will lack the knowledge to know the difference. For example, form documents and software to create wills have become quite popular, but many individuals may not require a will or may need some other type of protection, such as a living trust. There is also the risk that software will not keep up with changes in the law and may not recognize all of the distinctions and subtleties that an experienced professional could. Most current software incorporates "decision trees" that function well under clear rules and simple facts, but may break down under more complex fact patterns and legal ambiguities.[23]

There is also a concern that as lawyers lose ideological autonomy over their work, various nonmarket goals of legal work also will lose out (see Derber 1983).[24] For example, some authors question whether greater commoditization and bureaucratization will have a negative impact on legal ethics. Bureaucratic systems decrease ideological autonomy because personal ethics become subordinated to the organization's interest (see Derber 1983). A decline in technical autonomy brought about by more routinization and specialization also may lead to a decline in ethics. If tasks are highly atomized, it may be very difficult for any one attorney to even recognize there may be

---

[23] This is not to say that claims about potential risks in particular cases should be accepted at face value. Claims about protecting the public interest frequently mask the desire to protect professional interests (Hyman 2008).

[24] Derber (1983) recognizes that many professionals when surveyed indicate that the aspects of work they value most involve cognitive challenge and personal growth, not public service. Thus, the push toward serving public interests is frequently taken up by professional associations, professional schools, and law firms desiring to burnish their images.

an ethical problem. As reported in Chapter 6, Mitch told me that he had been told to essentially "bury" a document. If such a request lacks context, an attorney may not even recognize the request as problematic.

Increased unbundling also may lead to more conflicts of interest because cases will be shared among many more providers. More broadly, as legal services begin to be delivered increasingly by corporations (legal publishers and legal process outsourcing providers), some commentators are concerned that the profit motive may trump attorneys' professional judgment (e.g., Carson 1994). However, others note that law firms have always been profit-making ventures and, thus, proper regulation of corporate entities will continue to ensure that such entities follow appropriate ethical standards (e.g., Adams and Matheson 1998).

Some authors also wonder whether the proletarianization of lawyers will lead them to abandon service work and the pursuit of legal knowledge for its own sake. Derber (1983) suggests that pro bono work will suffer under increasing deprofessionalization. Others point out that the increase in size and complexity of large law firms has not led to the demise of pro bono work—in fact, in many cases, it has been strengthened. It is possible that even publicly traded law firms will retain an interest in providing pro bono services (see Farrell 2008). At the same time, the wide availability of commoditized legal services may actually reduce the need for some types of pro bono assistance.

Resisting Deprofessionalization or Ameliorating Its Effects

It appears that unbundling and commoditization promise such significant increases in efficiency that they will be very difficult to resist. Bar associations—to the extent that they are even able to agree to resist particular developments—may be outmatched by corporate and public interest groups that will welcome the efficiencies of these services. Legal outsourcing and offshoring are resistant to curtailment attempts because legal services are part of "commerce" and thus subject to the same constitutional protections afforded other types of services. They are also difficult to resist because powerful commercial interests, such as legal publishers, have entered the market. In addition, there may be lack of consensus within the bar, either because some attorneys will want to offer such services or because other attorneys believe that such services will benefit the public. For example, while the ABA took a position against lawyers being engaged in multidisciplinary practice, some attorneys sought such arrangements, and many legal scholars decried the ABA's position (e.g., Morgan 2002). Similarly, some attorneys advocate more use of paraprofessionals in the delivery of legal services to make such services more accessible and affordable to low- and middle-income clients (e.g., Rhode 1996).

Resisting Offshoring and Commoditization

State and local bar associations, as well as state legislatures, have so far generally placed relatively insignificant limitations on legal outsourcing and offshoring. A New York City Bar opinion is typical in finding that such services do not violate existing rules as long as the work is properly supervised by attorneys and ethical issues like confidentiality are properly addressed (see D'Angelo 2008). Legislatures also have not taken decisive action to limit offshoring of services, even though dozens of bills have been introduced. One commentator concludes that "the legal outsourcing industry is at no great risk from protectionist legislation. Bills that seek to limit outsourcing are either unlikely to pass, unconstitutional, or incompatible with international treaties" (Patterson 2008, 202). Even if such bills do pass and are found constitutional, they will have limited effect. Many of them deny government contracts to organizations that offshore services; this type of law will have a far greater impact on corporate entities than on law firms, which have relatively fewer government contracts.

There likely will be greater efforts by bar associations to control commoditization because it represents an apparently greater threat to legal monopolies. One recent example from Texas illustrates the challenges facing bar associations in "boundary maintenance" (Kronus 1976). Parsons Technology, a division of The Learning Company, introduced software to assist in the customized preparation of a variety of legal documents. The Texas Unauthorized Practice of Law Committee sued Parsons in 1997 over its offering of one such "do-it-yourself" product called "Quicken Family Lawyer," alleging that it violated Texas's UPL statute. A federal judge agreed and issued a summary judgment in 1999 in favor of the plaintiff (Biersdorfer 1999).[25] Response was swift and strong, with various publishers lining up to lobby the Texas legislature to amend the state's UPL statute to exempt legal software. The legislature quickly amended the statute, and the Court of Appeals

---

[25] The decision is: *Unauthorized Practice of Law Committee v. Parsons Technology,* 1999 WL 47235 (N.D. Tex.). The full text of the decision is available at http://www.bc.edu/bc_org/avp/law/st_org/iptf/exhibits/1999031701_uplc_v_parsons.html.

for the Fifth Circuit vacated the decision based on the amendment (see Lanctot 2002).[26]

However, we can score a victory for the lawyers in a battle on another front. For many years, bankruptcy lawyers and judges, and some consumer groups, complained about so-called "bankruptcy mills" that assisted in the preparation and filing of consumer bankruptcy petitions (see Mund 1994). These businesses were either run by nonattorneys or were headed by attorneys who had little participation in day-to-day operations and sometimes never met their clients. In many cases, petitions were filed in bad faith with the intent to temporarily forestall eviction or foreclosure but with no intent to reorganize or discharge assets. As part of more comprehensive bankruptcy reforms, the U.S. Congress included a provision that strictly regulated the preparation by nonlawyers of bankruptcy-related documents. See 11 U.S.C. §110 (2000). Among other things, the provision forbids nonlawyer preparers from offering legal advice, using the word "legal" in their advertising, and preparing any documents on behalf of their clients. There has been debate whether the statute was motivated by consumer protection or bankruptcy bar protection. In addition, the legislation may have had the apparently unintended effect of increasing reporting and other requirements for law firms (see Wann 2006).

Nevertheless, the apparent lesson to be learned from the revised bankruptcy statute and from the *Parsons* case is that legislatures are more likely to preserve attorneys' monopoly where the monopoly can be shown to at least arguably serve the public interest. Bankruptcy mills appeared to harm consumers and clog the courts in addition to taking away some of the bankruptcy lawyers' bread and butter. However, vague claims about potential consumer harm from overuse of legal software, in the *Parsons* case, were rebuffed by the Texas legislature.

---

[26] The Texas statute in early 1999 defined the "practice of law" as "the preparation of a pleading or other document incident to an action or special proceeding or the management of the action or proceeding on behalf of a client before a judge in court as well as a service rendered out of court, including the giving of advice or the rendering of any service requiring the use of legal skill or knowledge, such as preparing a will, contract, or other instrument, the legal effect of which under the facts and conclusions involved must be carefully determined" (Tex. Gov't. Code § 81.101 [Vernon's Texas Civil Statutes] 1998). The amendment provides: "the 'practice of law' does not include the design, creation, publication, distribution, display, or sale . . . [of] computer software, or similar products if the products clearly and conspicuously state that the products are not a substitute for the advice of an attorney." H.B. 1507, 76th Leg., Reg. Sess. (Tex. 1999). The *Parsons* case was included in a flurry of commentary regarding commoditization of legal services through software offerings (see, e.g., Brown 1999; Lanctot 2002; Scott 2003).

Making Commodity Legal Work Less Miserable

Susskind (2008) argues that a deprofessionalized and reprofessionalized legal practice of the future will require more innovative, imaginative, right-brained thinkers. This may be true for the relatively few attorneys who continue to offer truly customized services. It also may hold for those who design and market increasingly commoditized services. However, this research demonstrates that law still needs—and will need for the foreseeable future—a substantial contingent of workers to perform relatively deskilled tasks. Thus, it is important that organizations employing workers who perform these deskilled tasks attempt to make the work more tolerable.

This research shows that the work of document review possesses all three qualities of a "miserable job," as Patrick Lencioni (2007) describes. The first quality is "anonymity" (where management shows little interest in the employees), the second is "irrelevance" (employees have no idea that their work matters), and the third is "immeasurement" (employees have no objective way to gauge their performance). Until document review is significantly more automated, it may be difficult to reduce the overall tedium of the work. However, the three qualities of the "miserable job" could be ameliorated.[27] A sense of anonymity could be reduced by avoiding the use of the word "temp." Project attorneys could be treated more like valuable members of the "team" by informing them of developments in the case and asking for their input and feedback. Maya pointed out to me that the project attorneys have more knowledge of what is in the documents than do law firm personnel, so she would like to see the job "made more substantive" by firms asking for our input into "how to approach legal issues."

Law firms could also reduce "irrelevance" by making it clearer to project attorneys that their work is important in order to reduce the sense of disconnection, cynicism, and futility that project attorneys frequently feel. Roger told me: "It's frustrating, honestly, if you don't understand why you're doing something or why you've been asked to do something." Law firm partners could come by more frequently (if they come by at all) and tell the attorneys how the results of the document review were being used to assist the client. Kathy told me she would like to receive more information and suggested that the law firm could "at least let us know who the players are, what the deal is

---

[27] In addition, the work could be largely "delawyered" (Susskind 2008) by having document review performed by paralegals. However, many law firms appear to believe that licensed attorneys must perform document review. In any event, of course, handing over the task to nonlawyers would not make the job less miserable.

about, and why they're doing what they're doing, so at least we have some point of reference." Melinda said she wishes that firms would "make you feel like you're part of the case," adding that even if firms just kept the project attorneys up to date about what was going on in the case, she would feel like she's "part of the team, like [the document review] is really going to mean something."

Firms and agencies also could reduce "immeasurement" by setting clearer expectations about work product and by providing more feedback to project attorneys. Many of the attorneys I interviewed reported they got very little feedback from their law firms and agencies, and assumed they were doing a decent job if they were not told otherwise or if they were awarded further work. Ben said he would like "more information about how good a job you're doing, just a little more feedback."

Several attorneys also complained to me about the relatively low pay of document review, particularly when compared to the agency and law firm markups. One way to increase pay would be for law firms to directly hire temporary attorneys for the length of the project, cutting out the agency entirely. However, this may raise complex issues of recruitment and malpractice insurance coverage. Firms also could provide merit pay and bonuses, which additionally might serve to increase the quality of work and reduce review time. However, there are significant challenges to assessing the work product of document reviewers, especially on massive projects. The attorneys I interviewed told me also that the lack of benefits—particularly health insurance— was a significant worry for them. While some placement agencies have begun to offer limited health plans for their temporary attorneys, they tend to be expensive and rather limited in coverage. Other agencies offer vacation pay, provided certain minimum hours are met. These programs could be expanded.

Also, it is important that law firms provide clean, decent work spaces. One writer noted that "finding a place where contract attorneys can spread out and peruse documents has become its own separate challenge for law firms" (Jones 2005). Some firms have leased decaying, moldy office buildings or flea-infested warehouses, or stuffed the document reviewers into converted storage closets or crowded, smelly basement quarters of their own offices. Mitch told me:

> If the attorneys that we work for would just put our shoes on for a minute, and realize: "You know, I've gone through all of what you've gone through, I've jumped through the hoops you've gone through" . . . I mean, you wouldn't work this way. I mean, come on. And yes, I realize you're better than me. And that's fine. If you want to be better than me, be better than me, but, Christ sakes, you can't put me in a condemned building with a dangerous elevator and, you know, the fire

exits blocked, with no air-conditioning in July. Excuse me; I'm a professional here, too.

It is bad enough to have to perform a "miserable" job; doing it under miserable conditions makes it intolerable.

Greater Transparency

There is a need for greater transparency in the temporary attorney market. To begin with, the size of the temporary attorney workforce is difficult to estimate. There are dozens of agencies operating across the country, and attorneys are frequently registered at multiple agencies. The *American Lawyer* and the *National Law Journal* have published information about the number of temporary attorneys employed by firms; however, their surveys only cover the largest law firms and reporting is voluntary. There is a patchwork of ethics rules across state and local bar associations that provide for varying rules about disclosure to clients of firms' use of temporary attorneys. Only a few seem to require disclosure.

Bar associations and law schools could do more to insure transparency. For example, law schools could require all firms that recruit on their campuses to provide the number of temporary attorneys employed by the firm over the prior year. Bar associations could require law firms to disclose to clients their use of temporary lawyers. They also could require placement agencies to disclose and cap their fees. Staffing agencies generally do not charge an up-front fee to temporary workers; however, the size of their markup, which is a jealously guarded secret, is the functional equivalent of a fee (Gonos 2001, 2004). Greater disclosure and fee caps could lead to more competition among agencies and may ultimately increase the amount paid to temporary lawyers.

The legal and popular press also could do more to expose working conditions. Most articles have presented a one-sided depiction of legal temping as a "win-win" situation for lawyers and law firms. One exception involved reporting of a document review project run by the Washington, D.C., law firm Crowell and Moring (Triedman 2006a). Temporary attorneys there were paid $32 per hour plus overtime (potentially $50,000 over four months if the maximum hours were worked). Balanced against this was the working environment. Six hundred project attorneys worked in "near chaotic conditions. . . . Many showed up at 7 a.m. (breakfast buffet) and soldiered on until midnight (lunch and dinner provided). One temp from out of town lived in her car, taking showers at the gym" (Triedman 2006a).

Temporary attorneys themselves also could help to increase transparency. Only a handful of published articles have been written by temporary attorneys. One of them presents the work as "a degrading experience which does not promote working to the best of your ability, it promotes working to get a paycheck" (Snyderman 1998), while another says that "the work itself is mind-numbing" and the document review projects he was on were poorly managed and wasteful (Berman 1999). Over the last several years, Web sites have been created by or on behalf of temporary attorneys. Some have posted comments bitterly complaining about poor treatment by agencies and abysmal working conditions at some law firms. "Tom the Temp" is a blog that exposes "NYC Temporary Attorney Sweatshops" and solicits "horror stories" from other temporary attorneys.[28] Tom the Temp recently named one New York firm—Paul, Weiss, Rifkind, Wharton, and Garrison—"sweatshop of the year." One temporary attorney said that he had worked at the firm, putting in twelve-hour days six days a week in a windowless basement room with dead cockroaches and blocked exits. The managing partner of the firm was quoted as saying that its temporary attorneys do work on the "concourse level" and that some of the exits are blocked, but that "the firm complies with safety codes" (Triedman 2006b). Tom the Temp's Web site contains dozens of postings from disillusioned, frustrated temporary lawyers writing of deplorable conditions, unreasonable work demands, and dishonest firms and placement agencies. The site drips with sarcasm, cynicism, anger, and frustration. One person posted the following about a stint at a particular law firm: "Horrible. We were shoved into a tiny room with no a/c. Air was stale and hot. We were watched constantly, and leaving the building was extremely difficult, if not impossible. We were cheated out of overtime, and the woman that ran the project tried to deny us our food and transportation, even though we were initially promised the stipend and even though we were required to work past 10 p.m." Other posts malign particular law firms and placement agency personnel.

Certainly, these testaments bear little similarity to glowing reports in the legal press (cited in Chapter 2) about the flexibility and variety of temporary legal work. You will not find bloggers writing about temporary work as allowing them to spend winters in the Caribbean or as a means to writing the Great American Novel. It is too early to tell whether such public forums will lead to changes in practices or merely act as a venting outlet for the frustrated and demoralized.

---

[28] As of mid-2010, the Web site was located at: http://temporaryattorney.blogspot.com/.

Protection for Temporary Workers and Disincentives for Their Use

There have been many calls for increased protection of temporary workers. For example, Katherine Stone (2004, 2007) argues that employment laws should be updated to deal with an increasingly mobile and insecure workforce. As more white-collar workers and professionals join the ranks of nonstandard workers, we might finally see some legislation offering more worker protection. Some authors hope that a collective consciousness will emerge across a variety of high- and low-skilled occupational groups affected by increasing insecurity (e.g., Ross 2008). However, it is probably unrealistic to expect bold new government policies to provide protections for temporary workers or to reduce incentives for hiring them. The temporary employment industry has been quite successful in convincing employers of the benefits of using temporary workers (Parker 1994), while business interests have been able to limit new employee protections and water down existing ones (Crain 2004). Many corporations have supported the legal commoditization process, both within their own legal departments and in the law firms they employ, in order to reduce legal billings that have risen faster than inflation for many years (Zeughauser 1996). The use of temporary attorneys has been embraced by law firms as well, after initial concerns about ethical issues and quality.

Governmental agencies are perhaps even less likely to dictate employment relations in the context of legal services because the legal profession has always been highly self-regulating. And even some major changes that have been suggested to reduce the incentive to hire temporary workers generally may not be effective in the legal services sector. For example, some have suggested that providing universal, government-sponsored health care would reduce incentives to hire temporary workers. However, the avoidance of benefit costs does not seem to be a primary motivation for the use of temporary attorneys (or probably any other relatively highly paid professional); rather, law firms and corporations seem most interested in the flexible staffing that temporary attorneys allow.

One possibility is for state, national, and local bar associations to alter their ethics codes in ways that would provide disincentives to using temporary attorneys. For example, law firms could be required to treat the costs of temporary attorneys as a "pass-through" cost, eliminating any significant markup. Law firms might then be more inclined to make greater use of other alternatives such as hiring more permanent associates or staff attorneys, or creating dedicated document reviewers who would have more stable positions and would earn benefits. However, bar associations have been wary about creating strong regulations with regard to the employment of temporary attorneys and instead have crafted rather vague rules that allow a great deal of flexibility for law firms. Some tough early regulations by the New York City Bar were quickly withdrawn after a flood of complaints (Mansnerus 1989), and the American Bar Association crafted a set of rules that allowed a great deal of flexibility in using temporary attorneys (Sherman 1989). In addition, law firms may have difficulty resisting client demands that their projects be staffed with temporary workers.

Some law firms have decided to forgo significant use of temporary project attorneys. These firms have hired "permanent" document review attorneys directly and provided them regular, dedicated space (see Triedman 2006b). This would appear to reduce some inefficiency by eliminating the agency markup and reducing training time. It also would appear to present opportunities for better coordination and management of projects and provide attorneys with greater security in the form of a regular salary and benefits. However, only the largest firms would have the resources and the caseload to make such a dedicated firm "division" feasible, and such a system also creates a further, entrenched tier within the law firm.

Another possible way to avoid the use of temporary personnel is through the creation of legal service delivery firms whose customers are mostly other law firms (see Robinson 1996). Such firms could afford to employ their attorneys through standard work arrangements (i.e., offering salary and benefits) because work would be spread around to a number of clients, thus avoiding the up-and-down cycle of a single project within a single firm. Like dedicated document reviewers, this arrangement also further stratifies the profession; however, both scenarios at least remove the "surplus value" in the agency-temporary relationship (Gonos 2001), resulting in less client cost, more pay for the attorneys, or both.

Collective Organization

When I asked Larry how document review could be improved, he had one immediate, emphatic answer: "A union!" However, there are significant obstacles to temporary attorneys collectively organizing. First, attorneys have little history of unionization. Second, they face challenges similar to those involving other temporary workers because they are scattered across many workplaces (see Kalleberg 2000), although they do tend to be placed in groups. Finally, most temporary attorneys resist the label of "temporary," and also perceive this status to be short-lived. This lack of a collective, stable identity also militates against organization.[29] Greater commoditization and multi-sourcing of legal services will likely mean that more attorneys will be employed by corporate entities. The organization of this employment plus the nature of the work (unbundled, deskilled) perhaps makes unionization more feasible in the future.

Should the rise of the temporary attorney be resisted or embraced? After conducting this research, I was of at least two minds about this. I understood that for some attorneys (including me), the availability of relatively high-paying temporary work was a welcome option. The work provided employment to attorneys who were between jobs, seeking other career paths, or building a private practice. And there were even some attorneys who were making a "career" out of temporary work because they enjoyed the low pressure of the work arrangement. At the same time, most of the attorneys I interviewed were doing document review work "involuntarily" and would have preferred to be employed in a standard work arrangement. In addition, some of the projects we worked on were ineptly managed, we sometimes worked under poor physical conditions, and oftentimes we did not have the respect of law firm employees. Finally there were potential negative macrolevel effects: the general degradation of legal work and a deepening of existing stratification patterns.

Most project attorneys were resigned to their plight. Larry, like many others, told me he could not think of anything that would significantly improve the document review process:

No. No, I don't think that there is. People aren't in this job with hopes of advancement. I don't think anybody, after they've worked here for a couple of days, couple of weeks, thinks they're going to go and become an associate, and make that jump. It happens, but maybe one in ten thousand, one in a hundred thousand people. You know, you're here for a purpose, you're here as a stopgap—you're here because you don't want to be here, but it's a hell of a thing to have if you don't have anything else.

---

[29] One solution short of unionizing is creating "hiring halls," or even starting cooperative placement agencies run by the temporary attorneys themselves, as Bernice suggested to me. In fact, I was once recruited by a fellow temporary attorney to become part of such a cooperative, but the plans never materialized.

As commodity work becomes increasingly automated and much of it migrates offshore, temporary attorneys—many of whom are newly graduated, between jobs, or in transition—may find that the "stopgap" of temporary work may no longer be available. However, until the day when document review is fully automated, or until all of it is sent to India, the work of the project attorney—the leading edge of the new legal underclass—will continue.

Appendix A

Document Review Project Summary

	Industry	Dates Worked	Number of "Permanent" Attorneys in the Firm (as of 2009)	Nature of Matter	Maximum Number of Project Attorneys Employed (Approximate)
1	Telecommunications	04/2000 to 08/2000	More than 400	Private antitrust litigation	100
2	Consumer food products	04/01	More than 500	Second Request	6
3	Consumer food products	04/01 to 05/01	Same firm as #2	Second Request	150
4	Alcoholic beverages	05/01	More than 1,000	Second Request	50
5	Life insurance	06/01 to 08/01	Less than 100	Class action litigation	5
6	Financial services	08/01	Same firm as #2	Second Request	350
7	Electronics	12/01 to 01/02	More than 2,000	Second Request	120
8	Oil and gas	02/02 to 04/02	More than 1,000	Second Request	50
9	Manufacturing	06/02	More than 1,000	Private antitrust litigation	10
10	Electronics	07/02 to 08/02	More than 1,000	Second Request	20
11	Defense	08/02	Same firm as #7	Second Request	150
12	Manufacturing	09/02 to 11/02 and 01/03 to 02/03	More than 1,500	Private product liability litigation	8
13	Electronics	01/03	Same firm as #2	Discovery request involving merger of unrelated entity	15
14	Electronics	04/03 to 07/03	Same firm as #9	Second Request	50
15	Pharmaceuticals	08/03 to 05/04	Same firm as #10	State investigation	25
16	Defense	06/04 to 07/04	Same firm as #10	Second Request	50
17	Entertainment	07/04 to 08/04	Same firm as #10	Second Request	50

Appendix B

The Questionnaire

Interviews were conducted using a semistructured format. Questions were grouped in the following seven areas:

1. Demographics: Age, race/ethnicity, sexual orientation, marital status, residence history, parents' employment and education

2. Education History: Names and locations of high school, college, and law school attended; bar history (dates, pass/fail, and current membership)

3. Work History (nonproject work): Before and during law school, as well as after graduation

4. Attitudes toward the Law: Decision to attend law school; initial career plans; current plans; attitudes concerning identity as a lawyer; feelings about the practice of law

5. Experience on Projects: Initial entry; agency experience; reasons for doing the work; description of all projects worked to date; job security/flexibility; attitudes about the work (difficulty, repetitiveness); how the work is approached; number of hours worked; work habits of self and others; benefits; feedback

6. Relationships: Type and quality of relationships with agencies, coworkers, law firm employees; management of outside relationships and conflicts with work; disclosure about project work to others; search for permanent work

7. Miscellaneous: Attitudes about litigation and the antitrust process; connection to the case and outcome; likes and dislikes about project work; suggestions for improving the work

Appendix C

The Attorneys

Following are short biographical sketches of the attorneys who were interviewed for this project. Unless expressly updated, the information was accurate as of the date of the interview (between 2002 and 2004). Here and throughout the book, some personal information has been altered to assure the attorneys' confidentiality. In some cases, revealing even the attorney's ethnicity would likely have revealed his or her identity, at least to others with whom the attorney has worked. The law school rankings are from *U.S. News & World Report* (2009), which ranks each school based on various quantitative measures, and also places each school in one of four tiers, with 1 being the highest. (Note, however, that 100 of the 197 schools are in tier 1, and there are no schools in tier 2. Note also that rankings are disputed, are not authoritative, and have been criticized as overly reliant on certain quantitative measures that may have little to do with a graduate's success in the field.)

Susan is a single African American in her early thirties. Both of Susan's parents are professionals. She attended a private college in the West and a private law school (top twenty) in the East. After law school, Susan worked at a major law firm as a project associate and had two government jobs as well. As of 2002, she had worked on several temporary projects during the prior several years, and had worked on one project for nearly three years. She said her dream is to start her own business, and she has been saving money and making plans for several years. However, she also had recently reinitiated her search for a position in a law firm, in case her business plans do not pan out. Like most project attorneys, Susan finds document review work boring and tedious, but she tries to take a Zen approach to it to help get her through the day.

Michael is married, white, in his thirties, and has children. Michael's family of origin was middle class. He attended public college and a public law school (unranked; tier 4), both in the East. After law school, he took a job at a small law firm and then an in-house position with a corporation. Michael began temping in 2001, and when he was interviewed the following year, he expressed disappointment at not yet having found long-term, full-time work. He takes a "grin-and-bear-it" approach to project work, and finds that "humor and caffeine" get him through the day. Shortly after our interview, Michael found a permanent position with a small law firm.

Melissa is single, in her twenties, and is in a committed heterosexual relationship. Her father holds a college degree and works in the public sector. Melissa attended a public university and a public law school (unranked; tier 3). She quit a small law firm because she found the work repetitive and boring, having no idea she would wind up doing project work, which she finds much more tedious. She takes a very instrumental approach to the work, billing as many hours as she can in order to pay down her student loans. Melissa looks forward to finding more permanent employment with the federal government or a large corporation.

Larry is married, white, and in his twenties. He comes from a middle-class family where his parents were educators. He attended an Ivy League college and a private law school in the East (top twenty). At the time Larry was interviewed, he was rather dejected and felt he was "lacking for direction." He was considering entering a field other than law, although he felt he was "on the verge of becoming a career project attorney." Larry had worked in some of the worst physical project settings, and developed a keen appreciation for daylight and neutral air.

Betsy is white, married, and in her twenties. She comes from a lower-middle-class background. She attended a public university in the East and a private law school (unranked; tier 3) in the South. Betsy's only legal employment as of the date of the interview (two years after graduating from law school) was doing document review. She found the work tedious, but was proud of her work ethic and happy to have a relatively well-paying job. Later, she found a permanent government position for an agency in which she had always been interested.

Ben is an unmarried, Hispanic heterosexual in his thirties. His family of origin was middle class. He attended a public university and a private law school (top thirty), both in the East. Upon graduating law school, he planned on working for a corporation, but "more on the business side." At the time of the interview, Ben's only legal employment was in project work; however, he felt that the practice of law was probably rather uninteresting, given what his attorney friends had told him and what he saw at the law firms where he had been doing project work. At that time, he was looking for a government or corporate position.

Lynn is single, white, heterosexual, and in her thirties. Her background is middle class; neither of her parents attended college. She attended private college and a private law school (unranked; tier 3), both in the Midwest. Lynn had her own practice, and then began doing project work in 2001. She was one of the few attorneys I interviewed who could see doing project work long-term; she says that she became "burned out" having her own practice and likes the flexibility and variety of project work.

Mitch is divorced, white, and in his forties. He attended a private college and then obtained a master's degree from a public university. He was involved in a number of ventures before graduating from a private law school (top fifty) in the East. Mitch was one of several people who told me that he was not quite sure why he went to law school, and "didn't have a clue" as to what he would do when he got out. After graduation, he worked briefly for a large firm and also held a government position. He left to start his own practice, which was successful for many years. Mitch started temping shortly after that, and (like Lynn) is one of the few attorneys who told me they could see doing it indefinitely. Mitch's approach is to maintain the sense of control he had when he ran his own practice by treating agencies and law firms like his "clients." Unlike most of the interviewees, Mitch is "never worried" about getting assignments.

Frances is married, Asian American, and in her twenties. Both of her parents are professionals. She graduated from a private college and private law school (top one hundred), both in the East. She worked on several large-scale document review projects after law school, and also worked briefly for a law firm before being let go. Her dream was to become a partner at a large firm, but at the time of the interview, she said her future was cloudy, and added: "I'd take a job with anybody. I'm pretty desperate."

Bernice is white, divorced, and appeared to be in her sixties at the time of the interview. She comes from a middle-class family where neither parent finished college. She graduated from a private university and then held management positions in the private sector for a number of years before attending a public law school (unranked; tier 3). She began doing project work in the late 1990s. She took a job with the government, but left it because it was "too limiting," and also worked briefly for a legal services company until it went out of business. Bernice is still looking for permanent work, but fears that her age may make her unemployable.

Bill is single, African American, and in his twenties. His parents are professionals. He attended a private university in the East and then a public law school (top fifty) in the West. He was laid off from a small law firm after a year, and took his first project work in 2002, where he was interviewed. Bill believes that even working for a large firm, an attorney can only become "sort of upper middle class." However, he wants to be "rich," and feels the best way to do that is to start his own business or small law firm, where, he added: "I'd be directing a small staff that will afford me the ability to run around and act like I'm doing work when I'm really not."

Kathy is a single, Asian American heterosexual in her thirties. Her father owned a small business and her family was middle class. She attended a private college and a private law school (unranked; tier 4) in the East. After graduation, she worked as a lawyer in the public sector. She had loved the work, but moved to Washington, D.C., to be with her boyfriend. She told me she "had a delusion that it would be easy to find a job in D.C.," but for the last year Kathy had been doing project work. She misses the sense that she was doing important work in her former job, and looks forward to landing another permanent job, one where she hopes that she "can make a difference."

Evan is gay, white, in his thirties, and in a committed relationship. His father is a professional and his mother a technician. He graduated from a public university and a private law school (top forty), both in the West. Upon moving to D.C., Evan signed up with a legal placement agency because he thought it would be best to search for a permanent job only after he had passed the bar exam. At first, he was assigned a number of paralegal-level projects that he thought were well beneath his skill level. He switched agencies and began to receive better-paying assignments. Just before our interview, Evan accepted a position in the public sector and was looking forward to putting "temping" behind him. He added that he hopes to put in a few years in the public sector and then move to a private law firm.

Vince is gay, single, and in his thirties. His parents are professionals with advanced degrees. Vince received his undergraduate degree and master's degree from a university in the West, and a law degree from a public university (top ten). He was laid off from his government position and did project work for two years while looking for another public sector job. Vince was very unhappy doing project work and was dismayed at both the working conditions and the way that project attorneys were treated by law firms. In 2004, he accepted a permanent position in a federal government agency.

Debby is white, heterosexual, single, and in her twenties. Her family of origin was middle class, and her father has a college degree. Debby graduated from a private university and a private law school (top fifty). She was interviewed on her first project, where she claimed to find the subject matter fascinating but the work itself rather tedious. After working on several projects, she accepted a position in 2006 as a staff attorney at a medium-sized firm in the East.

Maya is a married Hispanic in her thirties and has children. Her family of origin was lower middle class. She attended a private university in the East, and then a private law school in the South (top seventy-five). She left a government position and began doing project work. She says that she is not in a hurry to find permanent work, but when she does, she would like the work to "mean something."

Roger is white, married, in his forties, and has children. Neither of his parents graduated college, and the family was middle class. Roger attended a private university in the Midwest and a private law school (top fifty) in the East. Roger worked for a law firm and also in-house for a small company. He was laid off from his last position and began doing project work. Although bored with the work, Roger is thankful that he has been able to get some relatively long-term assignments. Nevertheless, he is constantly worried about the insecurity that comes with temping, particularly with a family to support. He says he is resigned to doing project work "as long as my family needs me."

Julie is single, white, in her fifties, and avoided the sexual orientation question. Neither of her parents attended college and they held white-collar, middle-class jobs. Julie graduated from a private university and a private law school (top fifty), both in the East. She worked for law firms and had in-house positions as well. She retired and returned to project work to supplement her income, with no interest in returning to the practice of law. Julie prided herself on doing good work, and was quite colorful in her criticism of the work habits of other project attorneys.

James is a single, white, heterosexual in his forties. His father is a professional. He graduated from a private university in the South and a private law school (unranked; tier 4) in the Midwest. He worked for a small law firm and had an in-house position from which he was laid off. He then took up project work, while also pursuing other education and his hobbies. He finds himself unsure of his next career move and is satisfied doing project work until he knows more about what he wants professionally.

Rick is married, white, in his sixties, and has children. His father was a professional and his mother a technician. He attended an Ivy League university and a private law school (top seventy-five), both in the East. He spent many years as a partner in a law firm before taking a public service job. Since he left that position, he has been doing project work while also attempting to bring in other income streams to help support his family. Rick alternately expressed resignation and frustration at the thought that, given his age, he will never be able to find a permanent law firm job. Rick prides himself on his work habits and is disturbed to see some of the "shenanigans" that other project attorneys engage in.

References

Ackroyd, Stephen, and Paul Thompson. 1999. *Organizational* mis*behavior*. London: Sage Publications.

Adams, Edward A. 1992. "Temp" lawyers proliferate. *New York Law Journal,* November 23.

Adams, Edward S., and John H. Matheson. 1998. Law firms on the big board? A proposal for nonlawyer investment in law firms. *California Law Review* 86: 1–40.

Adler, Paul S. 2007. The future of critical management studies: A paleo-Marxist critique of labour process theory. *Organization Studies* 28 (9): 1313–45.

Adler, Paul S., Seok-Woo Kwon, and Charles Heckscher. 2008. Professional work: The emergence of collaborative community. *Organization Science* 19 (2): 359–76.

Agger, James. 1997. Laid off or stressed out associates find temping a viable career option. *Legal Intelligencer,* April 4.

Ainsworth, Earl. 2003. Huh? Legal work farmed out to India. *New Jersey Lawyer,* March 31.

American Bar Association. 1990. Formal opinion 90–357: Use of designation "of counsel." Chicago: American Bar Association.

———. 2006a. *Charting our progress: The status of women in the profession today.* Available at http://www.abanet.org/women/ChartingOurProgress.pdf.

———. 2006b. *Visible invisibility: Women of color in law firms.* Available at http://www.abanet.org/women/VisibleInvisibility-ExecSummary.pdf.

———. n.d. *Statistics about minorities in the profession from the census.* Available at http://www.abanet.org/minorities/links/2000census.html.

American Lawyer. 1988. Temptations of temping. March.

Anderson, Pauline. 2009. Intermediate occupations and the conceptual and empirical limitations of the hourglass economy thesis. *Work, Employment & Society* 23 (1): 169–80.

Androgue, Sofia. 2000. "Rambo" style litigation in the third millennium—the end of an era? *Houston Lawyer*, March/April.

Anleu, Sharon L. Roach. 1992. The legal profession in the United States and Australia: Deprofessionalization or reorganization? *Work and Occupations* 19 (2): 184–204.

Arron, Deborah, and Deborah Guyol. 2004. *The complete guide to contract lawyering*. Seattle, WA: Decision Books.

Associated Press State and Local Wire. 2000. Temps did much work in tobacco case, billing records show. June 29.

Atkinson, John. 1985. The changing corporation. In *New patterns of work*, ed. David Clutterbuck, 13–34. Aldershot, UK: Gower.

Bach, Pete. 2007. Outsourcing has its boundaries. *Appleton (WI) Post-Crescent*, January 2.

Barringer, David. 1996. The standby generation. *ABA Journal*, June.

Bell, Daniel. 1973. *The coming of post-industrial society: A venture in social forecasting*. New York: Basic Books.

Bellon, Lee Ann, and Kathryn C. Alexander. 1990/1991. Need seen for project attorneys. *National Law Journal*, December 31, 1990/January 7, 1991.

Bennett, Drake. 2005. Robo justice. *Boston Globe*, September 11.

Berkman, Barbara. 1988. Temporarily yours: Associates for hire. *American Lawyer*, March.

Berman, Geoff. 1999. Confessions of a temp. *American Lawyer*, October.

Bezanson, Thomas. 1998. Letter to the editor. *American Lawyer*, November.

Biersdorfer, J. D. 1999. Quicken legal-help software is banned in Texas by a judge. *New York Times*, April 25.

Black, Katherine D., and Stephen T. Black. 2004. A national tax bar: An end to the attorney-accountant tax turf war. *St. Mary's Law Journal* 36: 1–98.

Blodgett, Nancy. 1985. Temporary duty: Part-time option for lawyers. *ABA Journal*, July.

Bloomington Pantagraph. 1999. Attorney leaves practice for circus life. Bloomington, IL, September 3.

Blum, Andrew, and Gail Diane Cox. 1988. Bar curbs temps. *National Law Journal*, April 25.

Borgstede, James P. 2008. Radiology: Commodity or specialty. *Radiology* 247: 613–16.

Bowling, Jane. 1995. Temp firm enters legal market with the purchase of Attorneys Per Diem. *Baltimore Daily Record*, May 15.

Braverman, Harry. 1974. *Labor and monopoly capital*. New York: Monthly Review Press.

Brede, Scott. 1995/1996. The holiday crunch. *Connecticut Law Tribune*, December 25/January 1.

Brickley, Peg. 1996. Growing temp firm buys local company. *Fulton County Daily Report*, August 29.

Brock, David M. 2006. The changing professional organization: A review of competing archetypes. *International Journal of Management Reviews* 8 (3): 157–74.

Broschak, Joseph P., Alison Davis-Blake, and Emily S. Block. 2008. Nonstandard, not substandard: The relationship among work arrangements, work attitudes, and job performance. *Work and Occupations* 35 (1): 3–43.

Brown, William H. 1999. Legal software and the unauthorized practice of law: Protection or protectionism. *California Western Law Review* 36: 157–74.

Burawoy, Michael. 1979. *Manufacturing consent: Changes in the labor process under monopoly capitalism.* Chicago: University of Chicago Press.

Callahan, Denise G. 2005. Contract attorneys show they're more than temporary. *Michigan Lawyers Weekly,* October 31.

Cameron Gary. 1984. New businesses helping to bring up '80s babies: The new parents. *Washington Post,* August 27.

Carey, Malcolm. 2007. White-collar proletariat? Braverman, the deskilling/upskilling of social work and the paradoxical life of the agency manager. *Journal of Social Work* 7 (1): 93–114.

Carson, Cindy A. 1994. Under new mismanagement: The problem of non-lawyer equity partnership in law firms. *Georgetown Journal of Legal Ethics* 7: 593–635.

Carter, Regina Galindo. 1997. Alternative work arrangements. *Texas Bar Journal,* January.

Castells, Manuel. 1999. Flows, networks and identities: A critical theory of the information society. In *Critical education in the new information age,* ed. Manuel Castells, Ramón Flecha, Paulo Freire, Henry A. Giroux, Donald Macedo, and Paul Willis, 37–64. Lanham, MD: Rowman and Littlefield.

Cherovsky, Erwin. 1991. The use of temporary lawyers is on the rise in many firms. *New York Law Journal,* March 4.

Chudicek, Joe. 1996. Millionaire seeks her next dream. *Palm Beach Daily Business Review,* August 15.

Cohany, Sharon R. 1998. Workers in alternative employment arrangements. *Monthly Labor Review* 121 (11): 3–21.

Collinson, David L. 1988. "Engineering humor": Masculinity, joking and conflict in shop-floor relations. *Organization Studies* 9 (2): 181–99.

Compensation & Benefits for Law Offices. 2004. *CBLO* news briefs. October.

Connolly, James M. 2007. True confessions of a temporary lawyer. *Maryland Bar Journal,* July/August.

Coster, Helen. 2004. Briefed in Bangalore. *American Lawyer,* November.

Crain, Marion. 2004. The transformation of the professional workplace. *Chicago-Kent Law Review* 79: 543–615.

Crain's New York Business. 1987. Short-term arm of the law puts temp firm to work. June 8.

Crawford, Krysten. 1998. Chadbourne's missing paper trail. *American Lawyer,* September.

———. 2004. Outsourcing the lawyers. *CNNMoney,* October 15. Available at http://money.cnn.com/2004/10/14/news/economy/lawyer_outsourcing/index.htm.

Dale, Angela, and Claire Bamford. 1988. Temporary workers: Cause for concern or complacency? *Work, Employment and Society* 2 (2): 191–209.

D'Angelo, Carlo. 2008. Overseas legal outsourcing and the American legal profession: Friend or "flattener"? *Texas Wesleyan Law Review* 14: 167–95.

Davis, Ann. 1996. Temps use sparks ire in client ranks. *National Law Journal,* December 23.

De Cuyper, Nele, Jeroen de Jong, Hand De Witte, Kerstin Isaksson, Thomas Rigott, and René Schalk. 2008. Literature review of theory and research on the psychological impact of temporary employment: Towards a conceptual model. *International Journal of Management Reviews* 10 (1): 25–51.

Deger, Renee. 2003. Model behavior. *Recorder*, November 13.

Del Villar, Sandra Griffin. 1989. Lawyer offers an alternative through free-lance assistance. *Washington Post*, May 22.

Derber, Charles. 1982. The proletarianization of the professional: A review essay. In *Professionals as workers: Mental labor in advanced capitalism*, ed. Charles Derber, 13–36. Boston: G. K. Hall.

———. 1983. Managing professionals: Ideological proletarianization and post-industrial labor. *Theory and Society* 12 (3): 309–41.

Dick, Penny. 2005. Dirty work designations: How police officers account for their use of coercive force. *Human Relations* 58 (11): 1363–90.

Dinovitzer, Ronit, and Bryant Garth. 2007. Lawyer satisfaction in the process of structuring legal careers. *Law & Society Review* 41 (1): 1–50.

Ditton, Jason. 1972. Absent at work: Or how to manage monotony. *New Society* 21: 679–81.

Drell, Adrienne. 1997. Hired on trial. *Chicago Sun-Times*, July 6.

Drezner, Daniel W. 2004. The outsourcing bogeyman. *Foreign Affairs* 83 (3): 22–34.

DRI. n.d. *A career in the courtroom: A different model for the success of the women who try cases.* Available at http://www.abanet.org/marketresearch/pdfs/Women_in_the_Courtroom.pdf.

du Gay, Paul. 2004. Afterward: The tyranny of the epochal and work identity. In *Identity in the age of the new economy*, ed. Torben Elgaard Jensen, Ann Westenholz, and Paul du Gay, 147–58. Cheltenham, UK: Edward Elgar.

Duncan, Laura. 1994. Temporary work affords some lawyers time to grow, survey says. *Chicago Daily Law Bulletin*, August 24.

Eastin, Keith. 1997. As vulnerable targets, law firms need to be more aware of ways to prevent computer fraud and theft. *Washington, D.C., Legal Times. Supplement: Focus on Litigation Support*, July 21.

Edwards, Paul K. 1990. Understanding conflict in the labour process: The logic and autonomy of struggle. In *Labour process theory*, ed. David Knights and Hugh Wilmott, 125–52. London: Macmillan.

Edwards, Richard. 1979. *Contested terrain: The transformation of the workplace in the twentieth century.* London: Heinemann.

Ehrenreich, Barbara, and John Ehrenreich. 1977. The professional-managerial class. *Radical America* 11 (March/April): 7–31.

Eisenstein, James. 1978. *Counsel for the United States: U.S. attorneys in the political and legal systems.* Baltimore: Johns Hopkins Press.

Epstein, Cynthia Fuchs, and Arne L. Kalleberg. 2001. Time and the sociology of work: Issues and implications. *Work and Occupations* 28 (1): 5–16.

Espeland, Wendy Nelson, and Berit Irene Vannebo. 2007. Accountability, quantification, and law. *Annual Review of Law and Social Science* 3: 21–43.

Evans, Philip, and Thomas S. Wurster. 1999. *Blown to bits: How the new economics of information transforms strategy.* Cambridge, MA: Harvard Business School Press.

Evers, Michael D. 1992. Exploring temporary employment opportunities. *Chicago Daily Law Bulletin*, October 21.

Farrell, Arthur T. 2008. Public interest meets public ownership: Pro bono and the publicly traded law firm. *Georgetown Journal of Legal Ethics* 21: 729–38.

Fernandez, Roberto M. 2001. Skill-based technological change and wage inequality: Evidence from a plant retooling. *American Journal of Sociology* 107: 273–320.

Fernandez, Tommy. 2003. Lawyer temps give clients more power of attorneys. *Crain's New York Business*, July 21.

———. 2005. Temporary insanity. *Crain's New York Business*, June 6.

Fernandez-Mateo, Isabel. 2009. Cumulative gender disadvantage in contract employment. *American Journal of Sociology* 114 (4): 871–923.

Fevre, Ralph. 2007. Employment insecurity and social theory: The power of nightmares. *Work, Employment & Society* 21 (3): 517–35.

Filc, Dani. 2006. Physicians as "organic intellectuals." *Acta Sociologica* 49 (3): 273–85.

Filson, Glen. 1988. Ontario teachers' deprofessionalization and proletarianization. *Comparative Education Review* 32 (3): 298–317.

Flahardy, Cathleen. 2005. Overhyped, underused, overrated. *Corporate Legal Times*, July.

Fleming, Peter, Bill Harley, and Graham Sewell. 2004. A little knowledge is a dangerous thing: Getting below the surface of the growth of "knowledge work" in Australia. *Work, Employment & Society* 18 (4): 725–47.

Form, William. 1987. On the degradation of skills. *Annual Review of Sociology* 13: 29–47.

Foucault, Michel. 1977. *Discipline and punish: The birth of the prison*. New York: Pantheon Books.

Fournier, Valerie. 1999. The appeal to professionalism as a disciplinary mechanism. *Sociological Review* 47 (2): 280–307.

Fox, Kelly. 1994. Gone is lawyer staffing geared toward peak workloads. *Illinois Legal Times*, December.

Fraser, Jill A. 2001. *White collar sweatshop*. New York: W. W. Norton.

Freedman, David H. 1992. Is management still a science? *Harvard Business Review*, November/December.

Freidson, Eliot. 1977. The futures of professionalism. In *Health and the division of labor*, ed. Margaret Stacey, Margaret Reid, Christian Heath, and Robert Dingwall, 14–38. London: Croom Helm.

———. 1986. *Professional powers: A study of the institutionalization of formal knowledge*. Chicago: University of Chicago Press.

———. 1994. *Professionalism reborn: Theory, prophecy and policy*. Chicago: University of Chicago Press.

———. 2001. *Professionalism: The third logic*. Chicago: University of Chicago Press.

Frenkel, Stephen J., Marek Korczynski, Karen A. Shire, and May Tam. 1999. *On the front line: Organization of work in the information economy*. Ithaca, NY: Cornell University Press.

Frey, Jennifer. 1989. Temp-law agencies battle skepticism. *Manhattan Lawyer. Tri-State Support Staff Supplement*, September 19/September 25.

Friedman, Andrew L. 1977. *Industry and labor: Class struggle at work and monopoly capitalism.* London: MacMillan.

Friedman, Lesley. 1989. The use—and misuse—of temporary attorneys. *National Law Journal,* March 27.

———. 1990. Women lawyers eye part-time work. *New York Law Journal,* November 19.

Friedmann, Ron, and Joy London. 2006. Developments in legal outsourcing and offshoring. *LLRX.* Available at http://www.llrx.com/features/legaloutsourcing.htm.

Gallie, Duncan. 1991. Patterns of skill change: Upskilling, deskilling or the polarization of skills? *Work, Employment & Society* 5 (3): 319–51.

Gerth, Hans H., and C. Wright Mills. 1946. *From Max Weber: Essays in sociology.* New York: Oxford University Press.

Goffman, Erving. 1963. *Stigma: Notes on the management of spoiled identity.* New York: Simon & Schuster.

Golden, Lonnie. 1996. The expansion of temporary help employment in the U.S., 1982–1992: An empirical test of alternative models. *Applied Economics* 28 (9): 1127–42.

Golden, Lonnie, and Eileen Appelbaum. 1992. What was driving the 1982–88 boom in temporary employment? Preferences of workers or decisions and power of employers. *American Journal of Economic Sociology* 51 (4): 473–93.

Goldhaber, Michael D. 1999. Tempting work. *National Law Journal,* April 12.

Gonos, George. 1997. The contest over "employer" status in the postwar United States: The case of temporary help firms. *Law & Society Review* 31 (1): 81–110.

———. 2001. Fee-splitting revisited: Concealing surplus value in the temporary employment relationship. *Politics and Society* 29 (4): 589–611.

———. 2004. "Never a fee!" The miracle of the postmodern temporary help and staffing agency. *WorkingUSA* 4 (3): 9–36.

Gottfried, Heidi. 1994. Learning the score: The duality of control and everyday resistance in the temporary-help service industry. In *Resistance and power in organizations,* ed. John M. Jermier, David Knights, and Walter R. Nord, 102–27. London: Routledge.

Green, Francis. 2007. Temporary work and insecurity in Britain: A problem solved? *Social Indicators Research* 88 (1): 147–60.

Greene, Jenna. In brief. 2003. *Washington, D.C., Legal Times,* November 10.

Greenwood, Royston, and Laura Empson. 2003. The professional partnership: Relic or exemplary form of governance? *Organization Studies* 24 (6): 909–33.

Griffin, Keith. 2005. For temps, misgivings linger. *Connecticut Law Tribune,* January 17.

Gross-Glaser, Sheryl. 1990. Firing trends. *ABA Journal,* August.

Gutek, Barbara A. 1995a. Clerical work and information technology: Implications of managerial assumptions. In *Women and technology: Technological innovation and human resources,* ed. Urs E. Gattiker, 4: 205–28. Berlin: Walter de Gruyter.

———. 1995b. *The dynamics of service: Reflections on the changing nature of customer/provider interactions.* San Francisco: Jossey-Bass.

Harrison, Michael I. 1994. Professional control as process: Beyond structural theories. *Human Relations* 47 (10): 1201–31.

Hassard, John, John Hogan, and Michael Rowlinson. 2001. From labor process theory to critical management studies. *Administrative Theory & Praxis* 23 (3): 339–62.

Haug, Marie R. 1975. The deprofessionalization of everyone? *Sociological Focus* 8 (3): 197–213.

Hechler, David. 2004. Big firms growing, but by a thin 1.5%. *National Law Journal. Supplement: In Focus*, November 8.

Hecht, Jason. 2001. Classical labour-displacing technological change: The case of the U.S. insurance industry. *Cambridge Journal of Economics* 25: 517–37.

Heery, Edmund, and John Salmon. 2000. The insecurity thesis. In *The insecure workforce*, ed. Edmund Heery and John Salmon, 1–24. London: Routledge.

Heinz, John P., and Edward O. Laumann. 1982. *Chicago lawyers: The social structure of the bar*. New York: Russell Sage Foundation and American Bar Association.

Heinz, John P., Robert L. Nelson, Rebecca L. Sandefur, and Edward O. Laumann. 2005. *Urban lawyers: The new social structure of the bar*. Chicago: University of Chicago Press.

Heller, Jamie. 1991. Seasonal help. *Connecticut Law Tribune*. June 10.

Henson, Kevin D. 1996. *Just a temp*. Philadelphia: Temple University Press.

Hirschhorn, Larry. 1984. *Beyond mechanization: Work and technology in a postindustrial age*. Cambridge, MA: MIT Press.

Hochschild, Arlie Russell. 1983. *The managed heart: The commercialization of human feeling*. Berkeley: University of California Press.

Hodges, Jill. 1995. Legal community starting to accept contract lawyers. *Minneapolis Star Tribune*, May 21.

Hodgson, Damian E. 2004. Project work: The legacy of bureaucratic control in the post-bureaucratic organization. *Organization* 11 (1): 81–100.

Holmes, Andrew. 2008. *Commoditization and the strategic response*. Aldershot, England: Gower Publishing.

Hyman, David. 2008. Symposium: Challenges to the attorney-client relationship. *DePaul University Law Review* 57: 267–80.

Jacoby, Sanford M. 1985. *Employing bureaucracy: Managers, unions and the transformation of work in American industry, 1900–1945*. New York: Columbia University Press.

Janczak, Lynn M. 1997. Legal staffing alternatives in tomorrow's workplace. *Metropolitan Corporate Counsel*, September.

Johnson, Vincent R., and Virginia Coyle. 1990. On the transformation of the legal profession: The advent of temporary lawyering. *Notre Dame Law Review* 66: 359–442.

Johnstone, Quintin. 2008. An overview of the legal profession in the United States, how that profession recently has been changing, and its future prospects. *Quinnipiac Law Review* 26: 737–97.

Jones, Leigh. 2005. Faced with data explosion, law firms tap temp attorneys. *National Law Journal*, October 14.

Junge, Ember Reichgott. 2004. Commentary: Corporate counsel options change with the times. *Minnesota Lawyer*, January 26.

Kalleberg, Arne L. 2000. Nonstandard employment relations: Part-time, temporary and contract work. *Annual Review of Sociology* 26: 341–65.

Kalleberg, Arne L., and Cynthia Fuchs Epstein. 2001. Temporal dimensions of employment relationships. *American Behavioral Scientist* 44 (7): 1064–75.

Kalleberg, Arne L., Barbara F. Reskin, and Ken Hudson. 2000. Bad jobs in America: Standard and nonstandard employment relations and job quality in the United States. *American Sociological Review* 65: 256–78.

Kalleberg, Arne L., Jeremy Reynolds, and Peter V. Marsden. 2003. Externalizing employment: Flexible staffing arrangements in U.S. organizations. *Social Science Research* 32 (4): 525–52.

Kensik, Edward. 1998. Tepid attempts at temping. *New Jersey Law Journal*, July 27.

Kidder, Jeffrey L. 2006. "It's the job that I love": Bike messengers and edgework. *Sociological Forum* 21 (1): 31–54.

Kim, Young-Hwa. 2002. A state of art review on the impact of technology on skill demand in OECD countries. *Journal of Education and Work* 15 (1): 89–109.

King, Jennifer E. 1999. Chutes and ladders. *Corporate Legal Times*, May.

———. 2004. Legal specialists dominate in-house market. *Corporate Legal Times*, January.

Knotts, MichaelAnn. 2004. Outsourcing vs. job security. *New Jersey Lawyer*, June 14.

Krier, Dan, and William G. Staples. 1993. Seen but unseen: Part-time faculty and institutional surveillance and control. *American Sociologist* 24 (3/4): 119–34.

Krishnan, Jayanth K. 2007. Outsourcing and the globalizing legal profession. *William and Mary Law Review* 48: 2189–46.

Kronus, Carol L. 1976. The evolution of occupational power: An historical study of task boundaries between physicians and pharmacists. *Sociology of Work and Occupations* 3: 3–37.

Kunda, Gideon. 1992. *Engineering culture: Control and commitment in a high-tech corporation.* Philadelphia: Temple University Press.

Kunda, Gideon, Stephen R. Barley, and James Evans. 2002. Why do contractors contract? The experience of highly skilled technical professionals in a contingent labor market. *Industrial and Labor Relations Review* 55 (2): 234–61.

Kuntz, Esther. 1994. Attorneys on the cheap. *CFO*, March.

Kusterer, Kenneth C. 1978. *Know-how on the job: The important working knowledge of "unskilled" workers.* Boulder, CO: Westview.

Lanctot, Katherine J. 2002. Scriveners in cyberspace: Online document preparation and the unauthorized practice of law. *Hofstra Law Review* 30: 811–54.

Larson, Magali. 1977. *The rise of professionalism: A sociological analysis.* Berkeley: University of California Press.

Lee, Dwight R. 1996. Why is flexible employment increasing? *Journal of Labor Research* 17 (4): 543–53.

LegalZoom. n.d. http://www.legalzoom.com.

Lencioni, Patrick. 2007. *The three signs of a miserable job.* San Francisco: Jossey-Bass.

Lewis, Jonathan H. 2006. Finding the right staffing partner. *Metropolitan Corporate Counsel*, April.

Lewis, Theodore. 2007. Braverman, Foucault and the labor process: Framing the current high-skills debate. *Journal of Education and Work* 20 (5): 397–415.

Liecht, Kevin T., and Mary L. Fennell. 1997. The changing organizational context of professional work. *Annual Review of Sociology* 23: 215–31.

Littler, Craig R. 1978. Understanding Taylorism. *British Journal of Sociology* 29 (2): 185–202.

———. 1982. *The development of the labour process in capitalist societies: A comparative study of the transformation of work organisation in Britain, Japan and the United States.* London: Heinemann Educational Books.

Livingston, Kevin. 1998. Temp lawyers find freedom has its price. *Recorder,* August 12.

Loomis, Tamara. 1999. Contract lawyering catches on. *New York Law Journal,* October 22.

Lucas, Water. 1991. From 2-tier to per diem. *New Jersey Law Journal,* October 10.

MacEwen, Bruce. 2005. Milbank looks to India. *Law Technology News,* June.

MacLachlan, Claudia. 2001. Working by the hour. *Washington, D.C., Legal Times,* February 19.

Magnum, Garth, Donald Mayall, and Kristin Nelson. 1985. The temporary help supply: A response to the dual internal labor market. *Industrial and Labor Relations Review* 38 (4): 599–611.

Mandelbaum, Robb. 1995. Halfway in-house. *Connecticut Law Tribune,* October 23.

Mansnerus, Laura. 1989. Rule on temporary lawyers changes again. *New York Times,* June 2.

———. 1991. Lawyer layoffs. *New York Times,* May 3.

Marcotte, Paul. 1989. Temporary lawyer firms get OK. *ABA Journal,* March.

Marcuse, Herbert. 1964. *One dimensional man.* Boston: Beacon Press.

Marglin, Stephen. 1975. What do bosses do? *Review of Radical and Political Economics* 6 (2): 60–112.

Margolick, David. 1988. At the bar. *New York Times,* September 23.

Marx, Karl. [1889] 1967. *Capital: A critical analysis of capitalist production.* New York: International Publishers.

Massey, Douglas S., and Deborah S. Hirst. 1998. From escalator to hourglass: Changes in the U.S. occupational wage structure 1949–1989. *Social Science Research* 27 (1): 51–71.

McCracken, Jeffrey. 1999. A brief position for attorneys. *Crain's Detroit Business,* May 31.

McKinlay, John B., and Joan Arches. 1985. Towards the proletarianization of physicians. *International Journal of Health Services* 15 (2): 161–95.

McLean, Thomas R. 2006. Telemedicine and the commoditization of medical services. *DePaul Journal of Health Care Law* 10: 131–75.

Mertz, Elizabeth. 2007. *The language of law school.* New York: Oxford University Press.

Metropolitan Corporate Counsel. 1998. Meeting a need by matching jobs and talent. March.

———. 2001. Nancy Molloy: Offering an option for in-transition attorneys. September.

———. 2002. Partnering—DuPont legal model. July.

Miller, Brian. 2008. The ethical implications of legal outsourcing. *Journal of the Legal Profession* 32: 259–72.

Molloy, Nancy. 1997. Partnering-temporaries. *Metropolitan Corporate Counsel,* July.

Molloy, Nancy, and Jeffrey A. Heilman. 1999. Special Report: Staffing the new department. *Metropolitan Corporate Counsel,* May.

Morgan, Thomas D. 2002. Toward abandoning organized professionalism. *Hofstra Law Review* 30: 947–76.

Mulkay, Michael. 1988. *On humor: Its nature and place in modern society.* Cambridge, UK: Polity Press.

Mund, Geraldine. 1994. Paralegals: The good, the bad and the ugly. *American Bankruptcy Institute Law Review* 2: 337–51.

Murray, Kathleen M. 2000. Walking away from the law. *Washington, D.C., Legal Times,* November 13.

Muzio, Daniel, and Stephen Ackroyd. 2005. On the consequences of defensive professionalism: Recent changes in the legal labour process. *Journal of Law and Society* 32 (4): 615–42.

Myers, Bill. 2005a. Economic forces changing look of law biz. *Chicago Daily Law Bulletin,* April 7.

———. 2005b. Cost-cutting pushes lawyer jobs overseas. *Chicago Daily Law Bulletin,* April 8.

Nance, Sheryl. 1989. Five who divide their lives into law and something else. *New York Law Journal,* September 15.

National Association for Law Placement. 2004. *After the JD: First results of a national study of legal careers.* Chicago: American Bar Foundation.

———. 2009. *Salaries at largest firms peak in 2009.* Available at http://www.nalp.org/salariesjuly09.

National Law Journal. 2008. The *NLJ* 250. November 10.

Nelson, Robert L., and David M. Trubek. 1992. Arenas of professionalism: The professional ideologies of lawyers in context. In *Lawyers' ideals/lawyer practices: Transformations in the American legal profession,* ed. Robert L. Nelson, David M. Trubek, and Rayman L. Solomon, 177–214. Ithaca, NY: Cornell University Press.

New York Law Journal. 1993. Today's news update. September 1.

Nieuwenhuizen, Patricia, and David Priebe. 2000. The invaluable database. *New York Law Journal. Special Section: Litigation,* June 26.

Nolan, Jane P., Ines C. Wichert, and Brendan J. Burchell. 2000. Job insecurity, psychological well-being and family life. In *The Insecure Workforce,* ed. Edmund Heery and John Salmon, 181–209. London: Routledge.

Nollen, Stanley D. 1996. Negative aspects of temporary employment. *Journal of Labor Research* 17 (4): 567–82.

Norris, David. 1999. Anger at scheme for Internet "quickie" divorces on the cheap. *UK Daily Mail,* July 26.

Nuñes, Rodrigo. 2007. "Forward how? Forward where?" I: (Post)-operaismo beyond the immaterial labour thesis. *Ephemera* 7 (1): 178–202.

Ofstead, Cynthia M. 1999. Temporary help firms as entrepreneurial actors. *Sociological Forum* 14 (2): 273–94.

Oppenheimer, Martin. 1973. The proletarianization of the professional. In *Professionalization and social change, sociological review monograph,* ed. Paul Halmos, 20: 213–17. Staffordshire, England: J. H. Books.

Ors, Rose D. 1993. Contract staffing works for many legal departments. *Corporate Legal Times*, August.

Paonita, Anthony. 2006. Better living through automation. *Corporate Counsel*, May 26.

Parker, Robert E. 1994. *Flesh peddlers and warm bodies: The temporary help industry and its workers*. Camden, NJ: Rutgers University Press.

Parks, Ann. 2004. Attorney temping gains in popularity. *Baltimore Daily Record*, June 4.

Parsons, Talcott. 1970. Equality and inequality in modern society, or social stratification revisited. *Social Inquiry* 40: 13–72.

Partner's Report for Law Firm Owners. 2006. Staffing alternatives. November.

Patterson, Lee A. 2008. Outsourcing of legal services: A brief survey of the practice and the minimal impact of protectionist legislation. *Richmond Journal of Global Law and Business* 7: 177–204.

Patton, Paula A. 1996. Things are looking up. *National Law Journal*, August 19.

Paumgarten, Nick. 2007. The tycoon. *New Yorker*, July 23.

Peck, Jamie, and Nikolas Theodore. 1998. The business of contingent work: Growth and restructuring in Chicago's temporary employment industry. *Work, Employment & Society* 12 (4): 655–74.

Peña, Devon G. 1996. *The terror of the machine: Technology, work, gender and ecology on the U.S.-Mexico border*. Austin, TX: CMAS Books/University of Texas.

Penn, Roger, Michael Rose, and Jill Rubery. 1994. *Skill and occupational change*. Oxford: Oxford University Press.

Perin, Monica. 2005. Washington firm absorbs litigation boutique. *Houston Business Journal*, January 14.

Pessin, Jaime Levy. 2005. Growing ranks of contract lawyers try to make it work. *Chicago Lawyer*, January.

Pfeiffer, Sacha. 2007. Lawyers try to catch up in tech world. *Boston Globe*, December 31.

Phillips, Anne, and Barbara Taylor. 1980. Sex and skill: Notes towards a feminist economics. *Feminist Review* 6: 79–89.

Pickard, Susan. 2009. The professionalization of general practitioners with a special interest: Rationalization, restratification and governmentality. *Sociology* 43 (2): 250–67.

Polivka, Ann E. 1996. Into contingent and alternative employment: By choice? *Monthly Labor Review* (October): 55–74.

Prasad, Pushkala, and Anshuman Prasad. 2000. Stretching the iron cage: The constitution and implications of routine workplace resistance. *Organization Science* 11 (4): 387–403.

Pristin, Terry. 1998. Temp company acquired. *New York Times*, January 22.

Pulskamp, John. 2005. Proletarianization of professional work and changed workplace relationships. In *Labor in cross-cultural perspective*, ed. E. Paul Durrenberger and Judith E. Martí, 175–92. Lanham, MD: AltaMira Press.

Ramsey-Lefevre, Robert. 1997. More and more suburban lawyers find "temping" to be tempting. *Legal Intelligencer*, April 9.

Ramstack, Tom. 2005. Law firms send case work overseas to boost efficiency. *Washington Times*, September 26.

Reich, Robert. 1991. *The work of nations: Preparing ourselves for 21st century capitalism.* New York: Knopf.

Reisenger, Sue. 2003. General counsel cutting the fat. *National Law Journal,* March 10.

Rhode, Deborah L. 1981. Policing the professional monopoly: A constitutional and empirical analysis of unauthorized practice prohibitions. *Stanford Law Review* 34: 1–98.

———. 1996. Meet needs with nonlawyers. *ABA Journal,* January.

———. 2004. *Access to justice.* New York: Oxford University Press.

———. 2005. *Pro bono in principle and in practice: Public service and the professions.* Stanford: Stanford University Press.

Ritzer, George, and David Walczak. 1988. Rationalization and the deprofessionalization of physicians. *Social Forces* 67 (1): 1–22.

Robinson, David A. 1996. *Practicing law without clients.* Washington, D.C.: American Bar Association.

Rodrigues, Suzana B., and David Collinson. 1995. "Having fun?" Humour as resistance in Brazil. *Organization Studies* 16 (5): 739–68.

Rogers, Jackie Krasas. 2000. *Temps: The many faces of the changing workplace.* Ithaca, NY: Cornell University Press.

Roitblat, Herbert L., Anne Kershaw, and Patrick Oot. 2009. Document categorization in legal electronic discovery: Computer classification versus manual review. *Journal of the American Society for Information Science and Technology* 61(1): 1–11.

Rosenberg, Geanne. 2004. "Offshore" legal work makes gains. *National Law Journal,* March 29.

Ross, Andrew. 2008. The new geography of work: Power to the precarious? *Theory, Culture & Society* 25 (7/8): 31–49.

Rothman, Robert A. 1984. Deprofessionalization: The case of law in America. *Work and Occupations* 11 (2): 183–206.

Rubery, Jill, Kevin Ward, and Damian Grimshaw. 2005. Working time, industrial relations and the employment relationship. *Time & Society* 14 (1): 89–111.

Samborn, Hope Viner. 1994. Attorney available. *Legal Intelligencer,* October 12.

Sandburg, Brenda. 2000. Time out. *Recorder,* May 9.

Sawchuk, Peter H. 2006. "Use-value" and the re-thinking of skills, learning and the labour process. *Journal of Industrial Relations* 48 (5): 593–617.

Scheffey, Thomas. 1995. Rising temps. *Connecticut Law Tribune,* May 15.

———. 1995/1996. Kelly Girl, Esq. *Connecticut Law Tribune. 1995 Year in Review Issue,* December 25/January 1.

———. 1996. The real "new leverage." *Connecticut Law Tribune,* July 29.

———. 1998. Wallace's registry of discontent. *Connecticut Law Tribune,* September 14.

Schleef, Debra. 2001. Thinking like a lawyer: Gender differences in the production of professional knowledge. *Gender Issues* 19 (2): 69–86.

Scott, William A. 2003. Comment. Filling in the blanks: How computerized forms are affecting the legal profession. *Albany Law Journal of Science and Technology* 13: 835–63.

Sennett, Richard, and Jonathan Cobb. 1972. *The Hidden Injuries of Class.* New York: W. W. Norton.

Sewell, Graham. 1998. The discipline of teams: The control of team-based industrial work through electronic and peer surveillance. *Administrative Science Quarterly* 43 (2): 397–428.

Sharp, Elaine B. 1982. Street-level discretion in policing: Attitudes and behaviors in the deprofessionalization syndrome. *Law and Policy* 4 (2): 167–89.

Sherefkin, Robert. 1995. Legal trend: Lawyers as temps. *Crain's Detroit Business*, November 27.

Sherman, Rorie. 1989. Temp lawyers OK'd. *National Law Journal*, January 9.

Shiffler, D. Anne Slayton. 1998. Market opens for temporary attorneys in Austin. *Austin Business Journal*, February 27.

Skidmore, Sarah. 2006. Use of temporary doctors to fill gaps in staff growing. *San Diego Union-Tribune*, February 19.

Smith, Lisa R. 2004. Outsourcing: The next generation. *Accounting for Lawyers*, March 4.

Smith, Vicki. 1998. The fractured world of the temporary worker: Power, participation and fragmentation in the contemporary workplace. *Social Problems* 45 (4): 411–30.

Smith, Vicki, and Esther B. Neuwirth. 2008. *The good temp*. Ithaca, NY: Cornell University Press.

Snyderman, Marc Ian. 1998. A tale of a new attorney. *New York Law Journal*, April 2.

Socha, George, and Tom Gelbmann. 2008. A look at the 2008 Socha-Gelbmann survey. *Law Technology News*, August 11. Available at http://www.law.com/jsp/legaltechnology/pubArticleLT.jsp?id=1202423646479.

Sotirin, Patty. 2000. "All they do is bitch bitch bitch": Political and interactional features of women's officetalk. *Women and Language* 23 (2): 19–25.

Sotirin, Patty, and Heidi Gottfried. 1999. The ambivalent dynamics of secretarial "bitching": Control, resistance, and the construction of identity. *Organization* 6 (1): 57–80.

Spangler, Eve, and Peter M. Lehman. 1983. Lawyering as work. In *Professionals as workers: Mental labor in advanced capitalism*, ed. Charles Derber, 63–99. Boston: G. K. Hall.

Spenner, Kenneth. 1979. Temporal changes in work content. *American Sociological Review* 44: 968–75.

———. 1983. Deciphering Prometheus: Temporal change in the skill level of work. *American Sociological Review* 48: 824–37.

Standing, Guy. 1999. Global feminization through flexible labor: A theme revisited. *World Development* 27 (3): 583–602.

Sterling, Joyce, Ronit Dinovitzer, and Bryant Garth. 2007. The changing social role of urban law schools. *Southwest University Law Review* 36: 389–432.

Stone, Katherine V. W. 2004. *From widgets to digits: Employment regulation for the changing workplace*. Cambridge: Cambridge University Press.

———. 2007. A fatal mismatch: Employer-centric benefits in a boundaryless world. *Lewis and Clark Law Review* 11: 451–80.

Stone, Katherine V. W., George Gonos, Stephen Befort, and Michelle A. Travis. 2006. Employment protection for atypical workers. *Employee Rights and Employment Policy Journal* 10: 233–70.

Strahler, Steven R. 2005. Lawyers for hire in AT&T's case. *Crain's Chicago Business*, May 16.

Sullivan, R. Lee. 1995. Lawyers á la carte. *Forbes*, September 11.

Susskind, Richard. 2008. *Transforming the law: Essays on technology, justice, and the legal marketplace.* Oxford: Oxford University Press.

Sykes, Gresham M., and David Matza. 1957. Techniques of neutralization: A theory of delinquency. *American Sociological Review* 22: 664–70.

Szweras, Adam. 1993. Temporary work arrangements help law firms cope with "people crisis." *Lawyers Weekly*, July 2.

Taylor, Frederick W. 1911. *The principles of scientific management.* New York: Harper and Row.

Taylor, Pat. 1995. Going to market. *Washington, D.C., Legal Times. Supplement, Employment Guide: Focus on Temporary Help*, October 16.

Temes, Judy. 1990. No longer barred, temp agency thrives. *Crain's New York Business*, August 6.

Thompson, Paul, Chris Warhurst, and George Callaghan. 2001. Ignorant theory and knowledgeable workers: Interrogating the connection between knowledge, skills and services. *Journal of Management Studies* 38 (7): 923–42.

Thompson, William E., Jack L. Harred, and Barbara E. Burks. 2003. Managing the stigma of topless dancing: A decade later. *Deviant Behavior* 24 (6): 551–70.

Tilly, Chris. 1996. *Half a job: Bad and good part-time jobs in a changing labor market.* Philadelphia: Temple University Press.

Timmermans, Stefan. 2008. Professions and their work: Do market shelters protect professional interests? *Work and Occupations* 35 (2): 164–88.

Tope, Daniel, Lindsey Joyce Chamberlain, Martha Crowley, and Randy Hodson. 2005. The benefits of being there: Evidence from the literature on work. *Journal of Contemporary Ethnography* 34 (4): 470–93.

Torry, Saundra. 1996. Year-end rush keeps temps hustling and bustling. *Washington Post*, January 4.

Triedman, Julie. 2006a. Slaves of New York. *American Lawyer*, March.

———. 2006b. Temporary solution. *American Lawyer*, September 1.

Tucker, James. 1993. Everyday forms of employee resistance. *Sociological Forum* 8 (1): 25–45.

United States Department of Labor. 2007. *Occupational outlook handbook, 2008–09 edition: Lawyers.* Available at http://www.bls.gov/oco/ocos053.htm.

———. 2009. *Occupational employment and wages, May 2008: 23–1011 lawyers.* Available at http://www.bls.gov/oes/2008/may/oes231011.htm#(1).

United States Federal Trade Commission. 2002. *Comments on the American Bar Association's proposed model definition of the practice of law.* Available at http://www.usdoj.gov/atr/public/comments/200604.pdf.

Uribarri, Adrian G. 2007. Making a case for temp lawyers: A recruiting firm in the legal field fills a need for contract work. *Los Angeles Times*, April 25, C1.

U.S. News & World Report. 2009. Best Law Schools. Available at http://grad-schools.usnews.rankingsandreviews.com/best-graduate-schools/top-law-schools.

Van Hoy, Jerry. 1995. Selling and processing law: Legal work at franchise law firms. *Law & Society Review* 29 (4): 703–29.

Van Wijk, Ellen, and Peter Leisink. 2004. On becoming a freelance professional. In *Identity in the age of the new economy*, ed. Torben Elgaard Jensen, Ann Westenholz, and Paul du Gay, 99–121. Cheltenham, UK: Edward Elgar.

Vielmetti, Bruce. 1989. Temporary lawyer services gain acceptance in Tampa. *St. Petersburg Times*, May 8.

Wallace, Jean E., and Fiona M. Kay. 2008. The professionalism of practicing law: A comparison across work contexts. *Journal of Organizational Behavior* 29 (8): 1021–47.

Walsh, Mark. 1997. Attorneys for rent help firms cut costs. *Crain's New York Business*, October 27.

Wann, Robert, Jr. 2006. Note. "Debt relief agencies": Does the Bankruptcy Abuse Prevention and Consumer Protection Act of 2005 violate attorneys' first amendment rights? *American Bankruptcy Institute Law Review* 14: 273–300.

Washington Post. 2000. Microsoft to limit term of temporary workers. February 21.

Wells, Amy Stuart. 1987. Temporary workers are going upscale. *New York Times*, March 22.

Westenholz, Ann. 2004. Emerging identities beyond organizational boundaries. In *Identity in the age of the new economy*, ed. Torben Elgaard Jensen, Ann Westenholz, and Paul du Gay, 122–146. Cheltenham, UK: Edward Elgar.

Wheeler, Gerald R., and Carol R. Wheeler. 1980. Reflections on legal representation of the economically disadvantaged: Beyond assembly line justice. *Crime & Delinquency* 26 (3): 319–32.

Wiggins, Robert B. 2003. From boxes of documents to gigabytes and meta data. *Metropolitan Corporate Counsel*, December.

Wilensky, Harold L. 1964. The professionalization of everyone? *American Journal of Sociology* 70: 137–58.

Willging, Thomas, Donna Stienstra, and Dean Miletich. 1998. An empirical study of discovery and disclosure practice under the 1993 federal rule amendments. *Boston College Law Review* 39: 525–96.

Wolf, Mark. 1997. Short-term contract. *Rocky Mountain News*, November 3.

Yates, Charlotte, Wayne Lewchuk, and Paul Stewart. 2001. Empowerment as a Trojan horse: New systems of work organization in the North American automobile industry. *Economic and Industrial Democracy* 22: 517–41.

Yodh, Rahul D. 2004. Temporary solutions. *Washington, D.C., Legal Times*, May 10.

Zeughauser, Peter D. 1996. A new look at "full service." *New Jersey Law Journal*, December.

Zuboff, Shoshana. 1988. *In the age of the smart machine: The future of work and power*. New York: Basic Books.

CASES

Fadia v. Unauthorized Practice of Law Committee, 830 S.W.2d 162 (Tex. App. 1992).

N.Y. County Lawyers' Association v. Dacey, 234 N.E.2d 459 (N.Y. 1967).

State Bar v. Gilchrist, 538 P.2d 913 (Or. 1975).

Unauthorized Practice of Law Committee v. Parsons Technology, 1999 WL 47235 (N.D. Tex.).

STATUTES AND LAWS

11 U.S.C. § 110 (2000).
Tex. Gov't. Code § 81.101 (Vernon's Texas Civil Statutes1998).
H.B. 1507, 76th Leg., Reg. Sess. (Tex. 1999).

Index